∴ ∴ ∴

CHACO CANYON

Ancestral Pueblo McElmo Black-on-White pitcher from Chaco Canyon. Site unknown. AD 1100–1150. *Courtesy National Park Service Museum Management Program and Chaco Culture National Historical Park. Image CHCU 2048.*

∴ ∴ ∴

CHACO CANYON

Archaeologists Explore the Lives of an Ancient Society

BRIAN FAGAN

OXFORD
UNIVERSITY PRESS

2005

OXFORD
UNIVERSITY PRESS

Oxford University Press, Inc., publishes works that
further Oxford University's objective of excellence
in research, scholarship, and education.

Oxford   New York
Auckland   Cape Town   Dar es Salaam   Hong Kong   Karachi
Kuala Lumpur   Madrid   Melbourne   Mexico City   Nairobi
New Delhi   Shanghai   Taipei   Toronto

With offices in
Argentina   Austria   Brazil   Chile   Czech Republic   France   Greece
Guatemala   Hungary   Italy   Japan   Poland   Portugal   Singapore
South Korea   Switzerland   Thailand   Turkey   Ukraine   Vietnam

Copyright © 2005 by Brian Fagan

Published by Oxford University Press, Inc.
198 Madison Avenue, New York, New York 10016
www.oup.com

Oxford is a registered trademark of Oxford University Press

Library of Congress Cataloging-in-Publication Data
Fagan, Brian M.
Chaco Canyon : archaeologists explore the lives of an ancient society / Brian Fagan.
p. cm.
Includes bibliographical references and index.
ISBN-13: 978-019-517043-6
ISBN-10: 0-19-517043-1
1.   Indians of North America—New Mexico—Chaco Canyon—Antiquities.
2.   Chaco Canyon (N.M.)—Antiquities.
3.   Excavations (Archaeology)—New Mexico—Chaco Canyon.
I.   Title.
E78.N65F34 2005
978.9'2—dc22   2004023630

9 8 7 6 5 4 3 2 1

Printed in the United States of America
on acid-free paper

To
Gwinn Vivian

With thanks for his encouragement and
in honor of a life devoted to Chaco

and

in memoriam
Gordon Vivian

Chaco archaeologist and honored pioneer
of archaeological conservation

For I know some will say, why does he treat us to descriptions of weeds, and make us hobble after him over broken stones, decayed buildings, and old rubbish?

George Wheeler, *A Journey into Greece* (1682)

CONTENTS

viii ∴ *Contents*

∴ PART 4
MOVEMENT

12.   Readjustment   197
13.   Chaco's Legacy   214

Notes and References   231
Index   247

PREFACE

I had never thought of writing a book about Chaco Canyon, despite my many visits there. However, when members of the Chaco Synthesis Project (a National Park Service–supported project to synthesize current knowledge about the canyon) invited me to write a popular volume on Chaco, based on their work, I accepted at once, because the story of Chaco had long fascinated me. Had I known what I know now, I might well have refused! The task has been a daunting one, compounded by a great deal of contradictory argument and theoretical speculation, and by the cumulative legacy of more than a century's work in the canyon. Fortunately, Chaco boasts of a truly remarkable specialist literature, enshrined in books, edited volumes, and a great diversity of academic journals. The standard of technical publication is exceptionally high, even if the detail is sometimes downright mind-numbing even for the specialist. Some of the finest archaeological research in the world comes from Chaco Canyon and the San Juan Basin. It's been a pleasure to navigate through these academic waters, even if challenging shoals of controversy and strong disagreement beset one on many sides.

From the outset, I decided my story of Chaco would be straightforward, as we know it from the testimony of archaeology, the trowel, the spade, and the very latest in scientific technology. It's not, then, a story about archaeology or artifacts but a narrative of people going about their daily business, individuals and groups, living and dying, loving, raising children, living in plenty and in hunger, negotiating and quarreling with one another, pondering their cosmos, and facing the unpredictable challenges of drought. I draw on the researches of dozens of archaeologists and their writings in an attempt to tell a story of Chaco as a historical narrative based on archaeological research. This is a tale that obeys the Red Queen's advice to Alice: "Begin at the beginning, go on to the end, then stop!" And that is what I have done.

The story of Chaco is divided into four parts. Part 1, "A Canyon and Its Environs," introduces Chaco, tells the story of archaeology in the canyon, and describes the environment and climatic regimen of the San Juan Basin. The first three chapters provide the context of Chaco, for you cannot understand the canyon devoid of its history and setting. Part 2, "Beginnings," chapters 4 to 6, goes back to the earliest human occupation of the San Juan Basin, then describes the hunter-gatherer groups who visited Chaco for many millennia before farming began. Here, we'll meet the Basketmaker societies of the San Juan Basin and the first farming communities to settle by the Chaco Wash. Some remarkable archaeology has given us insights into societies that combined hunting and plant gathering with simple horticulture. Part 2 ends with the population movements that brought newcomers into Chaco and the beginnings of the great houses, a defining feature of Chacoan society. Movement, of individuals, households, and larger groups, is a pervasive element in Pueblo Indian philosophy and one of the dominant themes in the Chaco story.

Part 3, "Apogee," chapters 7 to 11, describes the dramatic events of the ninth to eleventh centuries, when Chaco's still little-known leaders presided over a rapidly growing society and an explosion in great house construction. We describe these developments through the lens of Pueblo Bonito, the greatest of all Chacoan great houses, excavated a century ago and now being reinvestigated with all the wizardry of contemporary science. It's easy to be mesmerized, indeed obsessed, with Chaco's great houses at the expense of the hundreds of households that built and supported them. Chaco teemed with smaller, inconspicuous settlements, unspectacular to look at and even less exciting to excavate. But the people who lived in them *were* Chaco, and were thus the engine that powered its growth. I have tried to redress a seeming imbalance in the story by stressing the importance of smaller Chacoan sites and of households, but if there is one aspect of Chaco that needs investigation, it is the smaller communities. Part 3 moves far beyond the boundaries of Chaco itself to examine the relationship between the canyon and the wider world of the San Juan Basin. Here, we explore the enigmatic roads that emanate from the great houses, the essential commodities and exotica that flowed into the canyon from afar, and the religious beliefs that may have sustained Chacoan society. Finally, I describe the lavish burials in the heart of Pueblo Bonito, which offer some clues about the identity of Chaco's shadowy leaders.

Part 4, "Movement," chapters 12 and 13, describes the readjustments in Chacoan society during the drought of AD 1130–1180, then takes us north of the San Juan River to a new center of gravity of Chaco culture at the Aztec and Salmon Ruins. By 1200, the northern San Juan prospers while the south is essentially depopulated. Then the great drought of 1280 descends on the northern Southwest, and the inhabitants of the pueblos of the Mesa Verde region respond by moving away to the south and east, where their descendants live today.

The Chaco story is a tale of people adapting to, and thriving in, one of the most demanding farming environments in the world. The Chacoans' lives were never easy, never predictable. This is a story of societies whose lives revolved around agriculture and religion, where the performance of ritual, of dance and chant, was as important as tilling the soil. Theirs was a world that required flexibility and patience, conservative farming methods, and an intimate knowledge of a harsh landscape. But in the final analysis, these remarkable Ancestral Pueblo societies knew that their rituals could not alter the eternal verities of localized, unreliable rainfall and severe drought cycles. Their greatness lay in their recognition of this fact, in their expertise at living within the limits of their world, and in their ability to recognize when it was time to move away. This is a story of strategies, successful and unsuccessful, of brilliant human opportunism, and versatility. We have much to learn from this story.

B. F.
Santa Barbara, California
August 2004

● ● ACKNOWLEDGMENTS

I am grateful to the participants in the Chaco Synthesis Project for their invitation to write this book, and for their ready acceptance of my conditions: the flexibility to find my own publisher and complete freedom to express my own viewpoints. I'm particularly appreciative of the support I've received from Steve Lekson, who directed much of the Project. He was able to find the subvention that allows the inclusion of a folio of color photographs in this book and was supportive at every turn, despite knowing that he and I are often in amiable disagreement. I have the highest respect for his archaeological expertise and profound knowledge of Chaco. I also wish to formally acknowledge a generous subvention from the National Park Service (NPS), Department of the Interior, for the color illustrations. The contents and opinions expressed in this book do not necessarily reflect the views or policies of the Department of the Interior.

My greatest debt is to Gwinn Vivian, widely acknowledged as one of the world's experts on Chaco Canyon. He was almost born there; his distinguished father, Gordon, worked in the canyon for many years. Gwinn has guided me to obscure (and not-so-obscure) references, and answered dozens of questions. He read the manuscript in first draft and corrected many factual sins. Obviously, we disagree on various points, but that has not inhibited a wonderful working relationship and a blossoming friendship. The least I can do is dedicate this book to him, and to the memory of his distinguished father.

This book went through a lengthy review process at draft stage. Steve Lekson, John Kantner, Joan Mathien, Lynne Sebastian, and Tom Windes read the entire manuscript and made trenchant and useful comments. Other specialists, too numerous to name, read selected chapters where their expertise was especially insightful. Dozens of colleagues and friends, some Chaco specialists, others involved with other fields, answered questions, guided me to references, and, on occasion, provided copies of unpublished work. I have a horror of long lists of acknowledgments, so I hope that they will accept a generic thank you. It has been a privilege working with such a close-knit and committed group of scholars.

Wendy Bustard was of immense help with the photographs for the book and opened the National Park Service Chaco Photographic Archives to me. Her assistance, and that of her assistant, John George, is gratefully acknowledged. Credits for individual photographs accompany the legends. I'm particularly glad to have had the opportunity to publish the Chaco work of George A. Grant, National Park Service photographer in the 1920s and 1930s, for the first time. Adriel Heisey took great pains to provide outstanding images from his aerial photographs of Chaco and its outliers taken from an ultralight aircraft.

On the literary side of things, Shelly Lowenkopf has been his usual critical and encouraging self. He was a wonderful sounding board, and he line edited the manuscript at draft stage. My debt to him is immense. Steve Brown drew the line art with his customary skill.

A word of thanks, too, to the editorial and production staff at Oxford University Press, New York, especially Elda Rotor and Cybele Tom, who have always been pillars of supportive encouragement. It was a pleasure working with them all. My wife, Lesley, and daughter, Ana, have lived patiently through the project, as have the rabbits and cats that add so much to our lives.

B. F.
Santa Barbara, California
September 2004

AUTHOR'S NOTE

All measurements are given in inches, feet, and miles, with metric equivalents.

Spellings of archaeological site names follow the normal usage in archaeological literature. Where there are differences, the most common spelling is used.

Place names are spelled according to current atlas usage.

The term Ancestral Pueblo is used in lieu of "Anasazi," commonly employed in archaeological literature.

Unless otherwise indicated, all radiocarbon dates are calibrated readings, following the convention of *Radiocarbon* 40(3), 1998. Following the academic literature on Chaco, the AD/BC convention is used.

∴ PART 1

A CANYON AND ITS ENVIRONS

There is no other place like Chaco. Some who go there find it remote, harsh, oppressive, and they leave quickly. Others return, pulled by a subtle yet unmistakable power captured within the canyon walls. Most acknowledge sensing the echo of those who once created a "Center Place" before time silenced their voices.

Gwinn Vivian and Bruce Hilpert[1]

1 ∴ MYSTERIOUS CHACO

Yellow butterflies,
Over the blossoming virgin corn,
    With pollen-painted faces
Chase each other in brilliant throng.

Korowista kachina song poem (Hopi)
translated by Natalie Curtis, c. 1906[2]

I walked upstream along the floor of the great canyon as the cool of evening
settled over Chaco. The sun cast the steep cliffs in deep relief. Pueblo
Bonito's weathered ruins glowed with a roseate orange as massing
clouds towered high above, dwarfing outcrop and site alike. As the
shadows lengthened, I gazed upward at the wide bowl of the heavens
and imagined the canyon nine hundred years ago. A chill wind sloughed
at my back as I sat down to enjoy the spectacular sunset. Chaco came
alive; I sensed the acrid scent of wood smoke carried on the evening
breeze, dogs barking at the setting sun. Flickering hearths and blazing
firebrands highlight dark windows and doorways on the terraces of the
great house that is Pueblo Bonito. People move between light and
shadow, dark silhouettes against the flames. The shrill cries of children
playing in the shadows, the quiet talk of men leaning against sun-baked
walls—the past comes alive in the gloaming. So does the most pervasive
sound of all: the scrape, scrape of dozens of grinders against dozens of
milling stones as the women prepare the evening meal.

The image faded as darkness fell, leaving Chaco in intense silence.
The brightly clothed visitors from our own world had long departed
in their cars. A few stars twinkled in the heavens overhead, but the

dark and stillness settled around me so tangibly that past and present seemed to merge. The ancient inhabitants of the canyon surrounded me and entered my consciousness, ancestral guardians of a once sacred place. They enticed me into their long-vanished world, into long winter nights where the dancers would perform underground in great kivas now open to the sky, wood smoke swirling from the fire as the chants and singing reached a crescendo. (Great kivas are large underground or semisubterranean structures with relatively standard floor features used for community-wide rituals.) I could imagine the nights when the fires at Pueblo Bonito and Chetro Ketl burned high, and the chants of the dancers echoed off the precipitous cliffs.

I sat for more than an hour in the dark as the past softly assaulted me with a vivid immediacy that I have rarely experienced during a lifetime as an archaeologist. Then I shivered in the chill, and the spell was broken.

Next morning I returned to my wandering, but the past was remote, almost beyond reach, a silent record of crumbling rooms and kivas open to the sky. It was as if no one had ever lived in the canyon. The ancient Chacoans had vanished on the wind, leaving only empty buildings behind them. I was reminded of the Victorian archaeologist Austen Henry Layard's memorable remark about his excavations of Assyrian cities in Mesopotamia: "The great tide of civilization has long since ebbed, leaving these scattered wrecks on the solitary shore. . . . We wanderers were seeking what they had left behind, as children gather up the coloured shells on the deserted sands."[3] Herein lies the great challenge of archaeology at Chaco—to assemble thousands of tiny clues into the story of a remarkable ancient society.

∴ ∴ ∴

From the air, Chaco Canyon appears to cut through the arid landscape like an arrow (see plate 1). On either side, the cliffs push northwest in sloping steps, defining the canyon and its great houses with dramatic flair. The zigzag meanders of the Chaco Wash wander across the flat floor like a giant serpent, shifting from side to side with downcuts that become shallower as you travel northwestward, downstream. The Wash and water seeping from the cliffs bring life to Chaco, where, for centuries, ancient farmers carved out a living from an unpredictable environment.

Chaco is a large canyon, dwarfed by the landscape on a grand scale that surrounds it—the vastness of the semiarid San Juan Basin, the hazy outline of the Chuska Mountains to the west, the scar of the Escavada

Wash flowing from the north and east to join the Chaco Wash at the western end of the canyon, and Huerfano Mountain crouching on the northern horizon. If you look closely, you can see traces of the ancient roads that emanated from Chaco, part of the much larger world of the canyon that once had cultural tentacles stretching to the far horizon and beyond. The visitor tends to linger within the familiar confines of Chaco itself, but this seemingly remote and isolated place once had an economic and spiritual power that extended far and wide.

Arriving by car, you come on the canyon suddenly, driving between high slopes pressing on the road. You emerge suddenly into another world, a flat valley defined by steep, golden cliffs and the deep gully of the Chaco Wash. The canyon floor itself is rather gentle, a place of soft colors, sand, and the subdued hues of sage and dried-up grass. Green is unusual, except in the patches of cottonwoods watered by the sporadic flow of the arroyo. You feel confined, yet high above the huge arc of the blue sky with its often towering white and gray thunderclouds brings hints of a much wider cosmos, of which Chaco was once a small part.

A walk in the canyon defines the heart of the Chaco world. You never forget the dramatic setting of steep, weathered cliffs that rise on either side. The southern-facing (actually southwestern) walls glow brilliantly in the late afternoon of summer, setting the side canyons in profound darkness. Deep shadows define the crumbling cliff faces, where huge chunks of sandstone teeter, ready to fall. The largest of all Chaco's great houses, Pueblo Bonito, backs up close to one such fractured, northern wall, as if awaiting its destruction by the forces of nature. At dawn, sunlight cascades into the canyon and brings less precipitous and much dissected southern cliffs into focus. In this direction, three distinctive mesas, flat-topped massifs, form the wall, separated by washes where small ancient house sites once flourished. These gaps brought precious water into the canyon during storms. You feel isolated from the outside world on the canyon floor, where unpredictable rainfall and patches of fertile soil defined existence. So too did complex rituals that commemorated the passing of the solstices, the seasons of planting and harvest, of life and death.

This is a place of remarkable beauty and stark dryness, where the ancient sites with their brown-hued walls seem to melt into their surroundings. You are almost upon them before you notice the serried rooms and crumbling walls of great houses vacated more than nine centuries ago.

AN ARCHAEOLOGICAL LANDSCAPE

The original Chaco Canyon National Monument covered some 32 square miles (83 sq km), but it is double that now. Chaco Canyon itself is, of course, much larger. Within the relatively small area of the old monument lie more than twenty-four hundred archaeological sites. Some of them are little more than a scatter of potsherds; others are the remains of small farming communities or agglomerations of a few stone-walled rooms. At the other end of the spectrum are the "great houses," also Chaco's spectacular kivas, which are world famous, dating to between the ninth and twelfth centuries AD. A walk through Chaco takes you through one of the most spectacular archaeological landscapes in North America. Small wonder some people call Chaco the "Stonehenge of America." I can only mention the highlights here; but it's important to visit at least one small settlement during your stay, as their less conspicuous houses form an integral part of Chaco's history.

Our walk downstream through the core of Chaco starts about halfway down (some 10 miles/16 km) from the head of the canyon and takes us first to the ruins of Pueblo Pintado (see plate 10), past other communities, then to the unexcavated ruins of Wijiji, nestled close to the north wall, one of the last great houses to be built in Chaco, between 1110 and 1115.[4] From there, you proceed to the confluence of the Fajada Gap, where the solid mass of Fajada Butte stands guard over one southern entrance to the canyon. As the floor opens up at Fajada, you pass the Gallo Wash and the ruins of two other great houses, Kin Nahasbas and adjacent Una Vida. The latter began as a small, slightly curved room block, then blossomed into a large arc of rooms after AD 930 (figure 1.1).

The weathered buildings are hard to see except at close quarters until you become familiar with the muted colors of the canyon floor, but after Una Vida your walk takes you into the heart of Chaco, past the most famous great houses of all, below the north wall. Hungo Pavi lies at the mouth of narrow Mockingbird Canyon. It shows how Chacoan great houses conformed to a basic pattern of growth, resulting in the classic D-shaped ground plan, with enclosed plaza and great kivas (see plate 7). This is an imposing structure that began in the early eleventh century as a narrow, rectangular complex of twenty-eight

---

Facing page
Figure 1.1a and b Maps showing archaeological sites in Chaco Canyon

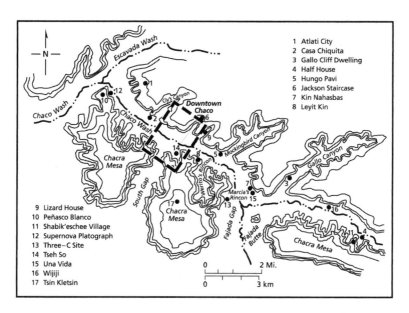

1 Atlati City
2 Casa Chiquita
3 Gallo Cliff Dwelling
4 Half House
5 Hungo Pavi
6 Jackson Staircase
7 Kin Nahasbas
8 Leyit Kin

9 Lizard House
10 Peñasco Blanco
11 Shabik'eschee Village
12 Supernova Platograph
13 Three–C Site
14 Tseh So
15 Una Vida
16 Wijiji
17 Tsin Kletsin

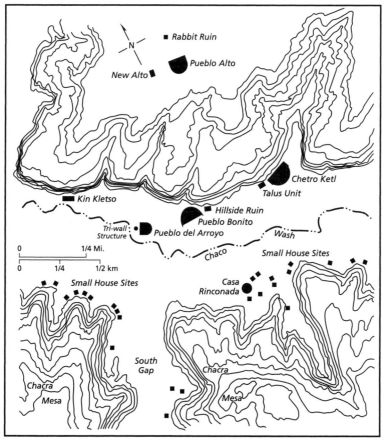

ground-floor rooms, with a second story above. Later on, the great house grew into a double row of two- and three-story rooms. A curved wall was added to the wings of the bracket shape, creating the D-shape and enclosing a plaza. The crumbled walls of today still stand 30 feet (9 m) high in places, and are up to 2.75 feet (.8 m) thick at the base.

One and three-quarter miles (2.8 km) downstream, you come to Chetro Ketl, a name of unknown meaning given to the site by a Mexican guide in the nineteenth century. This great house also began life as a rectangular room block, this time on the north side of an open space that eventually became an enclosed court (figure 1.2). You begin to acquire a sense of the scale of construction in Chaco's heyday—the straight north wall is over 450 feet (137 m) long, forming the long arm of an E-shaped great house. The long arm was constructed first. The entire structure has a circumference of 1,540 feet (469 m). A maze of kivas and other structures crowded the once-flat plaza in the heart of the site. A huge kiva 62.5 feet (19 m) in diameter, with benches, wall niches, and massive postholes for the roof supports, lies at the eastern end of the plaza. One of the pine logs survived for the excavators to find—26.5 inches (67 cm) in diameter, a huge timber to transport from

Figure 1.2   Chetro Ketl, looking southwest, in 1934. *Photograph by George A. Grant. Courtesy of NPS Chaco Canyon Historical Park. Negative 80076.*

afar into this treeless place. Chetro Ketl's fine masonry lies in magnificent courses of larger and thinner stone. One early archaeologist, Edgar Hewett, estimated that over fifty million blocks went into Chetro Ketl.

Chetro Ketl stands in the heart of Chaco, in what some archaeologists call "downtown Chaco," just upstream of Pueblo Bonito ("Beautiful Pueblo"), the most famous of all the great houses (figure 1.3; plates 1, 2, and 3). Pueblo Bonito was excavated in the early days of Southwestern archaeology. The work was adequate enough by the standards of the day, but the reports were inadequate, so any research there is a matter of careful detective work with old publications and incomplete field notes, piecing together a jigsaw of rooms, kivas, and construction styles. The best way to appreciate Pueblo Bonito is to look at it from above, standing on the cliffs overlooking the ancient town. There you can appreciate the semicircle of rooms pressing on the central plaza, the kivas that were an integral part of the site. It's a compact structure, with a south base line that measures more than 500 feet (152 m) and a maximum apex of 310 feet (94 m). We describe Pueblo Bonito's complicated history in chapters 7 and 8. Many kivas of various dates once lay in the plaza. As you wander among the ruins and the reconstructed

Figure 1.3   Pueblo Bonito in 1929. *Photograph by George A. Grant. Courtesy of NPS Chaco Canyon Historical Park. Negative 77420.*

rooms, you wonder how many people once lived at Pueblo Bonito. Some estimates are as high as a thousand, others a few dozen, except at times of major ceremonies and festivals. Herein lies one of the great Chaco controversies.

Across the canyon from Chetro Ketl and nearby Pueblo Bonito lies Casa Rinconada ("Corner House"), a great kiva dug into a sandstone and shale ridge bordering a dense cluster of small house sites (see plate 5). Casa Rinconada, built in the late 1070s, probably by great house masons, is more than 63 feet (19 m) in diameter. It displays all the standard great kiva features: an inner bench around the interior wall, a raised firebox, four pits for the great beams that supported the roof, and raised masonry vaults that served as foot drums (planks laid on them would resonate under a drummer's feet). Niches in the walls may once have held ritual objects. Rinconada has a unique 39-foot (12-m) underground passage that begins in a room in the northern antechamber and emerges in a narrow masonry trench sunk into the floor. It would have been possible for a dancer to make a dramatic appearance, seemingly from underground from this passage, if it were covered with planks or brush.

Clusters of small hamlets also lie opposite great houses throughout the canyon, from Pueblo Pintado to Peñasco Blanco, far downstream. No one knows how these two entities, the great house and the small settlement, functioned cohesively, one of the great mysteries of Chacoan society. Were the Chacoan great houses a form of public architecture, erected for specific political or religious purposes, or were they part of a much more complex social network that we have not yet deciphered? We simply don't know. But the association between great house and small sites extends over a much larger distance than just the very core of the canyon, so one cannot claim that it was unique to only a small area of Chaco.

Nine hundred and eight feet (276 m) downstream of Pueblo Bonito lies Pueblo del Arroyo opposite South Gap, begun in 1078, then expanded in a massive spurt after 1104–5 (see plate 6). Over the next quarter century, Pueblo del Arroyo developed into an E-shaped building, without the central limb, with a semicircular wall along the open side and the main block oriented north-to-south. The great house was multistoried, except for the front row of rooms, with the doorways perpendicular to the plaza.

On the bluff above Pueblo Bonito stands Pueblo Alto ("High Pueblo"), the most carefully documented of all Chaco's great houses (see plate 4). Several of Chaco's roads converge on the settlement, which lies at a central location, with easy access to the great houses below. Pueblo Alto is a single-story complex with eighty-nine rooms, eleven of which were excavated in the 1970s. Archaeologist Tom Windes found that only a few of Pueblo Alto's rooms were residential, as if the settlement had but few permanent inhabitants, perhaps as few as five households in the eleventh century, and twenty when the site was reused in the early twelfth century. Was Pueblo Alto a ritual link to the wide Chaco world? We do not know.

Our walk takes us next to Kin Kletso, one of the last great houses built in the canyon, between 1125 and 1130, which lies about half a mile (0.8 km) downstream of Pueblo Bonito (see plate 9). This compact, rectangular site backs up against the north wall, its simple masonry reminiscent of northern San Juan Basin pueblos. Some experts believe a community of northerners with a different architectural tradition moved into Chaco, perhaps dispersing some of its members into other great houses. Others attribute this difference to the availability of local limestone. The structure comprises two-room units, joined into a compact, rectangular building, with kivas nestling among the living spaces. Two of the original kivas had Chacoan features, but a two-story cylindrical room erected within a rectangular masonry enclosure over a huge boulder that served as the floor resembles a towerlike kiva typical of some great houses elsewhere than Chaco. There are no windows or openings, so the kiva looks like a solid rectangle attached to the second- and third-story house rooms at the west end of the site.

The Chaco Wash zigzags westward past Casa Chiquita, a small, late great house, again on the north side. Two miles (3.2 km) downstream, the Escavada Wash joins the Chaco on the north, overlooked by Peñasco Blanco ("White Bluff"), an unexcavated great house on the West Mesa, high above the canyon (see plate 8). Peñasco Blanco was founded between 898 and 917, an arc of eleven four-room suites built in tiers similar to those at Pueblo Bonito. The builders of Peñasco Blanco later added additional room blocks to create a great house with plaza and enclosure wall.

With Peñasco Blanco, we leave the heart of Chaco Canyon and its remarkable archaeological sites. The first time I walked from Wijiji to Peñasco Blanco, I became thoroughly confused by a jigsaw puzzle of different kinds of great houses and by the subtle differences in masonry and architectural styles. Just walking through the rooms at Pueblo Bonito left a sense of puzzlement. How many people lived in the great houses? Were all the suites at Pueblo Bonito occupied at the same time or was part of the site always unoccupied or under construction? Above all, what happened when? How and why did the great houses come into being? Even a short hike through Chaco makes the mystery seem even more profound, because the presence of small towns in this harsh landscape seems to strain credibility. Fascinating questions press upon the mind. How many people could agriculture in the canyon support? Did the great houses serve as vast granaries as well as community centers? The answers can come only from extremely detailed and taxing archaeological research, which elucidates such tricky questions as the sequence of room construction at Pueblo Bonito and the chronology of the different great houses.[5]

THE STORY OF CHACO

We have walked through a confusing palimpsest of great houses and smaller settlements, through a once densely populated canyon, depopulated abruptly in the early twelfth century AD. But Chaco's spectacular great houses and smaller hamlets are only part of a much longer history, which began thousands of years ago in the remote past, when the inhabitants of North America numbered in the few thousands (figure 1.4).

The foragers

Eleven thousand years ago, small bands of foragers flourished in the Southwest. A nomadic people, they subsisted on game large and small, and also off wild plant foods. We archaeologists call them Paleo-Indians, but know little about them, for they left an exiguous signature behind them. We know they traveled long distances in search of fine toolmaking stone. They made distinctive stone spear points, their bases thinned by removing a shallow, longitudinal flake on either side, so that the point could fit into the wooden shaft. These "Clovis" points, named after a Paleo-Indian site in eastern New Mexico, have never been found in Chaco Canyon, so we don't know whether Clovis people or later Paleo-Indians foraged in the vicinity.

For thousands of years, mere handsful of people lived in the San Juan Basin, constantly on the move in search of widely scattered plant foods. But the San Juan was an edible landscape, with all kinds of grasses, tubers, and edible nuts distributed at various altitudes and ripening at different seasons. The most valuable resource was permanent water—perennial rivers, springs, and small lakes—strategic places that served as the anchors for people on the move, especially during the dry months. Geomorphological studies of Chaco tell us that on

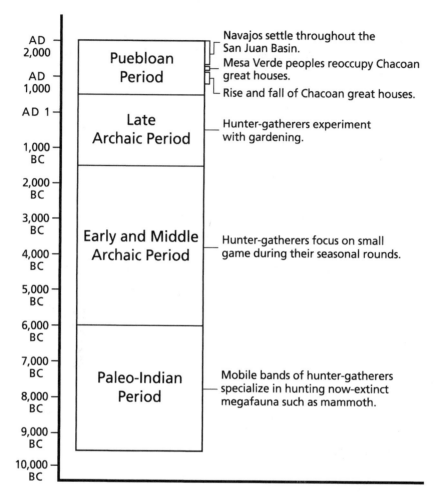

Figure 1.4   Generalized chronological table of developments at Chaco Canyon.

several occasions in the remoter past, a wind-accumulated sand dune blocked the mouth of the canyon, forming a shallow lake behind it. We know climatic conditions between about 3650 and 450 BC were dry, but nevertheless somewhat wetter than today. But, by two thousand years ago, the climate was more or less the same as today, with unpredictable cycles of wetter and much drier years. These rainfall shifts played a central role in Chaco's history.

Over many millennia, occasional visitors arrived at Chaco during the summer rains as part of their annual movements across large hunting territories. They were opportunists whose lives followed the constantly changing distributions of game and plant foods. These were conservative people; they had to be, for they had to adjust constantly to unpredictable conditions in a harsh land. The chronicle of their lives comprises little more than scatters of stone spear points and milling stones used to grind wild seeds and other plant foods. These people, known to archaeologists as members of the Oshara Tradition, scattered over an enormous area of north-central New Mexico and farther afield, were the remote, primordial ancestors of the Pueblo farmers of Chaco. They, in turn, may have been descendants of ancient Paleo-Indian groups well before 5500 BC. There was a deep historical continuity at Chaco throughout its history, going back to the earliest millennia of human settlement in the Americas.

The hunter-gatherers of the San Juan Basin foraged for foods of all kinds—piñon nuts at higher elevations, wild grasses on dune ridges, in river valleys, and on the banks of washes, and tubers and roots of all kind. They could read the landscape as though it were an edible encyclopedia, the subtle indicators of changing seasons when certain flowers bloomed or shrubs changed color. The very act of gathering vegetable foods led to unintentional tending of plants. Accidental seed dispersal and trampling of wild grasses can propagate more growth. Deliberate gathering of larger seeds at the expense of smaller ones could have unexpected genetic consequences, selecting against less desirable traits. These changes in plant genetics can be maintained over time, even if intensive human exploitation ceases. Long before maize and bean agriculture spread into the Southwest from Mexico, the people who visited Chaco Canyon had an encyclopedic knowledge of edible and medicinal plants of every kind.

The staffs of life

Some seven thousand years ago, hunter-gatherer groups in southern Mexico habitually gathered large crops of a tough, indigenous grass, teosinte (*Zea mexicana*), which grows in the region to this day.[6] This inconspicuous grass was the wild ancestor of maize. Teosinte has long branches tipped with tassels; its domesticated descendant, maize, has short branches tipped with ears. Over many centuries, the people harvesting teosinte may have gathered seeds of the preferred form, rejecting others that were less desirable. The repeated harvesting led to selective pressures for more harvestable forms of teosinte, where the original spiky branches shrank into more readily harvestable bunches, which made it hard for the seeds to scatter when ripe. As the hunter-gatherers began selective harvesting and planting these transitional forms, the grass became dependent on human intervention and genetic revolution followed. The qualities that made harvesting easier had a selective advantage. Thus was born *Zea mays*, Indian corn, the staff of life for Native American societies from the St. Lawrence River Valley to tropical South America.

Maize rapidly became a staple over much of Central America and flourished in northern Mexico long before it appeared in the Southwest, which is hardly surprising. Corn cultivation requires living in one place for long periods of the year, something incompatible with the nomadic existence of hunter-gatherers in an arid environment like the Southwest. We can assume that there were sporadic contacts with farming communities to the south, which meant that knowledge of maize, even gifts of seeds or seedlings, could have passed north into the hands of people who were well aware that a seed germinates when planted. The opportunity for adopting the crops existed long before anyone thought it worth doing so. But domesticated plants such as maize had one major advantage: they might not be highly productive, but they were predictable. The cultivator controlled the location and the availability of maize at different seasons by storing the crop. In an environment like the San Juan Basin with its uncertain rainfall and highly variable productivity, there were obvious reasons to cultivate maize in favored locations like Chaco with irregular but sometimes sufficient water and fertile soils. One could argue that the San Juan people accepted crops in order to become more effective foragers, not because they wanted to become farmers.

By 2000 BC, the human population of the Southwest generally had risen gradually—to the point where there may not have been enough food to go around, especially during the critical months at the end of winter and the beginning of spring. These may have been the circumstances under which maize cultivation took hold in societies with an expertise with plant foods and a toolkit of grinders and milling stones ideal for grinding not only wild seeds but corn as well.

The maizes that entered the Southwest were adapted to arid conditions.[7] The first corn to come north was the so-called *Chapalote* form, a small-kernel popcorn of great genetic diversity. This hardy, low-yielding form may have arrived in Zuni country to the southwest of Chaco Canyon as early as 1800 BC, being well established in the central and eastern Southwest during the first millennium BC. A radically different maize, *Maiz de Ocho*, was, however, the key to agriculture in later centuries. *Maiz de Ocho* is adapted to dry conditions and yields large, more productive, flowery kernels that are easily milled. No one knows exactly when *Maiz de Ocho* came into use in the Southwest, but, judging from kernels from southern New Mexico, it was by at least 1000 BC.

Even with larger-kerneled *Maiz de Ocho*, *Zea mays* is at the northern limits of its range in the San Juan Basin. Maize is intolerant of too-short growing seasons and weak soils, and vulnerable to crop diseases and strong winds. Soil moisture and regular water supplies were all-important in environments like the San Juan region, where the landscape was at best semiarid. Only a few locations allowed sustained maize cultivation. Chaco Canyon was sometimes one of them—as long as there was sufficient rainfall, but even then it was a challenge. Anyone who farmed in the San Juan Basin had to become an expert at seed selection, at choosing the right soils for cultivation, those with good moisture-retaining properties on north- and east-facing slopes that received somewhat less direct sunlight (figure 1.5). The farmers favored arroyo mouths and floodplains where the soil was naturally irrigated. They could divert water from streams, seepages, and springs to irrigate their crops. They were in the business of risk management, which was nothing new, because their ancestors had always lived conservatively, with many wild famine foods to tide them over from one summer to the next. The cultivators reduced risk by dispersing their gardens widely from one another to minimize the dangers of local drought or flood. They planted in different microenvironments, at diverse elevations, in any way they could devise to shorten the growing season and avoid severe heat. Few ancient farmers anywhere were as adept and resourceful as those who cultivated the soils of the San Juan Basin and its margins along the Chuska Mountains and elsewhere.

Two other crops completed the agricultural triad that formed the foundations of Southwestern agriculture. Squashes arrived in the Southwest by 1000 BC. They were used not only for containers but were also harvested for their seeds and fruit. Common beans appeared some centuries later and rapidly became a staple. They were an important crop, especially when grown with maize, for the two complement each other. Beans have a high lysine content, which aids in the effective digestion of the protein in corn. Furthermore, beans are legumes and can return vital nitrogen to soils that are depleted by maize. By growing maize and beans in the same gardens, Chaco farmers could maintain the fertility of the soil for longer periods. If we are correct in saying that beans arrived later than maize, this may be one reason why a considerable period of time elapsed between the first appearance of maize and significant dependence on agriculture.

Figure 1.5   Hopi maize field. *Photograph by William Bromberg, 1961.*
Courtesy of NPS Chaco Canyon Historical Park. Negative 100289.

By 200 BC, Southwestern hunter-gatherer groups everywhere had become less mobile as they adopted at least part-time cultivation. The sedentary way of life developed over many centuries, partly because agriculture was high risk in a region of such unpredictable rainfall. Cultivated food supplies may have varied more than wild plants and game did, restricting people in their movements. As time went on, every community relied more heavily on efficient storage and large storage pits to guard against shortages. Large villages appear in some numbers for the first time after AD 600, communities of individual oval-to-circular houses, often partially sunk in the ground to provide better insulation against extremes of cold and heat.

These early village communities, sometimes still grouped under the loosely defined archaeological term "Basketmaker," flourished throughout the northern Southwest.[8] Their culture owed much to earlier times, but soon the simple milling artifacts of the past developed into more elaborate slabs and troughlike grinders, worked with *manos* that required two hands to process maize more efficiently. Bows and arrows appeared for the first time. With more sedentary living came the first clay containers in about AD 200, vessels that allowed the farmers to boil stored maize and beans to maximize their nutritional value. Archaeologists bless this innovation, for changing pottery styles are a wonderful barometer of cultural changes in Southwestern sites. Pottery was commonplace throughout the Southwest within two centuries.

In the San Juan Basin and at higher elevations, the earliest villagers lived in pithouses, dwellings where part of the walls were formed from the sides of a pit excavated below ground, a thermally efficient way of heating or cooling them. Most were about 16.4 feet (5 m) across, their floors at least 1.6 feet (0.5 m) below ground. A framework of vertical poles set around the pit and stout posts supported a timber and brush roof. Sometimes low adobe walls or upright sandstone slabs subdivided the interior into kitchen and living areas, which could boast of sleeping platforms, or perhaps sacred space from less sacred space. Some of the villages were little more than two or three houses. Others contained as many as forty or more, with Shabik'eshchee Village in Chaco Canyon, with its many pithouses and well-built storage bins, among the largest with maybe as many as one hundred to one hundred fifty houses (see chapter 5).

This is the point, around AD 500, at which the story of Chaco Canyon really begins.

CHACO BLOSSOMS

The earliest well-documented Chaco farmers are Basketmaker people, known from their baskets and sandals, left in caves and rockshelters throughout the northern Southwest. Traces of their presence appear in Atlatl Cave in Chaco and at a few other places (see chapter 4, figure 4.4). These were semisedentary farmers, whose presence in the canyon is shadowy at best.

The portrait comes into focus in about AD 490, when Basketmaker farming began at Chaco in earnest, with the development of forms of maize well suited to local conditions. Two large striplike communities flourished on the mesa overlooking the Wash. The largest was Shabik'eshchee Village, a settlement of forty to sixty pithouses (see chapter 5, figure 5.1). The settlement clustered around a large kiva, which was the center of social and religious activities. The inhabitants were part-time farmers who stored their surplus corn and beans in storerooms (known to Chaco archaeologists as "cists") behind their pithouses.

By 750 to 800, the Chaco people enlarged their stone-lined store-rooms and linked them in rows of four or five behind their pithouses. Some time later, they erected shelters over the work areas in front of the storage compartments. Some generations afterward, the owners filled in the sides of the work areas with masonry, forming three-room residential units, actually suites, comprising a living room with two storage areas at the rear. The above-ground, three-room suites with kivas in front, occupied by nuclear families, became the building blocks for Pueblo architecture in the canyon and elsewhere for many centuries. By AD 800, the larger communities, almost all outside the canyon, had become crescent-shaped room blocks made up of four or five three-room suites, fronting on two or more subterranean kivas, the last vestiges of pithouses.

Small room blocks marked Pueblo communities throughout the Four Corners region by AD 800, even if they differed slightly from one area to the next. At a few sites on the north side of Chaco, the small room blocks of yesteryear became two- or three-story structures of fifty or more rooms. The builders now terraced the rows of rooms from north to south, so that everyone had the benefit of the winter sun.

At first the new architecture was tentative. On the south side, the farmers still lived in small room blocks, like those of their ancestors. The building of Chaco's great houses began during the ninth century. No one knows why such different structures rose on one side of the canyon and not the other. The archaeologist Gwinn Vivian has argued that the topographic and hydrological differences on the two sides of the canyon were conducive to two types of farming—dry farming using all manner of microenvironments near the south wall, and irrigated farming with densely packed gridded fields on the north side.[9] (There were some exceptions: some ditches and fields lie by Casa Rinconada on the south side.) This required different forms of agricultural labor, both dispersed and more focused, and hence both more dispersed communities and more nucleated ones. Whatever the merits of Vivian's hypothesis, by this time many more people were living within Chaco, requiring more sophisticated, more productive agricultural methods to feed more families. Were the newcomers immigrants escaping drought to the north during the 800s? Herein lies another of Chaco Canyon's most profound mysteries.

By 850 the Chaco population was growing rapidly. The canyon farmers must have been using more productive agricultural methods to feed themselves, perhaps diverting water from runoff over the cliffs during summer storms using dikes and ditches. It may be no coincidence that the three earliest great houses rose near major tributaries of the Chaco Wash. Whatever the methods used, agricultural productivity certainly increased. During the 900s, Pueblo Bonito mushroomed into an arced great house with three stories and over fifty rooms. Peñasco Blanco downstream grew rapidly into another arced structure, this time of sixty-five rooms. Una Vida also became an important great house.

The 1020s saw much more ambitious building programs that must have been planned for the long-term. The arcs of Pueblo Bonito were remodeled into rectangular lines during the 1050s. Three new great houses with now angular floor plans rose along a 6-mile (9.6 km) stretch of the north wall, also Pueblo Alto on the mesa to the north. Over a period of twenty years, hundreds of people quarried building stone from the cliffs above the canyon. The builders of the great houses moved from one site to the next, building major additions at Chetro Ketl, Pueblo Alto, and Hungo Pavi through time, resulting in almost constant building activity. The construction was a collaborative effort, planned carefully in advance, carried out without disrupting the seasonal routines of agriculture.

By this time, Chaco Canyon had become part of a much larger economic and social world. The building of the great houses required enormous numbers of tree trunks and timbers from distant forests, among them those in the Chuska Mountains to the west. The people imported fine painted pottery from afar, too. No less than 85 percent of the late eleventh-century clay vessels at Pueblo Alto came from outside the canyon.

All this elaboration required leadership and coordination, at least by a small number of people. Who these individuals were remains a mystery. Were they powerful chiefs, who governed a hierarchical society quite unlike any other in the Southwest of the day? Were they priests or tribal elders? Was this a society so distinctive and influential that its identity was known far from the canyon, an identity that the archaeologist Gwinn Vivian has aptly called "We the Chaco"? The nature of the society that engaged in these stupendous building activities is one of the greatest archaeological controversies over Chaco Canyon.

By the late eleventh century, several of Chaco's great houses had achieved their final D-shape, their plazas enclosed with an arc of rooms, kivas added. Each was unique, but they were all built according to a general convention that extended throughout the canyon. Now Chaco's influence had spread far beyond the confines of the canyon itself. Small and medium-sized great houses rose in many areas of the San Juan Basin, some as much as 120 miles (193 km) from the canyon, usually surrounded by small house sites and associated with a great kiva. A remarkable system of carefully constructed roads radiated out from Chaco toward these outliers, passing in straight lines across mesas and dry water courses, even up steep cliffs (see chapter 10, figures 10.4a and b). In places, four parallel sections of roads lie no more than 60 yards (55 m) apart. Some outliers had four-story tower kivas, conspicuous on the horizon, thought by some to have served as signal stations along the roads. The roads are incomplete, often hard to trace, and, on occasion, end in the middle of nowhere. Despite lengthy surveys and much scholarly debate, we do not know whether the roads were actual highways or simply symbolic paths that linked Chaco with a wider world sometimes claimed to be so large that it covered more than 60,000 square miles (155,388 sq km) in the early twelfth century.

The 1080s were when Chaco reached its zenith, at a time when a new generation of great houses rose in the canyon. New Alto, Kin Kletso, and Casa Chiquita, and many outlier great houses, were great houses with enclosed plazas but were really compact squares or rectangles, much smaller than their predecessors and built in a new architectural style without plazas, with the kivas among the rooms, using squarer blocks instead of the veneer of earlier times. But the Salmon site on the San Juan and the Aztec great houses on the Animas River, built at this time, were nearly as large as Pueblo Bonito and other classic Chaco great houses. The layouts conformed to the classic D-shaped ground plan at Chaco, at a time when there was a shift toward rectangular or square buildings.

READJUSTMENT

Chaco's influence expanded rapidly in the early 1100s. Then, seemingly at the height of its power, the Chacoans adjusted to new environmental conditions with astounding rapidity. By 1150 the canyon's great houses were empty. A modest population remained in the canyon until 1175–1200, but these inhabitants eventually left. Chaco's population scattered in all directions. Some moved north, to relocate in the Mesa Verde region and near the San Juan. Others, with their cherished oral traditions of Chaco, settled in pueblo communities along the Rio Grande, or at Acoma, Zuni, and Hopi, where their descendants live to this day.

The Chaco readjustment was one of the great controversies of American archaeology, until sophisticated research using ancient tree rings from living trees and ancient beams revealed the harsh realities of an epochal drought that settled over the San Juan Basin and the canyon between 1130 and 1170. Chaco's farmers were conservative and capable of surviving one, or even two bad drought years. But this particular drought persisted year after year. Agriculture became impossible to sustain, social obligations hard to maintain. Soon the outlying communities ceased to trade and share food with the canyon's great houses, forcing them to rely on their own already overstressed environment. The only recourse was one deeply ingrained in Pueblo philosophy even today—movement, using ties of kin to relocate in better-watered areas.

By the early 1700s, Navajo families settled within what had once been the Chaco world, close to the deserted canyon and great houses. Shortly afterward, in 1774, Chaco Canyon appeared on a Spanish map as an enigmatic place, named *Chaca*. It was not until 1823 that José Antonio Vizcarra, governor of New Mexico, rode into the canyon and drew the attention of the outside world to the desert great houses, "which are of such antiquity that their inhabitants were not known to Europeans." With his brief visit, the modern history of Chaco Canyon began.[10]

Now, two centuries later, we know much about the Ancestral Pueblos of Chaco Canyon, the chronology of their settlements, their technology, their great towns, and their architecture. But many questions remain. How did they manage to prosper in such a harsh, unpredictable environment? Who was responsible for the construction of the great houses and extended the influence of this remarkable place over such large distances? Was Chaco a great ritual center or a market place, or a symbolic hub of a much larger world? What was the relationship between the people of the canyon and those who lived in outlying communities? Above all, what was Chaco: A great civilization with connections as far away as Mexico, a truly unique Pueblo society with a system of governance unlike any other in the Southwest, or simply an isolated population of Pueblo farmers, who developed a distinctive way of adapting to the realities of their unusual environment—"We the Chaco"? There are myriad, and often conflicting answers to these questions, which we will explore. And herein lies the special fascination of Chaco Canyon.

2 ⋮ EXPLORERS, TREASURE
HUNTERS, AND
ARCHAEOLOGISTS

> This is Chaco Canyon, whose immense ruined
> pueblos, great kivas, earthen mounds, roads, and
> irrigation works have drawn the attention of schol-
> ars, tourists, vandals, and mystics for 150 years.
>
> Lynne Sebastian, 1992[1]

Every generation creates its own images of a famous place in the context of
its own times. Chaco Canyon is no exception. Archaeologists and explorers have puzzled over Chaco for more than two centuries. Their
adventures, ideas, and researches fill many bookshelves and the pages
of innumerable scientific journals. For better or worse, we live with their
legacy, some of it the result of casual observation and curiosity, some of
it little more than unscrupulous rummaging, much of it high-minded
research. Our own visions of the canyon and its ancient inhabitants are
defined in part by the explorations and researches of our predecessors.
We begin our exploration with their adventures and perceptions.

Few people inhabited the San Juan Basin at the time of the Spanish
entrada into the Southwest in 1540. Pueblo peoples had largely moved
out of the region two centuries before. Only handfuls of Navajo lived
near Chaco, mainly on the highlands to the northeast. As far as is
known, no Spanish explorers or military expeditions entered the Basin
until the late eighteenth century.[2]

There were vague echoes of the place. In about 1774, cartographer
Bernardo de Miera y Pacheco drew a map of the Spanish possessions
in New Mexico. Pacheco was a respected mapmaker, so much so that
he accompanied two Franciscan friars, Fray Atanasio Dominguez and

Silvestre Vélez de Escalante, on an abortive journey of exploration from New Mexico to Monterey on the Pacific coast two years later. His 1774 map marks the location of what we now call Chaco Canyon with a single word: *Chaca*. Almost certainly the two friars and their mapmaker never visited the canyon.

In 1823 José Antonio Vizcarra, governor of the Mexican province of New Mexico, entered Chaco with a small military party during a campaign against the Navajo. He was in a hurry and contented himself with the observation that the great houses were built by people unknown to Europeans.

The first published reference to the canyon comes from a popular writer, Josiah Gregg, who referred to the Chaco pueblos in his widely read book, *Commerce of the Prairies*, in 1844. He attributed the Casa Grandes ruins, the Hopi settlements, and Chaco to "founders" descended from Aztecs.[3] In this, he was merely following popular legend of the day.

JAMES HERVEY SIMPSON AT CHACO

By the 1840s, the Corps of Topographical Engineers of the United States Army was actively exploring and surveying the West. General Stephen Watts Kearny took over New Mexico for the United States in 1846. In early 1849, thirty-six-year-old Lieutenant James Hervey Simpson, a West Point graduate and topographical engineer, was assigned to the Navajo Expedition under Colonel John M. Washington, mounted "to make a movement against the Navajo Indians," who were attacking settlers. Simpson was charged with "making such a survey of the country as the movements of the troops will permit."[4] Fortunately for archaeology, Simpson was a methodical observer who kept a journal. He was accompanied by the Kern brothers—Richard, an artist, and Edward, a cartographer.

The party traveled southward from Santa Fe, mustered more volunteers at Jemez Pueblo, and passed onto "prairielike and rolling" terrain. They crossed the Continental Divide and then descended onto lower ground—into the Chaco Drainage. Five miles (8 km) farther on, they sighted "a conspicuous ruin" on "a slight elevation." Carravahal, the expedition's Mexican guide, called it Pueblo Pintado, "painted village," a name adopted by Simpson and used to this day (figure 2.1).[5] Colonel Washington pitched camp nearby, so Simpson and the Kerns had a chance for a leisurely examination.

Figure 2.1   Richard Kern's drawing of Pueblo Pintado, 1849. *Courtesy of NPS Chaco Canyon Historical Park. Negative 101391.*

The pueblo formed "one structure," and was "built of tabular pieces, of hard, fine-grained compact gray sandstone . . . to which the atmosphere has imparted a reddish tinge." The thin layers of masonry gave an impression of "a combination of science and art which can only be referred to a higher stage of civilization and refinement than is discoverable in the worlds of Mexicans or Pueblos of the present day." Simpson counted fifty-four "apartments" and commented on their small doorways, also the lattices of untrimmed roof beams that he imagined to have been covered with brush, bark, or stone slabs, then smothered with mortar. "At different points about the premises three circular apartments were sunk into the ground, the walls being of masonry. These apartments the Pueblo Indians call *estuffas* [kivas], or places where the people held their political and religious meetings." Darkness had fallen before they finished their examination, so they returned next day while the troops rode ahead. They dug hastily by the foundations, and commented on the brightly colored potsherds scattered on the ground, "the colors showing taste in their selection and in the style of their arrangement, and being still quite bright."

The expedition followed the Chaco Wash into what they called the Cañon de Chaco. Almost at once, they spotted "numerous small deserted and masonry habitations" within the sandstone cliffs, pausing at what Carravahal called Pueblo Weje-gi (now Wijiji) (figure 2.2). He did not have time to examine the pueblo thoroughly, except to appreciate the

Figure 2.2   Wijiji. *Photograph by Fred Wang, 1979. Courtesy of NPS Chaco Canyon Historical Park. Negative 765.*

fine view of the canyon with its rugged cliffs that seemed to converge in the far distance. Then Fajada Butte burst into sight, a striking mesa that Simpson greatly admired as the soldiers pitched camp in the heart of the canyon.

Next morning, Simpson and Robert Kern received permission to travel farther down the canyon while the troops took a more circuitous route. Carravahal and seven mounted Mexican soldiers accompanied them in a search for "more ruins of an interesting character." Two Native American guides went along, one from Jemez, and a Navajo named Sandoval, who provided Navajo names for the sites. A short distance down-canyon, they came to Una Vida ("A Life"), so named by their guide. There were at least four kivas, and two, if not more, room stories. One-and-a-half miles (2.4 km) farther downstream lay Hungo Pavi, where they counted seventy-two rooms on the ground floor.

Just under two miles (3.2 km) beyond lay yet another large pueblo that Carravahal named Pueblo Chettro Kettle (now Chetro Ketl), where Simpson counted at least 124 rooms on the ground floor, with walled-up windows, six kivas, and at least four stories stacked one upon the other. One room was remarkably well preserved. "The stone walls still have their plaster upon them. . . . The ceiling showed two main beams, laid transversely; on these, longitudinally, were a number of smaller ones in juxtaposition, the ends being tied together by a species of wooden fibre, and the interstices chinked in with small stones; on these again, transversely, in close contact, was a kind of lathing of the odor and appearance of cedar."[6] Several short lengths of rope hung from the beams.

Only a few hundred yards downstream was yet another large pueblo, destined to become the most famous of all the Chacoan great houses. This was Pueblo Bonito ("beautiful village"), the best preserved of Chaco's pueblos. Simpson had a passion for accurate measurement and precision. He counted 139 rooms on the ground floor but estimated there were once as many as 200. He located four kivas, dug deep into the ground and nicely walled with thin blocks of tabular stone. The masonry in many of the rooms was skillfully wrought with "alternate beds of large and small stones, the regularity of the combination producing a very pleasing effect."[7]

By this time the sun was low in the west, so there was little time to explore Pueblo del Arroyo a short distance farther on, or Pueblo de Peñasca Blanca (Peñasco Blanco) with its fine-banded masonry, "the largest pueblo in plan we have seen." Simpson's hectic day of observations involved not only 23 miles (37 km) of riding but also the examination of four large pueblos.

MONTEZUMA

Who, then, had constructed the pueblos? One common legend had it that Montezuma of the Aztecs was responsible, a tale so widespread that the Pueblo Indians themselves uttered it. Whether this was out of a desire to protect their own institutions from close scrutiny or from genuine belief is unknown. The Montezuma legend probably traveled north with Spanish colonists to become entwined with a universal Pueblo cultural hero, Poseyemu, identified with fertility and rain—the central concerns of the Pueblo world. According to Josiah Gregg, Montezuma was especially associated with Pecos Pueblo near Santa Fe, where he had instructed the people to keep a perennial fire going in one of the kivas "until he would return to deliver his people from the yoke of the Spaniards." The Montezuma legends gave Chaco and other pueblos a pervasive link to Mesoamerica, which still haunts

Chacoan archaeology to this day.[8] Then there were the Welsh under Prince Madoc, said to have colonized a "western land," a legend that came with British colonists to North America and somehow percolated to the Southwest.[9] Legends of Montezuma and the Welsh persisted until the late nineteenth century, in an era when almost nothing was known of Southwestern Indian culture, history, or archaeology.

WILLIAM HENRY JACKSON

After the end of the Civil War, a number of the civilian and military surveys included provisions for studying Native American groups in their "natural" state. Ferdinand Vandiveer Hayden, geologist, paleontologist, and physician, oversaw important surveys in Nebraska and Colorado, where his party included a teamster-and-stock-driver-turned-photographer, William Henry Jackson (1843–1942). Jackson became a celebrated chronicler of the West. He photographed Yellowstone; his photographs helped establish the nation's first national park. In 1873 Jackson visited Mancos Canyon in southwestern Colorado, where he described and photographed numerous "cliff dwellings," as well as stand-alone sites like Aztec Springs and Hovenweep. His photographs were a sensation at the Philadelphia Centennial Exhibition of 1876, while

Figure 2.3   W. H. Jackson's reconstruction of Pueblo Bonito, 1877. *Courtesy of NPS Chaco Canyon Historical Park. Negative 59499.*

his reports passed the term "Cliff Dweller" into common archaeological usage. Jackson came to Chaco Canyon in 1877 to photograph the ruins and to measure them with a view to making further models of the great houses (figure 2.3). He climbed out of the canyon, up "a line of steps and handholes hewn out of the rock, back of the Pueblo Chetro Kettle [*sic*] by which I easily gained the summit."[10] Today, the stairway is named after him (see figure 10.2).

RICHARD WETHERILL AT CHACO

Four years later a Quaker family, Benjamin Kite Wetherill, his wife, Marion, daughter Anna, and four sons arrived in the Mancos Valley of southwestern Colorado. They homesteaded land along the Mancos, running cattle in Mancos Canyon and atop the nearby Mesa Verde. The sons saw many archaeological sites as they tended their herds, and began exploring for others, having heard tales of "big ruins, high in the rocks" of the mesa. On a snowy December day in 1888, Richard Wetherill and Charles Mason, the husband of Anna Wetherill, saw a large ruin at the foot of a steep canyon cliff, climbed up to it, and named it the Cliff Palace, now one of the most famous archaeological sites in North America. Richard and John Wetherill created an informal partnership to dig for artifacts in the Cliff Palace and other Mesa Verde ruins. Burdened with a heavy mortgage, the Wetherills expanded their collecting activities and guided tourists to the Cliff Palace, among them a Swedish tourist and collector, Gustav Nordenskiöld, who assembled a large collection with the help of the Wetherills. By this time, there was considerable public outcry about the selling and export of artifacts from the pueblos, but, at the time, there was no legislation that forbade it. Back in Sweden, Nordenskiöld published his excavations and field notes in *The Cliff Dwellers of the Mesa Verde*, released in Swedish in 1893 and in English soon afterward. His scientific monograph (it was nothing less) set a standard for the next twenty years, with detailed studies of architecture and pottery—all artifacts from the sites. As Don Fowler points out, Nordenskiöld thought of the finds as documents of history, not just as curios. He was years ahead of his time and is one of the unsung heroes of Southwestern archaeology.[11]

In October 1895, Richard Wetherill and another Quaker family, the Palmers from Burdett, Kansas, traveled to Chaco Canyon. They spent a month exploring, also doing some digging in Pueblo Bonito and elsewhere with such productive results that Wetherill wrote to the Hyde brothers in Chicago, the wealthy sons of a prominent New York physician who had visited Mesa Verde with their father in 1892. The Hyde brothers and Wetherill had already formed the Hyde Exploring Expedition, with the two siblings providing the financial support. Their only condition was that the finds and site notes be deposited in the American Museum of Natural History in New York. In late 1893, and with Hyde backing, Wetherill and others had worked in the Grand Gulch region north of the San Juan, where they found human skeletons in a cave buried over 3 feet (1 m) below Cliff Dweller occupation. The people made no pottery but were expert basketmakers, were "a larger race" than the Cliff Dwellers, and possessed no bows and arrows. Talbot Hyde suggested that Wetherill call them Basket Makers, a name that Wetherill disliked, but it remains in use, as Basketmakers, today.

Excited by Wetherill's reports of Chaco, but anxious for their expedition to be a serious endeavor, they approached another archaeologist, Frederic Ward Putnam, recently appointed Curator of Anthropology at the American Museum, to lead it. Putnam agreed to be a nominal leader but did not visit the canyon until 1899. He put his assistant, twenty-three-year-old George Pepper, in charge in the field. George Herbert Pepper (1873–1924) was a brisk and witty man, filled with relentless optimism. He arrived at Mancos with "two cameras, a small truck filled with stationary and notebooks, the kindly instructions of Professor Putnam, and his own determination to make a name for himself."[12] He had absolutely no archaeological experience whatsoever, except for some youthful arrowhead collecting on Long Island.

Wetherill set up camp against the back wall of Pueblo Bonito (figure 2.4), while Pepper supervised local Navajos, who did the hard work.[13] The excavators searched for rich trash mounds and human burials. Two trenches across middens at Pueblo Bonito yielded little, so Pepper moved across the canyon to the area around Casa Rinconada. He unearthed thirty burials from small house site trash heaps near the kiva, but little else. Back at Pueblo Bonito, he trenched into the northern precincts. By the end of the season, Pepper and Wetherill had cleared thirty-seven rooms and recovered a railroad freight car full of artifacts. In one room in what we now know to be the oldest part of the great house, he found a large cache of clay vessels—114 jars and 22 bowls. Some burials with effigy figures, carved wooden wands, and a basket covered with an elaborate turquoise mosaic, came from nearby rooms. Inside the basket lay large numbers of turquoise beads and pendants, also nearly 4,000 shell beads and pendants. Wetherill was paid $600 for the season and complained that he lost money.

Figure 2.4 Pueblo Bonito in 1897. The Hyde Exploring Expedition Camp is by the back wall of the ruin. *Courtesy Department of Library Services, American Museum of Natural History, New York. Negative 412026.*

Over three more busy seasons, Pepper and Wetherill cleared rooms at Pueblo Bonito by the dozen. The latter had learned much from Gustaf Nordenskiöld, who had set a high standard. Despite constant suggestions to the contrary, their work was no better and no worse than most excavation of the day. In 1898 Richard Wetherill opened a trading post in Chaco Canyon, erected against the back wall of Pueblo Bonito, using beams from the ruin for the roof (figure 2.5). He stored his wares in nearby pueblo rooms. A little later on, he built a three-room structure just west of the ruins, again using beams from Pueblo Bonito as roofing material. The trading post soon became part of the Hyde Exploring Expedition, with Wetherill as the managing-but-minority party, receiving 10 percent of the profits. Within three years, the expedition supervised a small Indian trading chain of eight posts, a wholesale outlet in Albuquerque, even a retail store in New York City, this apart from dried fruit and harness enterprises.

The dealings of the expedition raised a red flag in archaeological circles. Archaeologist Edgar Hewett, then president of New Mexico

Figure 2.5   The Chaco Canyon Trading Company Store at Pueblo Bonito, 1929. This was a branch of the Matchin Trading Company of Crown Point, New Mexico. Managers Mr. and Mrs. Wade Smith stand in the doorway. A portion of Pueblo del Arroyo lies in the background. *Courtesy of NPS Chaco Canyon Historical Park. Negative 30765.*

Normal University in Las Vegas, and his colleagues in the newly formed Santa Fe Archaeological Society demanded a federal investigation; so did the governor of New Mexico Territory. Two government investigations in 1900 and 1901 exonerated the Hyde Exploring Expedition from charges that it looted ruins and sold artifacts, noting that the work was under the supervision of the American Museum. But political pressure continued, causing the commissioner of the Public Lands Office to issue an order in 1901, suspending further excavations. The order was made permanent in 1902.

Richard Wetherill had filed a homestead claim that encompassed 161 acres (65 ha), an area that included Pueblo Bonito, Pueblo del Arroyo, and Chetro Ketl, as well as the trading post. The federal authorities were deeply apprehensive of Wetherill, suspecting, with good reason, that he was using the Homestead Act to gain legal control of the ruins. After years of controversy, Wetherill was granted control over 113 acres (46 ha) but not over land where the ruins lay. Meanwhile Hewett and the Santa Fe Archaeological Society were lobbying for Chaco Canyon to be made a national park.

George Pepper did not get on well with Wetherill. He published little on their work, except for an illustrated elaboration of his field notes in 1920.[14] Interestingly, Pepper, and to some extent Wetherill, produced more records of their Pueblo Bonito work that Hewett ever did for his later excavations at Chetro Ketl. Nevertheless, Hewett was intent on shutting the Expedition down—and he ultimately succeeded.

MORE SCIENTIFIC INVESTIGATIONS

Frederic Ward Putnam visited Chaco Canyon briefly in 1899 and came to dig in 1901, when he excavated a site at the foot of Picture Cliff near Peñasco Blanco, west of Pueblo Bonito. He left behind two graduate students—Alfred Tozzer and William Farabee—with instructions to dig in some burial mounds and small ruins selected by Putnam and Wetherill. They set up camp 8 miles (13 km) west of Pueblo Bonito, laid out grids of 26-foot (8-m) squares, and cleared the first site in four days with the aid of four laborers. The same techniques were used on other sites. Tozzer subsequently carried out some ethnographic work among the local Navajos.

The figure of Edgar Hewett towers over the history of Southwestern archaeology and Chaco Canyon like a colossus. Edgar Hewett (1865–1946) was a pugnacious, stubborn man, known to his enemies as El Toro, who began his career as a teacher, became president of the New Mexico Normal University, was fired, and then became an archaeologist.[15] In the course of his long archaeological career, he directed the Museum of New Mexico and the School of American Research, and eventually founded the Department of Archaeology, later Anthropology, at the University of New Mexico. Hewett loathed Richard Wetherill and all he stood for, clashed constantly with the East Coast archaeological community, and was one of the leading forces behind the passage of the 1906 Antiquities Act, sponsored by Congressman John Lacey of Iowa, chairman of the House Committee on Public Lands. This provided a measure of protection to archaeological sites, like Chaco Canyon, situated on public lands. Chaco itself became a national monument in 1907.

Hewett considered the Southwest his domain, and a private reserve for western archaeologists. He was troubled by the constant influx of eastern archaeologists, many of them trained in new methods of recording and stratigraphic excavation that they called, grandiloquently, the "New Archaeology." In 1915 Nels Nelson of the American Museum, and a pioneer in stratigraphic excavation in the Southwest, visited Chaco Canyon. Finding few signs of federal stewardship, he reported that Pueblo Bonito had been "practically cleaned out" by Pepper and Wetherill. The pueblo walls were tottering dangerously. Nevertheless, careful stratigraphic excavations might yield valuable results, not only at Pueblo Bonito but also at other locations.

In 1916 the American Museum of Natural History in New York received a permit for excavations in the Southwest. Nelson carried out five days of excavations in a Pueblo Bonito midden, but failed to discover the stratigraphic sequence of pottery he sought. There were no signs of change in the pottery styles from top to bottom of the layered ash. He spent the rest of the summer exploring the country between Chaco Canyon and the Rio Grande in an attempt to explore the relationships between the ancient peoples of the two regions. Nelson was one of a small coterie of archaeologists who eschewed personal rivalries and worked cooperatively to develop a chronological approach to Chaco and other Southwestern sites, such as Aztec to the north, where the American Museum excavated from 1916 on.[16]

The rivalries over Southwestern archaeology pitted prestigious institutions against one another, with the American Museum using its political influence in Washington as others came into play. Anyone seeking to excavate in the region had to combine political acumen with carefully wrought professional alliances and secure funding. As far as Chaco was concerned, the Smithsonian Institution prevailed.[17]

In 1920 Alfred Kidder of Harvard University took a break from his Pecos excavations east of Santa Fe, described below, and joined three archaeological friends for an "exploration by wagon" of Chaco Canyon. The four men had worked together before, under Hewett in the Four Corners region. One of them, Neil Judd, drew on this common experience in asking them to help him with a preliminary survey of the ruins before excavations were to begin. The expedition by wagon was a memorable experience, quite apart from food and water shortages and a lot of gossip. They found one of Hewett's excavating teams working at Chetro Ketl. Judd boldly announced that the National Geographic Society was contemplating "extensive archaeological research" in the canyon. His announcement set off a political war of the first order between Hewett and his former student. Meanwhile, Kidder admired the great houses but puzzled over the issue of population. "If all of them had been inhabited at the same time, they might well have housed more than 10,000 people. But how so large a population could have supplied itself with the necessities of life, and still had time and energy left for the development of so remarkable a civilization has puzzled every observer who has visited the Chaco country." He added: "Definite answers to many of these questions will doubtless be provided by the new methods of research now being applied by Judd and his associates."[18] Years later, we are still puzzling over the same questions.

Neil Judd was a former Hewett student, but well schooled in the so-called new archaeology. He had started work at the Smithsonian in 1911 and had worked extensively in Utah by the time he was given a

National Geographic Society grant to survey Southwestern pueblos and villages. Despite Hewett's tireless efforts to derail him by lobbying in Washington, Judd started work at Pueblo Bonito in May 1921. During the next five years he completed the excavation and stabilization of Pueblo Bonito, then surveyed the ancient roads that radiated from the canyon for seemingly short distances. He speculated that they were used to transport the tree trunks used to fashion the roof beams and lintels in the pueblos. Years were to pass before he published the definitive account of his Pueblo Bonito excavations, which finally appeared in 1954–64, after his retirement.[19] In a *National Geographic* article, he called the great pueblo the largest apartment house in the world "until the Spanish Flats were erected in 1882 at 59th and Seventh Avenue, New York." His readers learned of "colorful clan ceremonies" that propitiated tribal gods, of wandering raiders so ruthless that Pueblo Bonito was walled in, the only access by a "ladder that could be drawn up." Potsherds from areas outside the canyon came from his excavations, evidence of the "cooperative efforts of people closely related."

While these events unfolded at Chaco itself, Earl Morris (1889–1956), known to his contemporaries as "the consummate dirt archaeologist," was digging the Aztec Ruins on the Animas River to the north for the

Figure 2.6   Earl Morris excavating at Aztec Ruins in 1917. *Courtesy Department of Library Services, American Museum of Natural History, New York.*

American Museum (figure 2.6; plate 12). Morris always told stories of how his father had given him a short-handled pick and shown him how to dig for artifacts at the age of three. After entering the University of Colorado in 1908, he encountered Edgar Hewett by chance on a train in 1911, worked for him for a while in the Southwest and in Central America, then had a falling out. He ended up working in New Mexico's Galisteo Basin with Nels Nelson, who taught him the basics of stratigraphic excavation both there and during his brief excavations in Chaco. In 1916 Clark Wissler of the American Museum of Natural History obtained $2,000 from J. P. Morgan and hired Morris to excavate the Aztec Ruin, which urgently needed scientific investigation and stabilization.

Morris was the ideal choice for Aztec. As budgets increased, so he expanded his work, becoming the American Museum's agent at the site in 1921. He remained there until 1934. Most of his excavations focused on the West Ruin, the largest complex at the site, in places three stories high, with more than 350 rooms, associated with a plaza and a great kiva. Generations of looters had rummaged Aztec, but there were still intact rooms, complete with roofs and artifacts in place. Morris excavated about three-quarters of the West Ruin between 1916 and 1921, which gave him enough stratigraphic data to identify two occupations. The earliest yielded architecture identical to that at Chaco and Chaco-style artifacts like those found in the canyon's great houses. Then there was a sterile layer of windblown sand and dust. Later, people with artifacts similar to those recovered in the Mesa Verde region to the north moved in, remodeled, and added more rooms.[20]

The stratified layers at Aztec were a discovery of the first importance, for they showed that Chacoan culture had spread far beyond the narrow confines of the canyon itself. The same excavation also revealed a later Mesa Verde–style occupation, replacing the earlier Chaco settlement. The Aztec excavations gave the first chronological dimension to Chaco.

Earl Morris had his own favorite field area between the La Plata and Mancos Rivers in southern Colorado. He returned to work there at intervals for many years after an initial visit in 1913.[21] Here he found very different sites from those of the Cliff Dwellers—small, circular, semisubterranean dwellings, some with burials of longheaded people, as opposed to the roundheaded skulls of Pueblo folk. The pottery from these sites was different, too. In 1921 Morris found similar sites south of Shiprock, New Mexico, while Kidder and Samuel Guernsey excavated rockshelters in the Tsegi Canyon area, where they unearthed small, vertical, slab lined "cists," for food storage. Others were considerably larger, so much so that they served as houses, like those found by another archaeologist, Jesse Nusbaum, at the Dupont Cave in southern Utah in 1920. A year before, Kidder and Guernsey had wondered if they had discovered a transitional stage from Basketmaker culture to the later pueblos. The kivas, they speculated, were "a ceremonial reminiscence of the earlier semisubterranean type of building."[22]

CHACO AND THE "PECOS CLASSIFICATION"

Basketmakers, "Pre-Pueblo," and Pueblo cultures: Chaco occupation at Aztec was replaced by Mesa Verde settlement, and by 1920 Chaco was part of a much larger archaeological jigsaw puzzle. By this time, the Harvard archaeologist Alfred V. Kidder had begun his seminal excavations into the deep middens at Pecos Pueblo, New Mexico, east of the San Juan Basin.[23]

Kidder excavated Pecos at intervals between 1915 and 1927, trenching into middens whose rich and unexploited cemeteries and ash heaps provided a chronological framework for the ancient Southwest that remains in use today, albeit with much modification. He found no fewer than six settlements atop one another at Pecos, which he used to develop a sequence of eight cultural stages that began with Richard Wetherill's "Basket Makers" and ended with the Spanish occupation. In 1924 Kidder published his *tour-de-force*, titled *An Introduction to the Study of Southwestern Archaeology*, where he both summarized his Pecos excavations and placed them in a wider context. He went even farther than that. Three years later, he arranged an informal conference of about forty archaeologists in his Pecos excavation camp to review work so far and to plot a chronological framework for future study. The meeting pooled data and techniques and laid the foundations for a unified system of nomenclature. The Pecos conference identified three Basketmaker stages, and five of Pueblos, the so-called Pecos Classification, dissipating much of the chaos that had surrounded the undisciplined archaeology of earlier years. Each year Southwestern archaeologists still gather for an annual Pecos conference, one of the revered gatherings of American archaeology. Five hundred of them attended the 1997 conference in Chaco Canyon.

The research of Kidder and others showed how thousands of years of human occupation had unfolded before Chaco's spectacular pueblos came into existence. Kidder thought of the time when Chaco reached its apogee as a period when the Pueblo people could balance opportunity and necessity. Then the Chaco people and their contemporaries fought hard against invading Toltecs from Mexico, whose pottery he claimed to have identified at Pueblo Bonito, but to no avail; the collapse of Chaco began, in Kidder's estimate, before AD 1100. In retrospect, Kidder was quite close in his estimate of the date when Chaco was depopulated, but his Toltec theory was nonsense, for there are no signs of their artifacts in the canyon.

The Pecos Classification was based on chronological guesswork, despite the participants' keen awareness of the potential of tree-ring chronology. Then, in 1928, Andrew Douglass filled the famous tree-ring gap between modern and ancient samples (see chapter 3) and produced a master curve for the past two thousand years. At a second Pecos Conference in 1929, participants discussed the implications of the new chronology, and, for the first time, pored over aerial photographs of Chaco, Pecos, and other major sites taken by Charles and Anne Morrow Lindbergh, who landed on a piece of "more or less cleared brush land" near Pecos, stayed overnight, and then photographed Chaco, among other areas.

FIELD SCHOOLS

The advent of tree-ring dating, described in chapter 3, revolutionized Southwestern archaeology. Neil Judd could now answer one of Chaco's most puzzling questions—how old were the pueblos? Their heyday proved to have been at the end of the first millennium AD and the beginning of the second. In 1929 Edgar Hewett resumed work at Chetro Ketl under the auspices of the School of American Research and the newly founded Department of Anthropology at the University of New Mexico. He regarded Chaco as a training ground for his students and established a summer field school in 1936, after the School of American Research largely withdrew from further Chaco research. Hewett called Chetro Ketl an ancient apartment house that would cover two modern city blocks. He also excavated the great kivas in the plaza and found an earlier one 12 feet (3.6 m) below it. Increasingly, he used Chaco as a training ground for graduate students, including Florence Hawley, Paul Reiter, and Gordon Vivian. The field school investigated a number of sites, including Tseh So (Bc 50) and Bc 51, small sites on the south side of the canyon close to Casa Rinconada and close to the base camp. Most fieldwork by the school was confined to eight small sites in this vicinity, also to a Basketmaker pithouse. Unfortunately, little of Hewett's research was ever published. Meanwhile, one of his students, Florence Hawley, refined an intricate pottery classification for the canyon, as well as carrying out important tree-ring research that put Chaco's chronology on a much firmer footing than that originally developed by Douglass. Her tree-ring and pottery studies established that some Chaco small settlements were contemporaneous with great houses.[24]

One of Hewett's students was Gordon Vivian, who was to devote his career to Chaco. In 1931 he was assigned to excavate Casa Rinconada, the celebrated great kiva on the south side of the canyon, which he and Paul Reiter described in a monograph on Chaco great kivas many years later, in 1960.[25] Vivian's Casa Rinconada work led to his developing a National Park Service ruins stabilization program in 1937. He became the Park Service archaeologist at Chaco in 1938 and remained there for his entire career. During this time he used stabilization and salvage programs to work on a wide range of Chaco sites, which he combined with research into the relationship between the small and large pueblos, as well as water-control systems, pottery styles, and later McElmo-style structures.[26] When flooding invaded Chetro Ketl in 1947, he salvaged the contents of unexcavated Room 93 that contained a large quantity of carved and painted wood (described in chapter 8).

Another important Vivian investigation involved the stabilization of Kin Kletso, which had been probed briefly in 1934. The Park Service was anxious to chronicle this great house to interpret late architectural developments at Chaco. Generally, Vivian's research, squeezed in between conservation and other duties, illuminated many details both of the early Pueblo occupation and of the late McElmo phase, as well as smaller sites. The publication of the Kin Kletso report by Vivian and Tom Mathews in 1965 marked the end of a long period of research by individuals such as Hawley, Frank Roberts, and others.[27]

THE CHACO PROJECT

By 1970 more than 370 sites had been found within the monument area itself. There was research on outlying Chaco sites as well. During the 1970s, Cynthia Irwin-Williams excavated the Salmon Ruins, described in chapters 12 and 13. She was so impressed by the scale of the Chaco world that she named it the "Chaco Phenomenon."[28] In 1969 the National Park Service launched a ten-year research initiative at Chaco in collaboration with the University of New Mexico, to look not at small details but at larger questions such as agriculture, the causes of the rise and collapse of Chaco, and the role of great houses. The initial fieldwork began in 1971. As interim director, Tom Lyons began the research.

The Chaco Center, headed first by archaeologist Robert Lister, then by James Judge, moved the project immediately out of the narrow confines of the canyon, combining wide-ranging survey with testing of undisturbed sites, including Pueblo Alto. By the end of fieldwork in 1982, the many people working on the project had located 2,538 sites, tested 27 of them, and collected more than 300,000 artifacts. Intermittent fieldwork continued after 1983, much of it by Thomas Windes, a National Park Service archaeologist. More than twenty volumes document the extraordinary researches of the Chaco Project.

This cutting-edge initiative did much to answer some of the major questions about Chaco. We know now a great deal about the relationships between great houses and small sites, about variations in Chaco culture. Tree-ring studies and architectural research have produced detailed studies of the development of great houses and their role in Chacoan history. Starting in 1969, Gwinn Vivian, son of Gordon, investigated the water-control systems of the canyon and triggered extensive research into Chaco roads, which had been forgotten for many years. Aerial photography and satellite imagery, collected and analyzed by the Remote Sensing Division, produced the first maps of the road system and focused renewed attention on Chaco outliers. Wide-ranging surveys identified many new sites, while selective excavations produced information on relationships between them.

The pace of fieldwork has slowed somewhat since the 1970s, except for innumerable surveys and small-scale excavations mandated by federal and state laws to record archaeological sites in the face of development. But the speculation about Chaco Canyon has intensified, a reflection of many more archaeologists who work on the canyon and its outliers, several hundred at last count. While some researchers like Thomas Windes continue to spend years on detailed investigations deciphering architectural histories of sites like Pueblo Bonito, others try to place Chaco in a broader context, grappling with the same questions that Kidder posed three-quarters of a century ago. How far did the Chaco system extend? Was it confined to the San Juan Basin or did its tentacles reach into northern Mexico, as architectural expert Steve Lekson believes?[29] Who were the authority figures who created and tended this short-lived but spectacular phenomenon? As we will see in coming chapters, every fresh piece of research raises new questions. The debates and speculations continue, as, one suspects, they always will.

We can understand them better if we take a brief look at Chaco Canyon in a broader environmental and chronological context, before we tell the story of its ancient inhabitants.

3 ∴ THE SETTING

The paleoenvironment of the Chacoan era . . . can
best be described as being characterized by the pre-
dictability of unpredictable weather and climate.

R. Gwinn Vivian and others[1]

"The view from the headwaters of the Chaco Wash . . . is of an empty landscape that seems to stretch for ever. Grassy hills fade into miles of an
unbroken expanse that ends in the faint blue curtain of the Chuska
Mountains."[2] Archaeologist Gwinn Vivian spent his childhood in Chaco
and speaks with authority of the vastness of the canyon's remote setting. This environment, and the unpredictable climate, defined the lives
of the Chacoans from the earliest times. The story of the rise and fall of
the society nestled in this remarkable place must begin with climate
and environment.

THE SAN JUAN BASIN

Chaco Canyon lies in the heart of the San Juan Basin, which covers
much of northwestern New Mexico and adjacent regions of Colorado,
Utah, and Arizona (figure 3.1).[3] The central part of the basin covers an
area of about 4,600 square miles (11,913 sq km), measuring about 100
miles (161 km) on a north–south axis and 65 miles (105 km) from east
to west. The landscape tilts to the northwest, so that most drainages
flow in that direction, with the highest altitudes of about 8,200 feet
(2,500 m) in the north, and the lowest, less than 4,900 feet (1,493 m), in

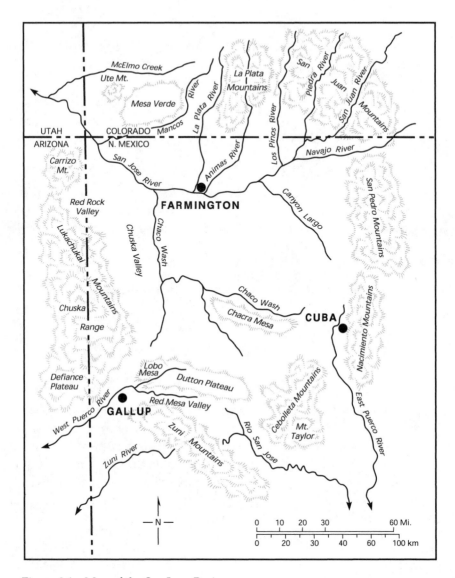

Figure 3.1   Map of the San Juan Basin

the west. Millions of years of erosion have produced a landscape of broad plains and valleys, where the relief is subdued. Small mesas, buttes, and short canyons define the Basin, the largest features being Chaco Canyon and Chacra Mesa south of the Chaco Wash. All basins have rims, in the case of the San Juan distinctive uplands that reach an altitude of more than 9,842 feet (3,000 m), uplifted mountains and plateaus formed during the Cretaceous Era over 65 million years ago. The wide, flat platforms between these uplifted areas include the Four Corners region, Chama, Acoma, and Zuni, at altitudes of more than 7,200 feet (2,200 m).

The Basin enjoys limited rainfall and has almost no permanent surface water, except for some perennial streams in the northernmost tracts. All other water flows in ephemeral arroyos and washes. The San Juan River drains most of the Basin. It flows across the northern Basin and empties into the Colorado River, having passed through an opening in the Four Corners. Not only perennial streams but also such transitory water sources as the Chaco Largo in the northeast and the Chaco Wash in the west flow into the San Juan. The Chaco Wash is sometimes called a river, because of the large area of the southern and western parts of the Basin drained by it, but this is a misnomer, for it flows irregularly. On a much larger scale, drainages in the southern San Juan Basin are affected by the Continental Divide. Those on the east flow into the Rio Grande and those on the west into the Colorado River.

Water in any form is in short supply in the Basin; the major aquifers are deep below the surface and do not produce springs. Only a few shallow ones produce water for crops, but these are of great importance. The quality of the groundwater depends on the soils. Coarser-grained sediments in the southwestern Basin soak up water quicker than the finer soils of the northeastern portions, which store water longer, with, however, the danger that minerals will collect, causing salinization. The ideal mix of 25 percent clay and more than 65 percent sand is best for agriculture, but this rarely occurs anywhere in the San Juan Basin. Chaco Canyon forms an approximate boundary between the two general soil types.

Four major air masses affect the climate of the Colorado Plateau and the San Juan Basin. During the winter months, cool, moist Polar Pacific air arrives from the northwest, brought down by cyclonic storms that move to the south and southeast. The rainfall from these storms comes mainly from mountain uplift, although some moisture comes from the convergence of local moist air with cold, dry, polar continental air masses that move from north to south. The pattern reverses during the summer, when air is drawn into the Basin from south to north. Summer rainfall comes from warm, moist tropical air from the Gulf of Mexico, with occasional incursions of tropical Pacific air that produce more rain than its Gulf relative. Summer rainfall also results from mountain uplift, from convergence with local air, and most commonly from convection from rising heat, which produces the intense, highly localized thunderstorms so characteristic of New Mexico summers.

A summer thunderstorm at Chaco is a memorable experience. Massive clouds darken the horizon as the sky turns an intense gray-black. Lightning flashes flicker as the storm nears with great drumrolls of thunder that threaten to tear the heavens apart. The wind picks up with vicious, unpredictable gusts. Sheets of rain cascade from the lowering clouds; arroyos suddenly flow with muddy floodwaters, boulders rush down normally dry streambeds. Then, suddenly, the rain stops and the storm is gone as rapidly as it arrived. Raindrops glisten on shrubs and trees, rocks shimmer briefly in the bright sunlight, and the floodwaters rapidly slow. Soon, it is as if the storm had never been except for the muddy water cascading down the Wash and the clinging mud that adheres to your boots.

San Juan Basin rainfall mirrors that of the Colorado Plateau generally. Summer rainfall comes mainly from thunderstorms, with a sharp peak between July and early September. The early fall is often dry, with gentler, if sporadic winter rains in the form of snow between December and March, followed by the driest months of the year—May and June. But only a small amount of rain falls each year, with considerable variation from year to year, and it is never predictable. Everything depends on the movements of air masses thousands of miles away from the Basin and on local topography. The amount of rainfall can vary significantly within a few miles in the compass of a single year.

The San Juan Basin lies on the edge of air circulation patterns to the north and south, receiving rain from both the cool north or the tropical south. Northwestern New Mexico, where Chaco lies, is on the edge of the summer circulation patterns of tropical air masses, while southwestern Colorado is near the southern limits of winter storm tracks. Thus, the people of the Basin farmed an arid environment where rainfall patterns varied considerably from north to south, and where even a minor shift in seasonal circulation could make all the difference between good rains and bad.

Quite apart from these variables, much of the Basin lies within rain shadows in the lee of mountain ranges to the west and south, in both summer and winter. Annual rainfall amounts tell the story. The northern mountains receive about 20 inches (50 cm) annually, while those to the south of the Basin receive about 17 inches (43 cm). The Basin itself averages about 8 inches (20 cm) annually, with slightly higher totals in the north as opposed to the south, also east to west, the amount of rainfall dropping by about .1 inch (0.25 cm) for every 100-foot (30-m) drop in elevation. Not only that, but the prevailing westerly winds, blowing over desert terrain, tend to keep humidity low.

Summers are hot, winters are cold. Over thirty years of observations at Chaco include a record high of 102°F (39°C) and a stunning winter low of –38°F (–39°C), with an average over the years 1941–1970 of 49.8°F (9.8°C). The growing season throughout the Basin is about one hundred fifty days, varying considerably according to elevation and topography, but the farming season in canyons and valley bottoms where the best soils lie is as much as thirty to thirty-five days shorter than on nearby terraces and mesas. Chaco had fewer than a hundred frost-free days during more than half the years between 1960 and 1982, and no year had as many as one hundred fifty. Back in 1983, the archaeologists William Gillespie and Robert Powers pointed out at the Second Anasazi Symposium that Chaco's growing conditions on a year-by-year basis, indeed those of much of the San Juan Basin, fell far short of the optimum for Hopi country of 9.8–11.8 inches (25–30 cm) of rainfall and one hundred twenty frost-free days.[4]

This was, and still is, a world where short-term major global climatic shifts such as El Niños can have a profound effect on agriculture on a year-by-year basis. This is because the San Juan Basin lies at the edges of circulation of four major air masses. Shifts in the jet stream and changes in the distribution of westerly winds play an important role in annual variations. Stronger westerlies shifting farther eastward bring cooler temperatures, with an accompanying southward shift of climatic conditions across the Basin. When the westerlies contract to the north, temperatures warm up and hotter climatic zones shift northward. The people of the Chaco world were at the mercy of these capricious and often subtle climatic shifts.

A CORE, A PLATEAU, AND SLOPES

Chaco Canyon and its outliers spanned an enormous area of the San Juan Basin, which still defies precise division into subareas. In any case, such classifications are of more value to specialist researchers than the general reader. Gwinn Vivian makes a broad distinction between the interior lowlands where the Chaco culture had its greatest impact, and the encircling uplands. Then he divides the zones into several large units based on drainage patterns in the lowlands and geological criteria on higher ground (figure 3.2).[5]

The San Juan Slope is part of the outer rim of the Basin, with drainages flowing south to the San Juan River. The mountainous terrain of the far north gives way to broken mesas and canyons in the south. The

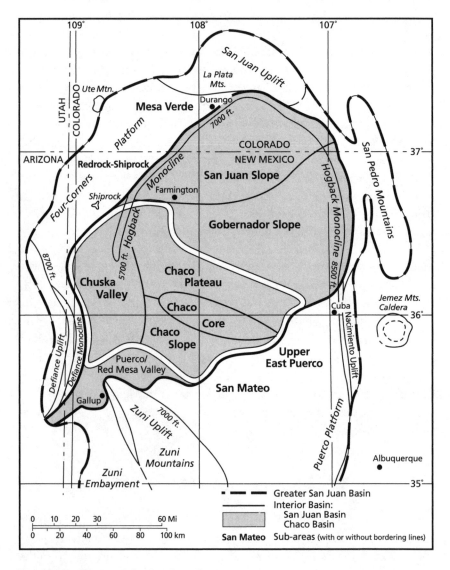

Figure 3.2 Zones of the San Juan Basin

higher elevations to the north enjoy higher rainfall, with dense wood-lands and coniferous forest about 6,900 feet (2,103 m) above sea level. Juniper, piñon, and oak woodland with valley grasslands cover the canyons and mesas of the south.

The Gobernador Slope rises from the opposite bank of the San Juan River, bounded to the east by the Hogback Mountains and to the south and west by the Canyon Largo and Chaco watersheds. The broad shal-low canyons on the western side of the slope give way to deep, narrow canyons as you approach the mountains. Again, rainfall rises as you move toward higher ground, with somewhat similar vegetation to that on the San Juan Slope.

The Chaco Plateau forms the northern half of the Chaco drainage basin. The northern and eastern boundaries follow the break between the Chaco and Chuska Valley watersheds. The Chaco River forms the southern and western boundaries. Here, rolling plains drained by wide ephemeral drainages form the landscape, with low sandy ridges and sometimes dune fields separating them. Mixed grassland covers most of the plateau, with only a few stands of juniper and piñon near rocky outcrops or along east-facing slopes.

The Chaco Core is the heart of the Chaco world, a strip of land about 10 miles (16 km) wide and 40 miles (64 km) long that extends along the Chaco Wash from its headwaters at the Continental Divide to its junction with the Kin Bineola Wash. You would expect Chaco Canyon to be the dominant landmark in the Core, but in fact it is not. That distinction goes to the Chacra Mesa, an uplifted stretch of higher ground as much as 5 miles (8 km) wide with a steep southern escarp-ment that rises between 400 and 500 feet (121–152 m) above the Chaco Slope to the west, and marked by a gentler slope to the east broken where the Chaco Wash has formed Chaco Canyon out of the underly-ing bedrock. Numerous deep canyons penetrate the Mesa, breaking through the southern escarpment in several places. The canyons de-bouch into Chaco Canyon about 15.5 miles (25 km) west of the Conti-nental Divide, cleaving the Chacra into the South and West Mesas that form the western boundary of the canyon.

CHACO CANYON

Chaco Canyon itself came into being when the Chaco Wash cut deep into Upper Cretaceous sandstones and shale, the upper strata of the Chacra Mesa formation. Few visitors realize that the canyon is about

18.9 miles (30 km) long and between less than a third to just under a mile (0.5–1.5 km) wide. From the head to the Fajada Gap, the canyon runs east to west, then turns northwest until it ends. The canyon bottom is flat, dropping a mere 5 feet (1.5 m) every sixth of a mile (.03 km). The dramatic canyon walls tower 295 to 590 feet (90–180 m) above the floor, but the effect is lessened by benching on both sides. The inner canyon walls attain nearly 100 feet (30 m) in a few places but are normally lower.

This is a relatively well-watered location within the Basin, largely because runoff flows through the canyon. The Chaco Wash can flow strongly after major storms, while tributary drainage basins pass into it both above and below the canyon. The conspicuous Fajada and South Gaps bring water directly into the heart of the canyon. So do small side canyons and bedrock cliff seeps on occasion. But the major water source is the Wash, which is wide and low above the canyon head, but flows up to 30 feet (9 m) below the floor in the heart of Chaco today. At the end of the canyon, where it joins the Escavada Wash, it becomes a broad channel of shallow waters with almost no walls. One tends to think of the deeply entrenched Wash as an unchanging watercourse, which meanders quite close to the walls in places, but, in fact, the course has changed considerably over the centuries.

Figure 3.3 Visitors at Pueblo Bonito in 1934. *Photograph by George A. Grant. Courtesy of NPS Chaco Culture National Historical Park. Negative 80061.*

Throughout the canyon, dependable water is always in short supply. There are a few cliff seeps in the contact zones between the shale and sandstone beds in both walls, and a handful of shallow, saline pools at the confluence of the Escavada and Chaco Washes, where the water table reaches the surface. A few rock potholes fill with rainwater or snowmelt, but they are soon gone.

By any standards, Chaco Canyon is a place with unpredictable water supplies. Herein lies the question of questions. How did people manage to build numerous large pueblos in a place where water supplies were at best exiguous, the growing season relatively short, and the temperature contrasts enormous? The question has exercised some of archaeology's best minds for more than a century (figure 3.3).

THE ASTRONOMER WHO LOVED TREE RINGS

Chaco Canyon is relatively well watered by the standards of the San Juan Basin, but hardly enough to support great houses like Pueblo Bonito. Was there, then, more rainfall in the past? Did a wetter climate coincide with warmer conditions and a longer growing season than those of today? Fortunately, a discovery by a University of Arizona astronomer nearly a century ago has provided some of the answers.

Andrew Ellicot Douglass (1867–1962) was an astronomer with an interest in the perennially fascinating topic of links between solar activity and global climate change.[6] Douglass moved to the University of Arizona in 1906, where he remained for more than half a century. Five years earlier, he had become interested in the annual growth of trees as a way of measuring sunspot activity. He knew that many species of coniferous and deciduous trees accumulated annual growth rings of cambial wood just beneath their bark and that these were an indication of age. Astrophysicists were actively studying the structure of the sun and fluctuations in solar radiation, as well as the 11.3-year sunspot cycle. Inevitably, they speculated about potential links between sunspot activity and climate on earth, but with no universal agreement. Douglass decided to test the idea by studying tree rings, which he saw as a potential chronicle of climate change over long periods of time.

Many earlier observers had commented on the tree-ring phenomenon. Some had even used tree rings as a way to date archaeological sites. The Reverend Manassah Cutler, a Massachusetts minister of somewhat dubious reputation, served as a land agent for retired Brigadier General Rufus Putnam's Ohio Company at Marietta, Ohio, in the

Muskingum Valley. Putnam planned Marietta with remarkable care, laying out a street grid conditioned partly by the presence of massive ancient earthworks. With enlightened forethought, Putnam surveyed the mounds and enclosures, setting some of them apart as public parks, the largest mound becoming part of the town cemetery. Cutler arrived at Marietta in 1788, just as the settlers were felling the trees on the mounds. Curious about the age of the tumuli, he counted the growth rings exposed in the trunks of some of the felled trees, one of which yielded a count of 463 rings. Thus, the mound where the tree grew had been built before AD 1300, perhaps much earlier.[7]

Cutler's prescient observations, which were not unique, foreshadowed what was to become a science in Douglass's hands. The Arizona astronomer knew that the sun's heat caused ocean water to evaporate. At the same time, the sun was the engine that drove the winds carrying water over land. It follows that variations in solar activity would affect rainfall and other weather phenomena on land. The trees of the Southwest depended for their growth not on ground water but on annual rainfall. Thus, he reasoned, a wide tree ring was a reflection of a good rainfall year, a thin one of drought conditions. If he could develop a record of tree-ring fluctuations over many centuries and link them with sunspot cycles, then he could examine the relationship between solar radiation and global weather patterns.

Douglass began collecting tree-ring samples in the San Francisco Mountains near Flagstaff in 1904, then from elsewhere on the Colorado Plateau, before moving on to California sequoias and redwoods. Five years later, he had developed a master tree-ring chart for the Colorado Plateau and knew that changes in tree-ring patterns could be traced across much of the desert West. By 1915 he had a chronology (he called it dendrochronology after the Greek "tree," and *chronos* "time") that extended back from 1900 to about 1400. A year earlier, the archaeologist Clark Wissler of the American Museum of Natural History read a paper by Douglass on estimating rainfall from tree rings. He promptly wrote to the astronomer, suggesting that he consider using wooden beams from ancient pueblos as a way of extending his master tree-ring chart back into the remoter past. At the same time, Wissler would have an accurate way of dating the same sites. Wissler used some of the funds donated for Southwestern research by the philanthropist Archer Huntington to support Douglass's work, while another American Museum archaeologist, Earl Morris, collected samples from Aztec Ruins and Pueblo Bonito in 1918. Douglass took tree-ring samples from beams at the two sites, and then compared the resulting ring sequences with his master tree-ring curve. He found that Pueblo Bonito was built about forty to forty-five years before Aztec. Not only that, but the Aztec beams were cut within two years of each other. Both Wissler and Douglass realized that this was a major breakthrough, both for archaeology and the study of Southwestern climate change.

For all this fascinating detail, the chronology "floated," without any anchor in modern times, in living trees. Douglass lacked the ring sequences to link Aztec, Chaco, and other ancient pueblos to his master chronology. Research accelerated, notably at Chaco Canyon, where Smithsonian archaeologist Neil Judd had started work at Pueblo Bonito with National Geographic Society support in 1921. He also organized three "Beam Expeditions" in the Southwest financed to the tune of $2,500 by National Geographic, which collected hundreds of wood samples from archaeological sites, historic pueblos, and early churches. Even these samples did not bridge an increasingly vexing gap between 1357, the earliest date on the master chronology based on modern trees, and the network of now cross-dated beams from Chaco, Mesa Verde, and other locations.

The National Geographic Society provided another $5,000 to support new research to close the gap. Douglass turned to two young University of Arizona archaeology students, Lyndon Hargrave and Emil Haury, who began by studying thousands of potsherds from ancient pueblos and putting them in a tentative chronological order, working back from known historical styles into the ever-remoter past. The research led them to ruins on the Mogollon Plateau in Arizona. On June 22, 1929, on the final Beam Expedition, Hargrave and Haury excavated a beam from the Whipple Ruin near Show Low, Arizona. Douglass arrived just as they were recovering the sample, compared it patiently to his master curve charts, and announced that the gap was closed. In fact, he had already closed it by using fragmentary samples, but he wanted stronger confirmation. For the first time, researchers at Chaco and elsewhere had an accurate way of dating not only entire pueblos but even their constituent suites. Douglass's student, Florence Hawley, continued to collect tree-ring samples at Chetro Ketl from 1930 to 1933. Her comparisons of dated masonry wall types and potsherds enhanced the ability of many Chacoan and Southwestern scholars to place their sites within current chronological schemes. Today, Chaco's chronology, from the late fifth to twelfth centuries, is among the most accurate of all ancient time scales, even if experts continue to refine its details down to the construction dates of individual rooms (see figure 3.4).

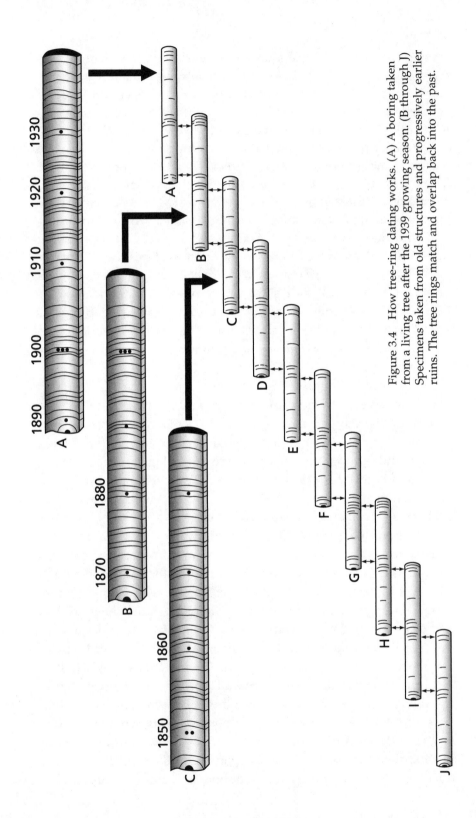

Figure 3.4 How tree-ring dating works. (A) A boring taken from a living tree after the 1939 growing season. (B through J) Specimens taken from old structures and progressively earlier ruins. The tree rings match and overlap back into the past.

HOW DENDROCHRONOLOGY WORKS

Everyone is familiar with the concentric growth rings that can be seen in the cross section of the trunk of a felled tree. These rings, formed in most trees, are of great use in the Southwest, where the seasonal weather changes markedly and growth is concentrated during a few months of the year. Normally trees produce two growth rings each year, which are formed by the **cambium** between the wood and the bark. Each year's growth forms a distinct ring that varies in thickness according to the tree's age and annual climatic variations. Climatic variations in the Southwest tend to run in cycles of wet and dry years, which are reflected in patterns of thicker and thinner rings on the trees.

The tree-ring samples are taken with a borer from living or felled trees. The ring sequences from the borer are then compared to each other and to a master chronology of rings built up from many trees with overlapping sequences tied to a known terminal date. The patterns of thick and thin rings for the new sequences are matched to the master sequence and dated on the basis of their accurate fit to the master sequence. By using the California bristlecone pine, tree-ring experts have developed a master chronology over 8,000 years back into the past.

Tree-ring experts have been able to develop an extremely accurate chronology for Southwestern archaeological sites that extend back as long ago as 322 BC. It was a difficult task, for they had to connect a prehistoric chronology from dozens of ancient beams to a master tree-ring chronology connected to modern times obtained from living trees of known age. The dates of such famed Southwestern sites as Mesa Verde's Cliff Palace and Pueblo are known to within a decade or less because tree-ring chronologies are accurate to within a year. Such precision even allows the dating of individual rooms within single pueblos. Tree-ring dating of pueblos requires care, since the builders sometimes reused much older timbers, which would give dates decades, even centuries older.

Dendrochronology has been used in other areas of the world as well—in Alaska and the American Southeast, and with great success in Greece, Ireland, and Germany. The bristlecone pine is to the Southwest as oaks are to Europe. European tree-ring experts have collected large numbers of tree-ring records from oaks that lived 150 years or so. By visual and statistical comparison they have linked living trees to farmhouse and church beams and to ancient trees found in bogs and prehistoric sites, providing a tree-ring sequence that goes back 10,021 years in Germany and 7,289 years in Ireland. Dutch tree-ring experts have even dated the oak panels used by old masters for backing their oil paintings as a way of authenticating paintings. And, in an elegant application of tree-ring dating, British archaeologists have used a ring sequence from the Italian Alps to date the spruce used to make a priceless Stradivarius violin called "The Messiah" to 1682. They also established that it was made from the same piece of wood as two other violins made by the master!

THE CLIMATIC YO-YO

Douglass was not an archaeologist but an astronomer with a passion for studying climate change. Once the tree-ring gap was closed, he returned to his original quest for ancient climatic trends. He founded the now world-famous Tree-Ring Laboratory at the University of Arizona in 1937 and continued to study tree rings and climate change until his death at the age of ninety-five.

Dendrochronology now does far more than merely date Chaco's pueblos. It provides a window into the intricate climatic history of the Southwest. Today, Jeffrey Dean and his colleagues work out of Douglass's revered Laboratory of Tree-Ring Research, located under the University of Arizona football stadium, focusing as much on climate change as on dating archaeological sites. They still work with Douglass's master chronology, developed by a scientist with rigorous standards of accuracy, which laid the foundations for the tree-ring science of today. Douglass and his contemporaries made all their comparisons by eye and with hand calculations. The eye is still important, but today, Dean uses computer-based analyses that allow the simultaneous analysis of scores of tree-ring and environmental variables over many centuries. These procedures have established consistent relationships between tree growth and environmental factors, allowing us to reconstruct climatic change throughout Chaco's history with remarkable accuracy.

Dendrochronologies for Ancestral Pueblo sites are now accurate to within a year—the most precise archaeological chronology anywhere. This means that even individual Chaco buildings can be dated, allowing the study of the complex architectural history of the great houses. At the same time, the Tree-Ring Laboratory has undertaken a massive dendrochronological study that has yielded a reconstruction of relative climatic variability in the Southwest from AD 680 to 1970.[8]

Now they are working on the first quantitative reconstructions of annual and seasonal rainfall, as well as of temperature, drought, and stream flow for the region. Such research is far more complex than anything Douglass undertook, involving not only tree-ring sequences but intricate mathematical expressions of the relationships between tree growth and such variables as rainfall, temperature, and potential crop yields. These calculations yield statistical estimations of the fluctuations in these variables on an annual and seasonal basis.

Using a spatial grid of twenty-seven long tree-ring sequences from throughout the Southwest, Dean and his team have compiled maps that plot the different station values and their fluctuations like contour maps, one for each decade. These maps enable them to study the progress of droughts, such as the so-called Great Drought of 1276–1299 from northwest to southeast across the region. The beginnings of the drought appeared in 1276 as negative standard deviations from average rainfall in the northwest, while the remainder of the Southwest enjoyed above average rainfall. Over the next decade, very dry conditions expanded over the entire region before improved rainfall arrived after 1299. This kind of mapping allows us to study the possible links between the abandonment of large and small pueblos and short-term climatic fluctuations.

Between AD 966 and 1988, the tree-ring stations in the northwestern region accounted for no less than 60 percent of the rainfall variance in the Southwest (figure 3.5). In contrast, stations in the southeastern portions accounted for a mere 10 percent. This general configuration, which persisted for centuries, albeit with shifts in the boundary between the two regions, coincides with the modern distribution of seasonal rainfall in the Southwest: predictable summer rainfall dominates the southeastern areas, while the northwestern region receives both winter and summer precipitation. Winter rains are much more uncertain, so the rainfall stakes were higher at Chaco and other Ancestral Pueblo locations than elsewhere.

Between 1250 and 1450, the long-term pattern broke down. The southeastern region remained stable, but there was major disruption

Figure 3.5 Areas of rainfall in the Southwest. The shaded line marks the frontier between the winter and summer rainfall patterns of the northwestern region and the more predictable summer rainfall of the southeastern area.

elsewhere. For nearly two centuries, the relatively simple long-term pattern of summer and winter rain gave way to complex, unpredictable precipitation and severe droughts, especially on the Colorado Plateau. As we shall see, this shift to an unstable pattern had a severe impact on Ancestral Pueblo society. Tree rings have shown us how the Chaco world danced to the tune of a harsh and unpredictable climatic drummer that never ceased playing. We can liken the relationship between the Chacoans and the climate as an intricate dance, a minuet of partners—the farmers and the endless gyrations of rainfall, temperatures, and growing seasons. The climatic partner set a quick, agile pace. Its human partner had to be nimble, quick to respond to hints from the land and sky, or else the dance would end in disaster. And the Chacoans were indeed responsive and flexible.

Jeffrey Dean makes some important distinctions about the relationships between human behavior and climatic change that are worth mention here. There have been no major changes in either the geological bedrock or the general climatic type in the Chaco region over the past two thousand years. But there have been low-frequency environmental changes such as those in hydrological conditions—cycles of erosion and deposition along stream courses, fluctuations in water tables in river floodplains, and changes in plant distributions. Such changes transcend generations and unfold over periods longer than a twenty-five year human generation. The Chacoans were probably barely aware of long-term change, for the present generation and their ancestors enjoyed the same basic adaptation, which we could call a form of "stability." But every Chaco farmer was only too aware of shorter-term higher frequency changes—year-to-year rainfall shifts, decade-long drought cycles, seasonal changes, and so on. Drought cycles, El Niño rains, and other such fluctuations required temporary and highly flexible adjustments, such as farming more land, maintaining two or three years' grain reserves, relying more heavily on wild plant foods, and, above all, moving across the landscape—mobility.

These strategies worked well for centuries, as long as the Chacoans farmed their land at well below the carrying capacity—the number of people per square mile it was capable of supporting. When the population increased to near carrying capacity, however, people became increasingly vulnerable to El Niños or droughts, which could stretch the supportive capacity of a local environment within months, even weeks. Their vulnerability was even more extreme when longer-term changes—such as a half century or more of much drier conditions—descended on farmland already pushed to its carrying limits. Under these circumstances, even a year-long drought or torrential rains could quickly destroy a local population's ability to support itself. When that happened, there was only one strategy for survival—movement. From the very beginning, the Chaco world was one where people lived on a climatic and environmental knife-edge that affected every aspect of their lives and the nature of society itself.

Tree rings are not, of course, the only source of climatic data from the past. Waterborne deposits from streams and canyons yield information of episodes of violent erosion or gradual accumulation, the latter sometimes caused by rising water tables, although these are often of only local significance. Fragmentary animal bones in archaeological sites represent the remains of ancient meals or are simply those of rodents that lived alongside humans. Some of these species, especially the smaller ones, are sensitive to drier and wetter conditions, and to temperature fluctuations.

In the early years of the twentieth century, a Swedish botanist, Laurens von Post, identified minute pollen grains from Scandinavian marshes and traced the vegetational history of northern Europe from them. He showed how the treeless steppe of the late Ice Age gave way to birch and pines, then deciduous forests. Since then, pollen analysis (palynology) has provided information on ancient vegetational changes and, by proxy, of climatic shifts in many parts of the world, including the Southwest. Pollens give local portraits of vegetation and provide a narrow view of a local environment, but, with enough samples from a wide enough area, one can obtain a reasonable picture of tree and plant cover. Packrat middens contain vegetational material that also provides information on local environments. Such middens and palynology have played a limited, but important, role in the Southwest, where tree rings remain the primary source of information about ancient climatic change.

By combining information from many sources, Jeffrey Dean and his colleagues have reconstructed the broad patterns of climate change in the San Juan Basin from about AD 250 to the present. One long-term trend was immediately evident—cycles of major dry periods of about fifty years' duration that occurred about every 550 years and lesser periods of aridity every 275 years that endured for about two decades. Increasing rainfall followed each dry period, which rose to a peak, then declined into another drought cycle. Every fifty to one hundred years, there were even more frequent swings in rainfall, to say nothing of local fluctuations.

Today, we have a year-by-year tree-ring record for Chaco Canyon from AD 661 to 1990, which can be used to reconstruct annual rainfall in the canyon (figure 3.6). The record speaks for itself, with a mean rainfall of 8.9 inches (22.6 cm) over the period, the lowest being 4.1 inches (10.4 cm) in 1748, the highest 14.2 inches (36 cm) in 1747. The tree-ring graph reveals slightly above or average rainfall during the eleventh century, except for a moderately dry spell between 1030 and 1060. A severe annual drought, with especially dry summers, occurred between 1130 and 1180, just as Chaco emptied. The arid summers were especially lethal. They brought rainfall failure during the critical warm growing months. Furthermore, tree-ring curves from long-lived and temperature-sensitive bristlecone pines in the San Francisco Peaks area

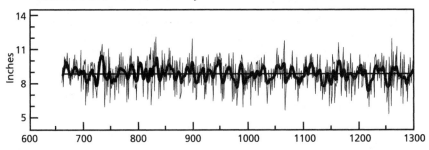

Figure 3.6 Rainfall in July/August at Chaco Canyon, AD 600–1300, reconstructed from tree-ring sequences from Chaco and Bloomfield.

reveal that warmer temperatures prevailed during the same dry intervals. Fairly wet conditions returned after the abandonment until the Great Drought of 1280, which caused people to leave the Montezuma Valley and Mesa Verde areas to the north. Interestingly, Chaco's climate has displayed considerably more unpredictability since 1550. Jeffrey Dean believes that the lesser variation in earlier centuries may have stabilized vegetation, also crop production, and allowed more precisely calibrated irrigation in the Canyon.

Identifying these cycles is one thing, establishing their cause is another. One commonly accepted theory argues that in about AD 750, the low-energy winter rainfall pattern gave way to a high-energy summer storm regime where summer rains fell with often great intensity for short periods of time, and with varying effects from one area to another. This summer dominant pattern continued until about 1050, when the winter cycle again became dominant. The history of Chaco Canyon spans two periods of higher rainfall and one of lower, with a particularly critical period from AD 750 to 1000, when the farmers had to live through not only a cycle of major drought from 850 to 900, but with unpredictable cyclical shifts in summer rainfall, which varied greatly in its intensity, frequency, and yield from one year to the next.

The Chaco people lived in a world where rainfall fluctuated wildly from one year to the next. No one could predict what the next growing season would bring. Theirs was a world governed by the passage of the seasons, by the solstices and the subtle signs of impending rain—massing thunderclouds, distant lightning flashes, showers dancing across the vast landscape. The margin between plenty and hunger, life and death was a knife-edge, manipulated by the farmer's skill and the proper observance of elaborate rituals that invoked the powers of the supernatural and the revered ancestors.

Far more than crops was at stake. At first, the people of Chaco were largely self-sufficient—in food, clay vessels, and timber. But they had an insatiable demand for timber of all kinds—for pueblo beams and also for firewood, both for domestic use and for firing clay pots. At first, the local juniper-piñon woodland provided much of their needs, but by AD 1000 the shortage was becoming apparent. Piñon vanished from newly built great houses, but continued in use in small settlements. Imported ponderosa from highland forests in the Chuska Mountains to the west assumed enormous importance in all construction. After 1090, spruce and Douglas fir, and perhaps aspen, came to the canyon in large quantities. The voracious appetite of the Chacoans for timber reduced the self-sufficiency of household and community and linked the canyon in webs of interconnectedness with a much wider San Juan Basin world. During the 990s, people began importing clay vessels from the Chuska region west of Chaco. The focus shifted during the twelfth century to the San Juan River region in the north. At the same time, toolmaking stone imports to sites south of the canyon shifted from the south to the west, then to the north.

Every ancient farming household was pragmatic and conservative in its doings, always ready for the year when the rains did not come and there was not enough to eat. The Chacoans were no exception. At a critical moment, they traded self-sufficiency for firewood, construction timber, and perhaps grain, making choices that were logical at the time, yet momentous in their long-term consequences.

The story of Chaco is the chronicle of a small population of subsistence farmers, who became enmeshed in an ever-expanding web of interconnectedness with communities and peoples near and far. The decisions they made were a reflection of the realities of survival in a harsh and capricious arid landscape. Chaco was far from unique in facing such a challenge, but the manner in which its people did so led to one of the most remarkable of all ancient American societies. And, in time, in a display of logical thinking that was entirely consistent with their earlier actions, they moved on when they could no longer sustain themselves by the Chaco Wash. In the pages that follow, we tell their story.

∴ PART 2

BEGINNINGS

I once heard a Zuni priest say: "Five things alone are necessary . . .
The sun, who is father of all.
The earth, which is the Mother of men.
The water, who is the grandfather.
The fire, who is the Grandmother.
Our brothers and sisters the Corn, and seeds of growing things."

Frank Cushing[1]

4 .∴. ULTIMATE ANCESTRY

> Agriculture is not to be looked on as a difficult or
> out-of-the-way invention, for the rudest savage,
> skilled as he is in the habits of the food-plants he
> gathers, must know well that if seeds or roots are
> put in a proper place in the ground they will grow.
>
> Sir Edward Tylor. Anthropologist, 1871[2]

A late spring afternoon at Chaco in 500 BC: The sun casts long shadows through the broken portion of the Chacra Mesa at Fajada Butte (figure 4.1). The northern cliffs glow with an orange hue, a cloudless sky high overhead. Dozens of jackrabbits feed on the grass along the sluggish-moving Vicente Wash, brown and gray dots between clumps of greasewood and against the green shoots of new growth. The feeding lagomorphs are oblivious to the fiber net strung between two large rocks slightly downstream, its base weighted with stones, erected at dawn by a small group of men and boys.[3]

Two bands, regular visitors to the canyon, have come together for the hunt. Quiet human figures flit softly up the wash and toward the canyon. They move into position, circling their prey, clubs and spears in hand. A soft whistle and the hunters move in slowly, waving sticks and deer hides. The jackrabbits circle and weave in confusion. Everywhere they turn, men and women club them down, and then fling carcasses aside. The hunters cast around them in a killing frenzy. Dozens of fleeing animals become entangled in the waiting net, where boys and girls spear them as they thrash. By sunset, dozens of carcasses litter the ground. The hunters gather them up quickly, then gut and skin them before cooking their prey in hot ashes. Much of the meat is dried for later use. . . . .

Figure 4.1   Fajada Butte. *Courtesy Russ Finley.*

For thousands of years, Chaco's ubiquitous jackrabbits were favored prey, especially in the spring, when a surging lagomorph population threatened to strip the landscape of precious edible foods. Jackrabbit hunts were as old as history in the San Juan Basin, especially in drier times when plant foods were more widely dispersed and in shorter supply.

∴ ∴ ∴

We begin with a basic question: Who were the ancestors of the Ancestral Pueblo builders of Chaco's great houses? Many people believe that the Chacoans' ancestry goes back deep into the remote past, even as far as Paleo-Indian times more than 13,000 years ago. Unfortunately, no one has yet discovered and excavated an archaeological site, like a cave, where they could trace this ancestry that far. We're left with an archaeological record of shreds and patches, with tantalizingly incomplete portraits of a primordial world of simple foragers.

One way of approaching the problem of Chacoan ancestry is to do what Alfred Kidder did at Pecos, begin by working back into the past from more recent times. In the case of Chaco, we begin not with the Ancestral Pueblo people themselves, but with their immediate predecessors, named Basket Makers by Richard Wetherill over a century ago. (Today they are called Basketmakers—one word.)

BASKETMAKER II (200 BC–AD 400)

Everyone agrees that the Basketmakers were the immediate predecessors of the Ancestral Pueblo and an ancient Southwestern culture that had strong roots in earlier hunter-gatherer societies.

About forty years ago, a veteran Southwestern archaeologist, Cynthia Irwin-Williams, investigated a cluster of archaeological sites near Arroyo Cuervo east of Chaco Canyon. Most of them were little more than scatters of stone choppers, projectile points, and milling stones used to process wild seeds. With painstaking care, Irwin-Williams pieced together the evidence for thousands of years of hunting and gathering near the arroyo. People based themselves there because of springs and natural seeps that provided reliable water supplies for the driest parts of the year. In 1973 Irwin-Williams used her Arroyo Cuervo researches to define a long-lived hunter-gatherer "Oshara tradition," within the local Archaic, which extended back to as early as 5500 BC and thrived until as late as AD 400.[4] Here, also, she claimed to have documented "long slow progress from small bands of hunters and gatherers to fully sedentary agricultural villages."[5] This claim was based on progressive changes in stone projectile point styles, like potsherds, one of the most useful artifacts for archaeological detection available to Southwestern fieldworkers (figure 4.2).

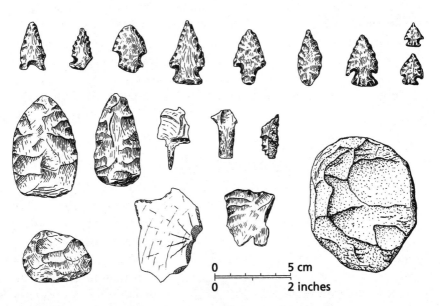

Figure 4.2   En Medio stone artifacts from the Arroyo Cuervo region.

The study of projectile point forms is a field of inquiry unto itself, which some people pursue with obsessive passion. Such studies have many uses, among them tracking the appearance of bows and arrows in the Southwest around 300 BC, marked by a distinctive form of small, stemmed arrowhead. These do not tell us much about the cultures who made them, or about the relationship between Archaic hunter-gatherers and later Chaco societies. But most experts tend to agree with Irwin-Williams and derive the new, more sedentary societies of 200 BC and later from Oshara roots. The changes took hold slowly, over at least five centuries, which makes it doubly hard to identify them. After 200 BC, hunter-gatherers who had once dabbled in maize cultivation gradually became more-or-less fulltime agriculturalists, using new, more productive strains of maize. These transitional cultures are known generically as Basketmaker II.[6]

The culture changes were slow and subtle, in part the result of climatic shifts, in part due to inexorable population growth. By 200 BC, rainfall had improved throughout the Basin, which led to lower-risk farming and more permanent settlements in places like Chaco. Nevertheless, there were occasional droughts, which made people very cautious about relying more heavily on agriculture. At the same time, groups in the north settled on the San Juan Slope around Durango, Colorado, and Bloomfield, New Mexico, a region sparsely settled by Archaic hunter-gatherers. The differences between the sites occupied by these people and those to the south in Arroyo Cuervo and other areas are sufficient to identify at least two Basketmaker II groupings in the San Juan region by 200 BC, one north of the San Juan River apparently well engaged in farming, the other to the south still relying heavily on plant gathering. Clearly, the actual picture was more complicated than this; future research is bound to reveal more cultural diversity over these centuries.

Los Piños

Wood smoke hugs the ground on a gloomy summer day by the Pine River in AD 200. Gray clouds obscure the hills and canyon slopes. Curtains of rain drift across the low terrace above the arroyo where the village lies. There's little to see except a row of low, irregular humps that protrude slightly above the ground. Two men watch the muddy flow of the river as the cascading waters rise slowly after hours of rain. They use stone choppers and digging sticks to channel rainwater into a small garden by water's edge. On the terrace, a woman crouches over an open storage bin, quickly gathering seeds into a weathered basket. She replaces the lid, scurries quickly back to her house, and vanishes through a low entrance. The scraping sound of stone against stone is barely audible against the sound of the rising creek. The arduous work of preparing food never ceases. . . .

∴ ∴ ∴

A distinctive form of Basketmaker II culture, named the Los Piños phase, flourished from just north of Durango, Colorado, to the San Juan River and as far south as the Navajo Reservoir area northeast of Chaco Canyon.[7] Most Los Piños sites lie between the Animas and Pine Rivers at elevations between 5,900 feet (1,800 m) and 7,200 feet (2,200 m) above sea level. Here piñon-juniper woodland and ponderosa pines grew in an environment where the growing season varied between 115 and 150 days a year. The Los Piños people settled on well drained terraces and slopes close to, or in, canyons with small floodplains. Perhaps some three hundred people lived in the present-day Navajo Reservoir area, the larger settlements being villages of about thirty people with outlying homesteads housing extended families.

Elsewhere, the settlement pattern varied considerably. Along the Animas River, for example, people lived in houses set on small terraces dug into natural slopes, so villages tended to be linear, with storage pits, work areas, and other features scattered between them. It's difficult to know how large individual villages were, because the inhabitants built, rebuilt, and abandoned their dwellings at different times. At least thirty-five house floors survive at one village near Durango; another at the Navajo Reservoir has eleven. Two large villages in the Navajo area had oversized structures, one with red-painted interior walls that may have served both as a residence and a gathering place for religious ceremonies.

For thousands of years, people had lived in temporary brush shelters. The Los Piños people constructed more permanent dwellings based on shallow, saucerlike depressions dug into the soil, then lined with clay. The average house in the north was about 29 feet (9 m) in diameter, but some were considerably larger, with antechambers that served as interior storage rooms. Each had walls constructed of horizontally placed logs, the chinks between them filled with brush before they were covered with mud. A domelike roof of logs, brush, and mud, supported by floor poles, completed the houses, which crouched low to the ground, a design which provided excellent insulation against extremes of summer and winter weather. These people took storage seriously, constructing pits and clay domes both inside and outside their dwellings.

All Los Piños groups subsisted off maize, wild plants, and hunting. No question, wild seeds were still of great importance—amaranth, tansy mustard, sunflowers, and wild vetch come from rockshelters of this period on the Animas River. Along the Pine River, milling tools represent as much as a third of the toolkit. At the same time, you find more and more trough-shaped grinding stones and grinders, used to produce maize meal. The rest of the toolkit was simplicity itself—stone projectile points, crude axes and scrapers, and many stone choppers used for woodworking. You find large numbers of bone awls, used for basketmaking, for Los Piños people were experts at the craft (figure 4.3). They were also skilled weavers. The dry layers of the Falls Creek rockshelters in the Animas Drainage have yielded twilled and cross-woven sandals, woven bags, tule reed matting, and many baskets made by expertly coiling fibers.

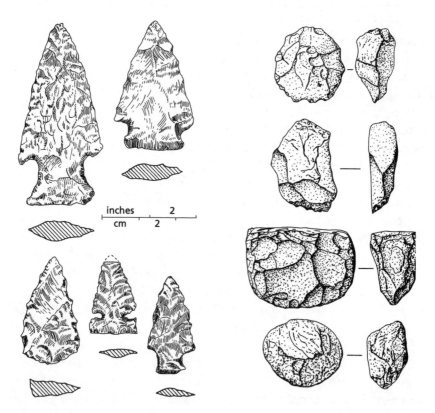

Figure 4.3   Los Piños artifacts, including projectile points, from the Navajo Reservoir District.

None of these communities were self-sufficient. From the Durango region southward, we find imported objects of many kinds—hornstone, greenstone beads, and seashell ornaments in the north, toolmaking stone like obsidian (volcanic glass) and chert in the south. Frank Eddy, who surveyed and excavated the Navajo Reservoir sites in the 1950s and early 1960s, believed that the particular groups also imported food-stuffs because they built so many storage bins and pits.[8] An inconspicuous cobweb of kin ties, social obligations, and trade already linked small communities many miles apart.

En Medio

Arroyo Cuervo—a dry season day in fall, AD 200. The rolling landscape is parched, the cloudless sky light blue and dusty. A small cluster of domelike brush dwellings lies close to the water seeps at the foot of the dunes. Three women and their daughters sit outside the crude shelters, picking through trays of dusty wild seeds. Deftly, they flick out the husks and small stones, then turn handfuls of seeds onto waiting milling stones. Nearby, a man sits on a boulder, shaping a stone arrowhead with delicate thrusts from a fragment of well-worn deer antler. He pauses again and again, weighing the tanged head in his hands. Satisfied at last, he binds the head to a fine wooden shaft, sighting along the arrow to check that it will run true. As the sun nears the horizon, he slips out of camp in search of deer (see fig. 4.2).

∴ ∴ ∴

In the south, the rhythm of hunter-gatherer life still unfolded seamlessly, year after year. We've already mentioned Cynthia Irwin-Williams's investigations at Arroyo Cuervo, where she claimed that she discovered evidence for continuity between hunter-gatherer and Basketmaker societies. She named this critical transitional stage En Medio, after a rockshelter of that name, dating it from 800 BC to AD 400, with the Basketmaker portion of En Medio dating to after 100 BC.[9] En Medio is earlier, and longer lasting, than Los Piños, with sites distributed widely over the San Juan Basin, most of them in or near broad river valleys like Arroyo Cuervo and the northern Chuska Valley. A number of sites lie in Chaco Canyon. These people occupied a considerably drier environment than their Los Piños neighbors, so much so that they anchored their settlements to reliable water supplies. Life continued much the same as it had been in earlier hunter-gatherer times, with territories ranging over mesa tops and canyons, also into dune areas. Some groups also engaged in occasional maize cultivation.

Even so, many En Medio groups were constantly on the move, dwelling in temporary encampments. No area of the central and southern San Juan Basin had enough water or food resources to allow people to settle within a small area for long periods of time. In the north, Los Piños bands exploited much smaller territories, were more sedentary, and relied more heavily on maize. In the south, people also cultivated maize, but the population had risen somewhat, so groups responded by exploiting larger areas, especially near larger arroyos. At the same time, they increased their storage capacity, a strategy that allowed more people to live together during fall and winter. The Arroyo Cuervo people used larger winter camps, but elsewhere such locations may have served as temporary collecting points for people who spent most of the year exploiting large areas of the Basin.

We know almost nothing about En Medio settlements. Many people dwelt in brush shelters. Some groups used domed shelters with oval floors. They stored food in bell-shaped pits, often lined with clay or stone slabs. There are roasting ovens, too, used for roasting cacti such as yuccas.

Some El Medio groups were cultivating maize as early as 1000 BC, because pollens have come from their sites. (Such tiny spores are, however, very hard to date, as they move easily from one layer to another.) Maize is securely dated to as early as 1200 BC in the nearby Rio Puerco Valley. We get the impression that cultivation in any form was just part of the annual round. Significantly, most grinding tools found on En Medio sites are of the form used for processing wild seeds. Long lists of wild seeds, everything from yucca to hackberry and numerous grasses, come from such sites, species collected from several ecological zones.

By AD 200 there was a significant Basketmaker II population in the Rio Puerco Valley near Arroyo Cuervo. Several habitation sites occur along ridges adjacent to the river floodplain. House forms are circular to oval, semisubterranean structures, some with antechambers, and probably made of brush and earth. They range from 9.8 to 16.4 feet (3–5 m) in diameter. Some have numerous and fairly elaborate exterior storage features similar to those at Los Piños sites. These facilities and occasional finds of maize fragments suggest that agriculture was more prevalent among En Medio groups than once thought.

At the same time, the simple toolkit of earlier En Medio times changes little in Basketmaker II levels, except for minor changes in grinding tools attributable to more use of maize. But the innovations are strikingly minor. We know the people fashioned baskets, but, again in contrast with Los Piños settlements, the evidence of interconnectedness with other communities is less conspicuous, being confined to exotic toolmaking stone and apparently nothing else, not even food. This does not mean that there was no interaction between neighboring bands, or that reciprocal obligations between kin were not in play. But longer distance trade, interaction with a much wider world, seems to be missing.

These were times when the San Juan Basin was a diverse cultural landscape. In the Rio Puerco and other favorable areas, there were both groups cultivating maize, and hunter-gatherers who had some knowledge of agriculture but depended little on maize and other crops.

CONTINUITY OR DISRUPTION?

What, then, are we to make of what appears to be a fairly striking dichotomy in the San Juan world of two thousand years ago? If there were two populations in the region, the one dwelling in relatively permanent pithouses, the other in temporary shelters, the one cultivating maize on some scale, the more southerly still heavily involved in foraging rather than farming, which one was the ancestor of the Ancestral Pueblo of Chaco?[10] Was Irwin-Williams correct in assuming a fundamental continuity between earlier hunter-gatherer and Basketmaker societies? If correct, then the institutions of Pueblo society should be visible in archaeological sites left by Archaic and Basketmaker II cultures. Was there a smooth transition between En Medio and Los Piños (Basketmaker II) and later Basketmaker III society, which is generally agreed to be part of the ancestry of Ancestral Pueblo society?

En Medio remains shadowy, largely because almost all known sites left by these people were occupied but once, making it difficult to study changes in their culture through time. The only barometers of cultural change are imprecise indicators such as projectile heads. What is striking, however, is the seeming lack of change in En Medio sites generally, and the overwhelming persistence of wild plant foods in the diet long after Los Piños communities in the north were cultivating corn. Well-documented climatic changes, such as drought cycles or increased rainfall, do not appear to have disrupted En Medio life or led to dramatic changes in ways people made their living. In recent years, a dramatic expansion in cultural resource management investigations has produced radiocarbon dates from individual sites that will, in time, produce a more accurate chronology for En Medio and its contemporaries.

Los Piños is a different matter. Los Piños and En Medio were partially contemporaneous, but there are signs that the Los Piños occupation was an abrupt change from earlier lifeways. Los Piños, apparently a more complex society, came into being six centuries later. Furthermore, there are no signs that Los Piños developed from earlier hunter-gatherer traditions in the area; earlier sites are almost nonexistent in the Los Piños culture area. Los Piños appeared abruptly, but no one knows why this sudden change took place. Gwinn Vivian and others believe that the new culture was a response to population pressure and a climatic shift to wetter conditions. As a result, the people relocated to higher elevations near permanent streams, where they had access to wild plants and game, as well as land suitable for simple maize cultivation. Eventually, the expanding population dominated neighboring areas and was able to develop multiple and essentially simultaneous ways of acquiring food. This, in turn, accelerated the rate of culture change without radically changing its direction. In another scenario, Michael Berry believes there was never a transition from hunting and gathering to agriculture on the Colorado Plateau. He theorizes that Los Piños populations entered the area abruptly from southern Arizona and New Mexico.[11]

Are we correct in attributing these changes to climatic change? Tree rings tell us there were five centuries of unpredictable rainfall from 500 BC to AD 1, which may have led to more regular experimentation with maize and other crops—activities that required a much greater investment of time in securing food. Large corncobs and new corn types appear in archaeological sites of this period. Camp sites are larger, some even occupied more-or-less permanently, with more extensive storage facilities. At this point, some Los Piños communities were moving toward a more sedentary lifeway, which depended on a great deal more daily labor.

Around AD 1, precipitation increased, water tables rose, and there was more intermittent stream flow, sufficient to support small-scale agriculture. A combination of more reliable water supplies and fertile soils allowed for small-scale agriculture—a much more reliable food source than the patchy supplies of earlier times. As a result, farming activity intensified in some places, with a corresponding increase in the use of storage facilities. A more sedentary lifeway and permanent settlement provided a more stable domestic environment, and the opportunity to have more children, for more people on the ground could increase food supplies by jump-starting agricultural productivity. After several centuries, farming became the dominant subsistence pattern and hunting and gathering faded to lesser importance. Then, as later, cycles of drought and rainfall, as already noted, played a vital role in San Juan history— and in the unfolding saga of Chaco Canyon.[12]

Basketmaker II was a time of experimentation. Between AD 1 and 400, nascent farming communities in the north established pithouse settlements at higher elevations overlooking lower ground near streams and intermittent washes with their fertile soils. In other places, people still lived in brush shelters, especially in dune areas, where they still processed wild seeds as their predecessors did. These two forms of site may represent fall and winter pithouse settlements, and spring and summer foraging camps at lower elevations. More changes came with the appearance of pottery between AD 300 and 400, which must have brought a revolution in cooking, allowing the boiling of beans and corn.

Between AD 400 and 700, pithouse settlements became larger on the uplands. By the 500s and 600s, population increases led to the establishment of such villages in lower, more open areas such as Chaco Canyon. Perhaps people from the north moved southward along such natural routes as the Chaco Wash, seeking places where they could combine farming with the foraging that had always sustained them. As we shall see in chapter 5, by AD 800, there was no going back. The people of Chaco and elsewhere were locked completely into economies based on maize and bean cultivation.

BEFORE THE BASKETMAKERS
(6000–800 BC, PERHAPS EARLIER)

After 800 BC, there was increasing cultural diversity throughout the San Juan Basin, even if few details of how it came into being have survived. From then on, we have a reasonable knowledge of the culture changes that led to the flowering of Ancestral Pueblo society in later centuries. But what was the ultimate ancestry of the Basketmakers and the hunter-gatherers from which they apparently descended?

Basketmaker's roots lie in the six thousand years or so of Cynthia Irwin-Williams's Oshara tradition, identified over an enormous area throughout the San Juan Basin and from the Rio Grande Valley in the south into south-central Colorado and southeastern Utah. There's an almost numbing similarity between the toolkits of Oshara groups thousands of years apart, and over vast distances. For all these six millennia, people were thin on the ground, were on the move constantly, and lived out their lives in small family bands. Over most of this time, human existence had little changed, the only discernible cultural shifts being in projectile point design—and we do not know what, if anything, most of these small changes signify.

During these long millennia, people lived life on the move: they had to, because their food supplies were scattered over a vast, yet edible, landscape. Each band's territory covered hundreds of square miles, except in places like Chaco where food supplies were unusually diverse. One expert has estimated that the hunting bands visiting Chaco exploited a territory with a radius of about 6 miles (10 km), but this is merely a guess. The basic rhythm of life underwent little change from one year to the next, as the people adjusted to cycles of drier and wetter years, to seasons of good piñon harvests and years of hunger. Survival depended on ingenuity, opportunism, and, above all, minimizing the risk of starvation. This was the basic theme of life in Chaco. Everyone traveled light, with the simplest of toolkits—spears and atlatls (spear throwers), clubs, and, above all, light milling stones and grinders. Such toolkits make for unspectacular archaeology. They leave little trace on the ground, but we should not be deceived by the seeming simplicity of technology, low population densities, and the constant mobility. These were people with a sophisticated, encyclopedic knowledge of their environment, who could read it literally like a book. They did so with brilliant success for more than seven thousand years.

Archaeologist Alan Simmons is one of the few fieldworkers who has searched for the earliest Chaco settlers and tried to decipher the dynamics of their lives.[13] He believes that the canyon, and perhaps Chacra Mesa, sustained the local bands during the winter, whereas from spring onward they dispersed into neighboring areas. Unfortunately, both surveys and limited excavations in rockshelters in Chaco itself have yielded meager data to support his theory. By examining the artifact scatters from small camp sites just north of the canyon, Simmons identified locations where people processed plants, pursued game, and manufactured tools. There were no large base camps, perhaps a reflection of the diverse foodstuffs available in or near Chaco Canyon, so people did not stay in the same place exploiting a specific food for a very long time.

For thousands of years, Chaco was a stopping place, perhaps during winters, for hunter-gatherer bands who never numbered more than a couple of dozen people. These bands were small in numbers, moving over a wide area. They were aware of a much wider world beyond their own loosely defined territories, but it was a world that impinged little on their lives. In the course of a year, most people never encountered more than a few dozen members of neighboring bands at occasional gatherings for major ceremonies and other social transactions like arranging marriages.

Had you flown over the San Juan Basin five thousand years ago, you would have seen few signs of human activity—perhaps the white smoke of a campfire rising into the still air from a river bank, or a tiny cluster of brush shelters atop a low mesa. And perhaps a couple of times you might have seen a line of people walking along a game path, tiny dots almost lost in the vastness of semiarid land. On the ground, the silence would have been complete except for the sloughing of a soft westerly wind, an occasional dust devil raising fine sand from a dry watercourse, or a solitary deer starting up from the brush. But, had you approached a human encampment, you would have smelled the acrid scent of wood smoke and heard the endless scrape, scrape of milling stone against grinder readying the evening meal.

More than seven thousand years of exploiting an edible landscape, little apparent change in either toolkits or the ceaseless search for food, lives lived in egalitarian bands where only experience and consensus governed daily life—these were people who defined their world with chants and shaman's performances, with vivid myths and intricate oral traditions of people interacting with mythic beasts and the supernatural. We know this not because we know of their beliefs and rituals, but because all hunter-gatherer societies everywhere define their lives by such rituals. The earliest Chacoans were no exception. Then, some time in the second millennium BC, came change—in the form of maize.

Maize arrived in the Chaco region some time during the second millennium BC. The exact date eludes us, but some time afterward the Chacoans first come into more intimate focus. Alan Simmons found three sites with maize pollen during his survey of early sites, and another one that yielded a carbonized maize cob, radiocarbon dated to about 900 BC.[14] This was a time when visitors to the canyon also used convenient rocky overhangs as temporary camps, one of which yielded hunting artifacts, and also maize and squash. People certainly visited Atlatl Cave near the head of a small canyon within a mile (1.6 km) of the western end of Chaco, excavated not by Simmons but by the Chaco

Figure 4.4   Atlatl Cave, Chaco Canyon. *Courtesy of Gwinn Vivian.*

Project (figure 4.4). The shallow, sandstone rockshelter contained a hearth, but no signs of dwellings and only thin garbage deposits. Radiocarbon dates place the occupation in the tenth century BC. Numerous wild plant remains came from Atlatl Cave, as did fragments of rabbit fur, basketry, pieces of a yucca sandal, and part of a small, flat atlatl.

Atlatl is an especially important site, because it yielded perishable foods and artifacts, whereas nearly every other known Archaic site in the canyon is in the open and little more than a scatter of stone tools. At the time when Atlatl was in use, people also camped on nearby dune ridges, where stone artifact scatters and telltale fire-cracked stones from cooking were found.

At this time, Chaco was a place you merely visited. The larger base camps of fall and winter lay elsewhere, near canyon heads with ample water supplies and nearby bottom land for simple cultivation. So far, no one has located such a settlement in the Chaco core, or upstream of it, but they may well come to light in the future. The inconspicuous signature left by these visitors is hardly surprising, for the overall human population of the San Juan Basin was still no more than a few hundred people.

Yet, for all their shadowy presence, these Archaic hunter-gatherers were ancestors of the Pueblo peoples of a later time.

AN EVEN EARLIER ANCESTRY?
(6,000 TO 11,000 YEARS AGO OR EARLIER)

No one knows whether the roots of the ancient Oshara tradition went back into Paleo-Indian times, before 6000 BC and back to the still little-known earliest chapter of Southwestern history before thirteen thousand years ago when the descendants of the first Americans visited the San Juan Basin. The border between Paleo-Indian and Archaic times is hazy at best, with the latter adapting to drier climatic conditions and exploiting a far wider range of foods. Many experts believe that the genealogical roots of Southwestern society do indeed go back very far into Paleo-Indian times, in an arid world where things changed little over thousands of years.

No one knows when the first human being set foot in Chaco Canyon, but, judging from finds of Paleo-Indian stone projectile points elsewhere in the San Juan Basin, it was at least eleven thousand years ago. For thousands of years, Chaco's inhabitants were only a fleeting presence. They were foragers, probably never more than a few dozen people at a time, who camped briefly on mesa tops and by water sources on the canyon floor. At the time, the human population of the San Juan Basin was tiny, most of it anchored to natural water seeps and springs, such as those in the Arroyo Cuervo region southeast of Chaco.

The long history of Chaco Canyon began with willow-wisps of human occupation over eleven thousand years ago. When we admire the serried rooms of Pueblo Bonito and other great houses in the heart of the canyon, it's well to pause and contemplate the deep cultural roots of the people who built them. They came from an ancient tradition of human existence in arid lands, their culture forged from thousands of years of flexibility, mobility, and opportunism. These qualities served the Basketmakers and their successors well, allowing them to adapt to a vastly more complicated economic and political world. We describe the beginnings of this changing world in chapter 5.

5∴ SHABIK'ESHCHEE AND THE FIRST PUEBLOS

> Long ago in the north below from the Place of Emergence everybody came out. Now when those who are everyone's chiefs came out they all went out. They went down south. . . . They went along coming from the north and they began to make towns.
>
> Cochiti origin myth[1]

Chaco Canyon, early fall, AD 550: The men move slowly down the slope above the village, juniper poles slung between their shoulders. Below them, the pithouses nestle against the ground on either side of a small drainage. Some are in use, smoke drifting idly from their roofs. Others lie in ruins, little more than ovals filled with collapsed roof brush and clay, the posts carefully salvaged for use elsewhere. The men turn toward two broad ovals dug out of the ground—pithouses in the making. Wearily, they drop their logs by one of the depressions, next to heaps of brush piled up some distance away. They watch as the owner of one of the houses and his son dig out deep postholes for the roof uprights, sweating in the hot fall sun. The piñon trees have yielded a good harvest this year. While the men tip a stout post into one of the floor holes, their wives and daughters are sorting the newly harvested nuts and packing them into stone-lined bins.

Down by a side canyon, the village's gardens bake in the afternoon sun, the still unharvested maize stalks withering in the heat. No rain has fallen for weeks and the Chaco Wash is dry. An old man sits in the shade and contemplates the dry landscape. Fortunately, the piñon harvest has been bountiful, so the group will not go hungry. . . .

∴ ∴ ∴

Between AD 400 and 700, the San Juan Basin enjoyed considerably more rainfall, three centuries of adequate moisture interspersed by only occasional droughts. Rising water tables, more rainfall, and consistent filling of washes and river channels with fertile alluvium encouraged numerous communities to plant crops away from the traditional flood-plain areas. At the same time, wild plant foods became more abundant. It was now possible to accumulate substantial food surpluses to tide one over from one season to the next. This advantage was offset at least partially by rising population densities and less frequent, but longer droughts that forced communities to draw down on stored foods, or to revert to more foraging. Overall, however, climatic conditions favored a shift from hunting and gathering to a more sedentary farming life. Had drought conditions been more severe, there's no question that the changeover would have been delayed for several centuries.

BASKETMAKER III

Because the San Juan Basin has a diverse landscape with widely varying rainfall patterns, it's hardly surprising that the changeover to farming occurred at different rates and at different times through the region. Archaeologists know the new farming cultures generically as Basketmaker III. In the northern Basin, the Los Piños Basketmaker II culture developed into two local Basketmaker III variants, of which the largest and most important is often called La Plata. La Plata settlements cover a large area, from Mesa Verde and the La Plata-Animas drainage in the north to the Chaco core and Lower Chuska Valley, as well as the southern portions of the San Juan Basin. Quite how La Plata originated is unknown because, as is so often the case, we have no sites that document the transition from earlier Los Piños. But there's reason to suspect that Los Piños Basketmakers who were part cultivators, part foragers, may have moved out of highland regions on the northern edge of the San Juan Basin into areas to the south where they could find favorable places for simple cultivation. There they adapted to new environmental conditions, settling near piñon-juniper woodlands and locating their villages on higher ground above local drainages. Nearly 70 percent of the La Plata sites in Chaco Canyon lie on knolls, ridges, or slopes below mesa rims, but there are also some settlements buried deep below the alluvium on the canyon floor.

Almost all La Plata communities lived in pithouses, some of them forming quite large villages. By AD 500, at least two Basketmaker III (La Plata) communities were well established in Chaco Canyon, in villages that were occupied for several centuries.

SHABIK'ESHCHEE VILLAGE

In 1926, archaeologist Frank Roberts investigated what appeared to be a large pithouse village atop Chacra Mesa, 9 miles (14.5 km) east of Pueblo Bonito. Roberts was working for Neil Judd's National Geographic expedition at the time and only had time to excavate two pithouses and several storage bins. He returned the following year to clear eighteen houses, a large kiva, and forty-eight storage bins on a knoll slightly to the west.[2]

Roberts named his new site Shabik'eshchee, obtained a few tree-ring samples, and documented changes in the house styles from circular and oval to a rectangular style from a later time. The dwellings originally had antechambers, which later evolved into ventilators instead. The pithouses were semisubterranean, mostly roughly circular or rectangular. Their sandstone slab walls were covered with plaster. Each pithouse had four timber roof supports and a domed roof of sloping side posts covered with a layer of twigs, bark, and earth. The storage bins—similar to pithouses, with slab walls, plaster floors, and dome roofs, but were much smaller—had no hearths or other interior features. Shabik'eshchee's kiva covered 1,022 sq. feet (95 sq m). A low bench surrounded the entire interior wall. Roberts identified Shabik'eshchee as a pre-Pueblo, Basketmaker III site, one of the earliest settlements in Chaco Canyon, but he also detected signs of a later occupation.

Much has happened at Chaco since Roberts's day. We now know of numerous Basketmaker III settlements in Chaco Canyon and its surroundings.[3] Most are of small size, with no more than one to twelve pithouses, so Shabik'eshchee is much larger than the average Basketmaker site in the Chaco area, covering nearly 20 acres (8 ha). The village lies on the northern end of a narrow mesa that overlooks the Chaco Wash, bordered on three sides by steep cliffs. New surveys and excavations have added to the pithouse count at the site, which now total between forty and sixty, distributed almost equally on the southeastern and northwestern sides of a small drainage that runs through the settlement.

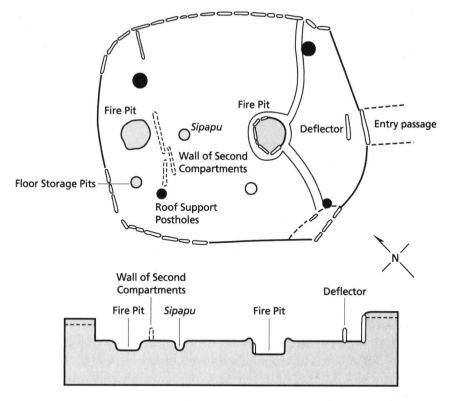

Plan and Profile of House M, Shabik'eschee Village.
Illustrating Typical Features

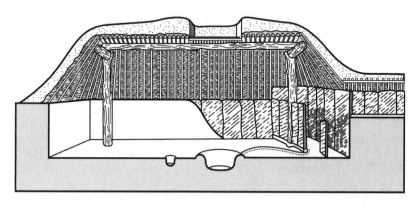

Cross Section of Idealized Pithouse Showing
Method of Construction and Features

Figure 5.1   Plan of Shabik'eshchee pithouse.

How big was the village in its heyday? Superficially, the settlement seemed to be of considerable size, but excavation methods were less sophisticated in Roberts's day than they are today—and he was a good excavator for his time. We also know much more about pithouses from extremely precise tree-ring studies of these dwellings throughout the Southwest. Tree-ring sequences from individual houses tell us that most of them were only in use for between ten and fifteen years—a figure that agrees well with modern-day studies of pithouse equivalents such as Navajo hogans and Plains earth lodges.[4] After about a decade or so, vermin and structural decay took their toll and most of the houses were abandoned (figure 5.1).

Rodents and decay are common to such structures everywhere in the world. I remember visiting farming villages in Central Africa's Zambezi Valley, where mud and thatched dwellings were constantly being rebuilt, extended, or repaired, and often abandoned, while a new house rose a short distance away. They were compact but "untidy" settlements. The original village was laid out according to some informal plan. People built their huts close to fellow kin, sometimes near friends. But, as time went on, people moved between houses, got married, nuclear families dispersed. The original relatively orderly settlement became something less ordered and quite different, an agglomeration of new houses and old, of collapsed ruins, and even dwellings destroyed by fire. Of course there were always villages where social hierarchy and other considerations were important and the layout rarely changed, but, for the most part, there was no formal order to the settlement. This seems to have been the case at Shabik'eshchee.

Shabik'eshchee is still poorly dated, but was probably in use over about two-and-a-half centuries from AD 500 to the early 700s.

VILLAGERS OR VISITORS? OR BOTH?

For generations Chaco archaeologists have assumed that the appearance of pithouses meant that the people settled in permanent villages for the first time, as they became full-time farmers. In recent years this assumption has been questioned, even for many post-Basketmaker settlements. As the Los Piños sites show us, maize cultivation was combined with foraging, and the same may have been true for Chaco Basketmaker people. Many years ago, the University of Michigan archaeologist, Kent Flannery, studied the origins of agriculture in Central America.[5] He pointed out that people can eat well off wild grasses, but they can do so only if they store them on a large scale for use for months after the harvest is over. Such storage acted as a form of tether, which tended to favor a degree of permanent village life, or "sedentism" as archaeologists call it. This in turn creates a problem for the now-tethered foragers, who still have to acquire a proportion of their food from elsewhere. There were various solutions, principal among them being the notion of caching food for later use, as many Great Basin groups did in caves and rockshelters. Obviously, the farther you need to travel to find additional food, the harder it is to monitor storage back at base.

The large numbers of storage bins, pits, and other such facilities at Shabik'eshchee struck both Frank Roberts and later investigators. There were so-called antechambers attached to pithouses by small tunnels or passageways. These could hold about 60 cubic feet (1.7 cu m) per house; Roberts excavated one that had "considerable carbonized corn on the floor." Circular and oval clay-plastered bins, or "cists," made of stone slabs and covered with wickerwork, mud, and earth, lay above ground between many of the houses, similar to those used in Basketmaker caves in other areas such as southwestern Colorado. They had a mean volume of 56 cubic feet (1.6 cu m).

A large storage capacity, you might think, but one that appears to have been handled in different ways. Pueblo households today store their maize and other foods in cool, dry rooms, which are entered daily as part of preparing meals. The pithouse antechambers may have been facilities like these, owned by individual households. The bins out in the open were free-standing, separated from one another and the houses, and only accessible through a small opening at the top. They were completely sealed, limiting the exposure of the contents to the air and to humidity, something essential to prevent premature germination of the seeds inside, which were essential to the next year's planting. (With adequate sealing, maize seeds can be germinated after many years of storage.)

The bins were certainly used to store maize, but they may have had another function, too: caching food. They were sturdy structures, hard of access, used to store food for long periods of time. To reach the food at the base of a bin may have involved partially dismantling it, for they were as much as 4 feet (1.2 m) deep. Because the bins were out in the open, highly visible, and none of them associated with specific houses, archaeologists Wirt Wills and Tom Windes theorize that they were group-owned, in sharp contrast to the privately owned storage rooms inside the pithouses.

Thus, Shabik'eshchee may represent a new form of settlement, where a core group of families resided permanently and monitored the commonly held storage, while a large number of people congregated at the site when local conditions allowed for enough food to do so. If this theory is correct, then we are witnessing a major shift away from thousands of years of communally shared supplies on the part of hunter-gatherer societies. Now there was a new emerging social order, where notions of reciprocity of mutual obligation, which dominated hunter-gatherer life, while still important were being replaced by household ownership of food.

Wills and Windes believe that two variables were at play—the local availability of wild plant foods and periodically favorable conditions for agriculture. In Shabik'eshchee's heyday, piñon-juniper woodlands flourished near the settlement, and more abundantly at a distance. The piñon averages one good harvest every four years, perhaps the interval at which Shabik'eshchee's population grew temporarily larger.

All of this implies that Basketmaker subsistence in the San Juan Basin involved two strategies. The typical Basketmaker III group was probably about one to three families, who occupied several small settlements in the course of a year or more, just like modern Navajo used to do. There were, however, places with unusual environmental variability like Chaco Canyon, where larger populations sometimes gathered for short periods of time, especially in the fall after the nut harvest. At the time, annual planting might not have been feasible because of unpredictable rainfall, so long-term storage caches were extremely advantageous.

There are two distinct linear clusters of Basketmaker III sites in the canyon, one at Shabik'eshchee, the other at a large settlement labeled 29SJ423 that lies on a rocky promontory overlooking the canyon far downstream. 29SJ423 includes another large kivalike structure, associated with at least twenty-four storage bins built at various times during the occupation of the site in the 550s. Wills and Windes believe that 29SJ423 functioned in the same way as Shabik'eshchee Village. In both cases, the linear clusters run from the top of Chacra Mesa down to the canyon edge, where the two major sites lie at strategic high points above the canyon floor. The 10 miles (16 km) between the two sites contain no dense clusters of Basketmaker sites, just a few scattered settlements.

Interestingly, both the larger sites lay close to similar environmental features—fertile soils, large local watersheds, and piñon groves. We don't know whether the two locations were occupied at the same time, but they both lie in places where the same pattern of a small resident population, caching, and occasional larger populations would have been feasible. Such larger Basketmaker settlements are known from other areas far from Chaco Canyon, but they are never common. Here, as in later times, Chaco seems to have been an unusual place, where a diversity of subsistence activities were possible and where there were relatively predictable water supplies. As a result, in good piñon harvest years, the population of the canyon may have risen considerably for a few weeks, even months, while large food caches were carefully maintained there year after year.

We have no reliable means of estimating how many people lived at Shabik'eshchee and other pithouse settlements. In the 1930s, the great anthropologist Julian Steward, who was an expert on desert hunter-gatherers, estimated that each Shabik'eshchee pithouse housed a family of 5.5 people. He based his estimate on analogies with modern Plains earth lodges.[6] A figure of five people has been widely accepted but is almost certainly unreliable, since there is no evidence that nuclear families were in fact associated with the pithouses.

How many of the pithouses were in use at one time? Frank Roberts estimated that 1.6 pithouses were intact, relative to each dismantled pithouse. Thus, about 42 houses at the site were in use at the same time, with a floor area of 8,234 sq. feet (765 sq m) and a population of 76.5 people. Factoring in a hypothetical ratio of two adults to three children, we get an estimate of about 15.3 families. This must be a maximal figure, because we know almost nothing of the changing size of the site, which may have grown significantly over time.

The 15.3 (families) figure applies only to Shabik'eshchee, not to the many smaller Basketmaker settlements of one to three pithouses, which cannot have had more than five to fifteen people each. Whatever the estimates, it seems that the basic population of Chaco during the Basketmaker centuries was tiny, perhaps as few as a hundred most of the time. But the number of people increased dramatically, perhaps to two or three times that number for short periods of time, especially during good piñon and maize harvest years.

BASKETMAKER SOCIETY

By AD 700 Chaco Canyon's permanent population was perhaps a hundred people or so, increasing occasionally to several hundred. If Wills and Windes are correct, the dynamics of Chaco society were now very different from those of earlier millennia, when only the occasional foraging band visited the canyon. The ancient rhythm of hunting and plant harvest still followed the repetitive cycle of the seasons. At the same time, the hunter-gatherers were also cultivators, anchored for several months to their maize gardens. Maize is a demanding crop, which requires water and constant weeding in addition to protection against birds and other predators. During the critical growing months, even a modest plot required daily attention, long after the farmers had gambled on the timing of rainfall and planting. Then there was the problem of food storage, in earlier times communal, now apparently a combination of ancient practice and individually owned rooms or bins.

Basketmaker society was made up of individual households, linked to one another by kin ties, with many communal interests, and reciprocal obligations. Such social dynamics worked well when numbers were small, and individuals and families could handle disputes. I believe the long periods of aggregation, when people came together, changed the dynamics. There were advantages in numbers. Such gatherings offered excellent opportunities for exchanging information about food supplies and water supplies scattered widely over a vast area. They were also times when marriages were arranged, when neighbors traded with one another, and communal rituals were performed. But the dangers of conflict between people thrown into close juxtaposition for weeks and months at a time were dramatically heightened.

This situation arose everywhere in the world where people settled in permanent villages, or lived close alongside others for long periods of time. For example, at Abu Hureyra in Syria's Euphrates Valley, some of the world's earliest farmers of 10,000 BC lived in a dense cluster of mudbrick houses separated by courtyards and narrow alleys. The Abu Hureyra settlement flourished for more than four thousand years, a clear sign that the people had developed effective ways of defusing social tensions and settling disputes. Shabik'eshchee and other growing Basketmaker communities faced the same problem, which could only be solved by social change. Studies of modern-day village societies suggest that the critical point came in settlements with six to eleven households—forty or more people. At that point, the nuclear family was no longer sufficient to resolve even simple disputes, and the authority of the extended family, of the kin group, came into play. Both the large Chaco Basketmaker sites of AD 600 boasted of permanent populations well above this critical threshold.

Shabik'eshchee was five times the size of the average Chaco Basketmaker III settlement, with over seventy inhabitants. The technological innovations were minimal, but for such a community to function, someone had to coordinate a large number of important decisions. Who was to forage for piñons on higher ground to the east in fall? Who would organize hunting expeditions, arrange rabbit drives before crops were planted? Who would handle relations with other groups and serve as point person for communal rituals? Just the logistics of storage required levels of consensus that transcended the narrow confines of the individual household.

Who, then, were those who had such authority? Were they elders or kin leaders, or people with unusual supernatural powers? There is little consensus among the experts.

Many years ago, University of Michigan anthropologist Marshall Sahlins studied chiefs in Pacific Island societies.[7] He identified what he called "big men," able, entrepreneurial individuals who combined ritual powers with an expertise at trading, and an ability to attract loyalty among their followers, which they cemented with generous gifts of the food and other goods they acquired—a process of redistribution. Sahlins pointed out that these big men could not pass their authority on to their children or others. Their effectiveness was measured by their success, their generosity to their followers. Directly they died, this following evaporated, their loyalties transferred to others.

The big man model has long seduced archaeologists in many parts of the world. It's an elegant and convenient solution to the authority problem. Was it valid in Chaco's Basketmaker communities? Two well-known archaeologists—Kent Lightfoot and Gary Feinman—argued that big men oversaw the larger villages.[8] They pointed to the private storage rooms and the bins associated with the pithouses as evidence for redistribution. Unfortunately, there is no evidence for more substantial houses where big men might have lived at either of the two larger sites, nor are there definite associations of larger storage facilities with specific dwellings.

What, then, are the alternatives?[9] First, there is the seeming flexibility of Shabik'eshchee and site 29SJ423, where populations ebbed and flowed, where food was stored for long periods of time in both private and communal settings. Unquestionably, there was some form of group decision-making process at more than the household level. The presence of kivas at both the large sites strongly hints at such a mechanism, places where people from all households could meet, or where fellow kin could deliberate. The most logical individuals to be involved in what must have been periodic consultations were heads of individual households or kin leaders who would come together on the occasions when communal decisions were needed, especially in times of stress. Large gatherings of Basketmaker people were the exception rather than the rule. For the most part, then, decisions were made, as they always had been, at the household level. The larger settlements were occupied sporadically, each occupation being a specific episode in Chaco life. The people who gathered there shared common territories and fields, but there are no signs that they had the close ancestral ties to farming land that were commonplace in later centuries and are typical of farming societies in every part of the world.

No question that a few talented individuals did indeed rise to prominence for short periods during their lifetimes, but there are no signs that this prominence was anything but transitory. Certainly, the few Basketmaker burials that we know of show no signs of lavish decoration or individual prestige. Basketmaker society was egalitarian, kin based, and cemented together not by big men but by consensus reached between households in the quiet setting of a kiva, where the rituals unfolded that, then as now, underpinned life at Chaco.

Did this need for consensus produce a system of chiefs in the San Juan Basin, one or more of them living in Chaco? An argument for chiefs leans heavily on the assumption that no Basketmaker III community was self-sufficient. Apart from anything else, each one required marriage partners to remain viable. We know this because La Plata, and other Basketmaker II sites, contain many more exotic objects such as obsidian, turquoise, and marine shells from the Gulf of California. Such objects had already passed from hand to hand over long distances for many centuries. As anthropologist David Stuart points out, there were two rainfall patterns in the San Juan Basin. In the west, winter snowfall and summer rains provided two wet portions of the year. In the east and southeast, spring and mid- to late summer provided the rain. Chaco was on the boundary between these two areas (see figure 3.5). As result, he believes the Chacoans became brokers in trade in such commodities as pottery between these areas.[10] But had this exchange now become more formalized in the hands of newly emergent community leaders?

If Wills and Windes are correct, then sites like Shabik'eshchee were simple, if quite large, settlements, marked by relatively few permanent residents and a constantly shifting social landscape. I think this implies a lack of any form of social hierarchy, of any chiefs. Rather, kin groups and households made decisions, by a process of consensus, while long-distance exchange remained a minor background noise in lives where many people were still on the move for much of the year. But the increase in exotic objects foreshadows later centuries, when the tentacles of long-distance trade extended far from the canyon, at a volume unimaginable generations earlier.

To succeed, any strategy, be it for waging war, selling automobiles, or of survival, has to have an edge. The moment it loses that intangible edge, it's no longer effective. Herein lies the rub—realizing when change is imperative. Such a realization depends on instinct and leadership, on an ability to weigh risk. Such a moment came to the people of Chaco during the eighth century. For more than a thousand years, their ancestors had combined simple cultivation with hunting and plant gathering. They were hunter-gatherers as much as farmers during centuries when, for the most part, there was good rainfall. But, for all the greater moisture, there were still unpredictable droughts when crops withered in the gardens and the people fell back on stored food, deer and rabbits, and their edible landscape. As Wirt Wills and Tom Windes point out, large foraging territories were essential for people cultivating gardens in small, scattered locations some distance from their villages. They conclude: "the most common Basketmaker III settlement strategy probably was dispersal."[11]

Basketmaker III was a time of experiment, of cautious innovation with simple cultivation. On the whole, the new strategies were successful, so much so that populations rose. By the eighth century, the semiarid landscape of Chaco was near capacity—close to the ability of the land to support its human population. With this population growth came a much higher risk of hunger. Chaco Canyon offered some insurance against drought—its inhabitants could collect water, both from drainages flowing into the canyon and from summer storms that enter Chaco through breaks in the Chacra Mesa. The same mesa provided game and wild plant foods, firewood, and, at any rate initially, beams for house construction. In many respects, Chacra Mesa was more important than the canyon itself in Basketmaker III times, when people spent much of their time away from Chaco foraging for wild plant foods. Interestingly, both Shabik'eshchee and site 29SJ423 lie on benches of Chacra Mesa on the south side of the canyon, close to piñon nuts and other foods.

After AD 900, considerably more people lived at Chaco than in earlier times. Some households shifted their villages from the mesa to the south edge of the Chaco Canyon floor, where most smaller Chacoan settlements are to be found. The south side was close to Chacra Mesa with its terrace benches that were ideal for small maize gardens, as were the soils in the bottoms of short side canyons nearby. In addition, winter snow melts more slowly on the southern side of the canyon, where there is more shade. The melting snow percolated slowly into the soil, providing vital moisture for seed germination in the spring. Small sand dunes also provided convenient places for growing beans, introduced into the Southwest centuries earlier. No settlements of these centuries lie on the north side of the canyon, presumably because farming was harder owing to less favorable runoff conditions and more rapid snowmelt, and lack of runoff deposits.

Within a few centuries, as rainfall became more irregular and life less predictable, the Chacoans embarked on a cultural trajectory that melded ancient traditions with new ideas that were to crystallize into a brilliant and short-lived Southwestern society.

6 ∴ A WORLD OF MOVEMENT

> Understanding the emergence of the Chaco system
> may be like mapping a maze; we may have to look
> for its beginnings on the outside to help understand
> how to get to its center.
>
> Richard Wilshusen and Ruth Van Dyke[1]

A huge bank of black thunderclouds masses on the far horizon, mocking the bright sunlight bathing the canyon cliffs. The air is heavy and still, weighing upon the small figures weeding between the corn shoots along the canyon floor. Despite the heat, the methodical weeding continues, even as hurricane-force wind gusts burst suddenly through the canyon. A few fat raindrops form deep holes in the sandy soil as a wall of gray rushes between the cliffs. Suddenly, the deluge hits, a dense curtain of rain, pummeling, soaking. The farmers take shelter under a nearby rocky overhang. Cliff gullies become waterfalls; the canyon bed becomes a muddy torrent, sweeping boulders before it like ninepins. Then, just as abruptly, the downpour ends, as if switched off by a distant faucet. The gray world evaporates. Canyon walls glisten in bright sunlight. Incandescent raindrops reflect brilliantly on the green maize shoots. As the shadows lengthen, the precious moisture soaks into the cultivated ground while the weeding continues.

∴ ∴ ∴

By the eighth century, the better watered areas of the San Juan Basin were becoming densely populated. As farming activity intensified and people relied more and more on storage for survival, storage facilities became larger and universally moved above ground. This was the time when the first room blocks, the very first pueblos, appeared, ushering in a period of profound social tension, population movements, and political change, known to Southwestern archaeologists as Pueblo I.

PUEBLO I

In AD 800 Chaco was not a center of power, nor even an important place. Between 800 and 875, the main centers of economic and social power in the San Juan drainage lay around the edges of the Basin, not in its center. Only after 1050 did Chaco's great houses rise to prominence. How and why they acquired such importance remains one of the great historical enigmas of Chacoan history. Fortunately, much new research outside the canyon has yielded rich dividends and intriguing answers. Chaco itself was a frontier zone for many centuries, a place where Basketmaker traditions from north and south had coexisted and mingled. It was a place where egalitarian groups made most of their decisions within the compass of the household or the extended family, depending on the number of people living in a village during a specific season.

By the late 700s, drought cycles were more frequent. All kinds of changes in Basketmaker society were now under way. The dynamics of the annual round changed completely. For centuries, every community had switched effortlessly from cultivation to foraging, from sedentary living to mobility. Only a few villages had reached any size, and those were base camps as much as permanent settlements—Shabik'eshchee is a classic example. Even the largest villages were dispersed communities of people living in pithouses, and increasingly, in above-ground room suites—small pueblos. These changes, and an increasing reliance on agriculture, ushered in the three centuries of Ancestral Pueblo occupation at Chaco. But there's good reason to believe that the canyon's population remained very small until the late ninth century.

The changes were cautious ones, those of people feeling their way in a time of uncertainty. As villages became more permanent, so households deepened their pithouses, which also became smaller. At the same time, the bins and storage pits of earlier times became arcs of small, insubstantial rooms, usually fronted by *ramadas*, sheltered work areas with hearths, where food was processed. By 900 the arc of small rooms had become room blocks, with a larger front room with a hearth and often food processing equipment, while two much smaller back rooms served for storage. Each household occupied a three-room suite, which faced an area where one or more pit structures lay, some of them exhibiting some of the features found in later kivas. Over a century and a half, the informal pithouse settlements of the Basketmakers became modular settlements of above-ground rooms clustered into small communities, a few of which reached a considerable size. The above-ground pueblo with its room blocks and numerous storage compartments was born, most likely among communities in both the northern and southern San Juan Basin.[2]

During the ninth century, most Chacoans still lived in small communities of a few households. Between 875 and 900, large Pueblo I communities arose rapidly in the southern San Juan Basin. In the northern San Juan region, also, much of the population now lived in substantial farming villages made up of above-ground room suites. Their inhabitants relied almost entirely on maize and bean cultivation, and, in dry years on stored food and supplies traded from elsewhere. Pueblo I villages flourished far north of Chaco—in Utah or along the Utah-Colorado border by 770 and 830.[3] Soon afterward, villages appeared at Mesa Verde, along the Mancos River, and in the Durango area of southern Colorado. By 825–850, few northern villages had less than fifteen households, many between thirty and fifty. The Pueblo I population had swelled rapidly, not as a result of people moving their villages but from immigration. Judging from the pottery, much of the growth resulted from in-migration from the south and west, often from places as much as 60 miles (96.5 km) away where conditions were drier. By 840–880, Pueblo I villages formed a continuum from Mesa Verde to the northern part of the Montezuma Valley. At least a third to a half of the known population of the Ancestral Pueblo world then dwelt in the northern San Juan region.

The Pueblo I settlements of the north had a single room block inhabited by between ten and thirty households, with smaller room blocks surrounding the core, almost invariably within about 160 feet (50 m) or so of the main block. A village of about three to eighteen room blocks covered an area of 24–37 acres (10–15 ha). Many villages consisted of linked or multiple room blocks, usually with a U-shape. Apparently, the villages were occupied all at one time, probably for about thirty to forty years rather than over several centuries, as earlier investigators once thought.

How many people lived in these villages? One estimate, based on a sample of twenty-one Pueblo I sites, estimates an average size of about forty-eight households, all of them living in permanent, substantial villages in the true sense of the word, a far cry from the highly flexible

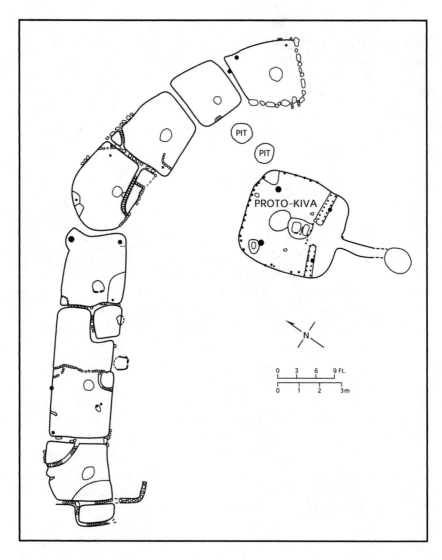

Figure 6.1   A northern San Juan Plateau house unit with a "proto-kiva" from Wetherill Mesa, Mesa Verde, Colorado.

pithouse settlements of a few centuries earlier (figure 6.1). These estimates agree well with historic figures for villages outside the influence of modern civilization, which lasted about twenty-five years and ranged in population from between about seventy people to as many as six hundred fifty, or one hundred thirty households.

The Pueblo I farmers of the north lived in high-density settlements, so much so that they placed new demands on the surrounding landscape for fertile agricultural land, firewood, construction lumber, wild plant foods, and drinking water. As Richard Wilshusen and Ruth Van Dyke have pointed out, the sheer proximity of these newly permanent, large settlements made for a potentially volatile social and political environment, at a time when there was little common social and religious unity between neighbors and apparently no mechanism that exercised authority over communities and their neighbors for the common good.

Hundreds of archaeological sites, large and small, chronicle village life in the north between 800 and 880. Then, suddenly, there are virtually no sites at all. Archaeologist Mark Varien plotted the cutting dates for all known Pueblo beams in the Mesa Verde region between AD 400 and 1300. His data shows an extraordinary drop in the archaeological tree-ring record between AD 880 and 1020, despite investigations of hundreds of sites in the region. There's no way investigators would have missed such sites. Nor do any trees cut down during this period show up in later sites as reused timber. Most later settlements in the region date to between 1000 and 1150. Almost certainly, the northern San Juan region was virtually depopulated in the tenth century. The people had moved away as abruptly as they had arrived. The question is—where did they go?[4]

The northern villagers may have come from the south and west, which meant that many of them could have come from south of the San Juan River. Here, the Pueblo I population was sparse, with none of the substantial villages that were so commonplace in the north. Basketmaker III and Pueblo II settlements are relatively commonplace in the south, but Pueblo I sites are scarce, and large villages virtually nonexistent. Many years ago, archaeologist Earl Morris of Aztec Ruin fame excavated a Pueblo I room block of twenty-two rooms at Bennett's Peak on the Chuska Slope south of Shiprock, a site dated to AD 799–850.[5] There are some Pueblo I villages on the Tohatchi Flats, again in the same general time range, found during a pipeline survey, but none of them approach the size of northern communities. Where there are larger sites, room blocks of three to six compartments are dispersed over an area of as much as a third of a square mile (0.7 sq km). Larger

villages were the exception. The overall population density of the southern San Juan Basin was probably about the same as the north, but is
little known from archaeological surveys. Unlike the north, most settlements were little more than small hamlets of two to three households,
compared with the fifteen to forty households of northern villages.
These were almost invariably located along small and ephemeral drainages, where cultivation was possible. Not until about AD 880 are there
signs of more sites and of dramatic population increases.

Chaco was still sparsely populated. Pueblo I sites are relatively
uncommon; few have been excavated.[6] Site 29SJ627 in Marcia's Rincon,
south of the Chaco Wash, was founded some time between 780 and 910,
a small settlement of ten to fourteen storage rooms and a work area—a
small room block with two or three contemporary structures occupied
for only ten to thirty years and on several occasions. Site 29SJ724 in
nearby Werito's Rincon dates to about 760–820, and was occupied on
only one occasion, when eleven surface rooms and work areas and a
single pithouse were constructed. Both these sites, two of the largest
Pueblo I settlements south of the San Juan so far excavated, are mere
hamlets when compared to the villages of the northern San Juan, but
much larger ones are known to exist.[7] Pueblo I sites are known to exist
in the south, among other places in the Red Mesa Valley, but they remain largely uninvestigated.

A Pueblo I settlement lies in the South Fork and may date to about
AD 875–1120.[8] Tom Windes mapped twenty-five to twenty-seven small
hamlets within this South Fork community, each with an average of two
households and very limited midden deposits or residential architecture (see figures 6.2 and 6.3). Most lie within line of sight of two adjacent
Pueblo I houses within a small part of the valley. Almost certainly, a
great kiva lies just below the two masonry houses. Another cluster of
Pueblo I sites is known from the next drainage to the west, making for
about fifty to seventy households living within this limited area.

Tom Windes, who has spent his entire career working at Chaco, believes that most Pueblo I occupation in the canyon took hold in the
mid- to late ninth century, much later than in the north. He attributes
the sudden increase in human settlement to a population movement
from outside, which may have coincided in part with the appearance
of the first great houses in the canyon.[9]

Everyone studying Chaco Canyon agrees that the first great houses
appeared in the canyon in the late ninth and early tenth centuries. The
earliest were Peñasco Blanco, Pueblo Bonito, and Una Vida, each constructed at the confluence of a major tributary flowing with the canyon.

Figure 6.2   Excavating Room 8 at a small Chaco site, 29SJ629. *Photograph by Earl Neller, 1975. Courtesy NPS Chaco Culture National Historical Park. Negative 10618.*

Figure 6.3   Site 29SJ629. A pithouse after excavation. *Photograph by Robert Greenlee, 1976. Courtesy NPS Chaco Culture National Historical Park. Negative 12327.*

These locations are where some of the best-watered agricultural land lies. Unfortunately, it's very hard to date the founding of these great houses, for they were constantly remodeled during their heyday and the earliest deposits are, in any case, buried deep below later occupation. A few early tree-ring dates from each of the three great houses place their founding in the late ninth and early tenth centuries. Only Pueblo Bonito has more than a few dates between 820 and 950, which we discuss in more detail in chapter 7. However, it seems that one portion of Pueblo Bonito was constructed as early as the 860s. Three other possible great houses—Kin Nahasbas (800s–900s), and Chaco East Community (900s), also Casa del Rio (late 800s) just west of the canyon—may date to the same period of time.[10] Almost certainly, other great houses appeared in the canyon at about the same time, but their earliest occupations remain undated, among them Pueblo Pintado (figure 6.4).

By the early ninth century, the northern San Juan population was on the increase, while that in the south was at best steady and probably declining.[11] By about AD 850 the population of the Mesa Verde region was in the order of eight thousand people, whereas the south was home to only about two thousand to four thousand, with no more than five to ten households living together anywhere.

Figure 6.4   Kin Bineola (Navajo: "house in which the wind whirls") lies in the southwestern Chaco Core, about 12 miles (19.3 km) southwest of Pueblo Bonito. Its founding date is unknown but may lie in the mid-900s. *Courtesy NPS Chaco Culture Historical Park. Slide 199.*

Then the picture changed dramatically. Between 900 and 925 the population of the north dropped rapidly, at the very moment when the first great houses appear in Chaco Canyon, along the Chuska Slope, and in other areas of the southern San Juan.

What, then, does this sudden shift mean? Chaco's population between 800 and 850 was probably in the hundreds, with scattered concentrations in other regions such as the edge of the Chuska Slope. In contrast, the northern San Juan was packed with between twenty and forty large villages and hundreds of hamlets. To argue, as some have, that we simply haven't found the equivalent village sites in the south stretches credibility after more than a century of often intensive archaeological surveys.

Over the past few years, archaeologists working in the north have acquired a mass of new chronological data, which allows them to look outside the narrow confines of a single site and to trace population movements. Originally, there was so little survey data that people tended to think that the farmers had moved within the confines of individual drainages, shifting their villages as arroyos cut down their courses. Now they suspect that the population movements both in and out of the north covered much larger areas, not merely tens of miles. During the ninth century, the newcomers arrived with their own southern architectural and pottery traditions that we can identify in archaeological sites. The data on these movements comes from a database of no less than forty-five hundred Pueblo sites in southwestern Colorado and over twenty-three hundred in northwestern New Mexico.

When the large villages of the northern San Juan were abandoned in the 880s, new communities with many of the same features appeared close to the San Juan River. The new settlements were of simple design, occupied for no longer than five to fifteen years—less than a generation. By the AD 910s, these villages with their fifteen to forty houses were burned down and abandoned. They seem to have been halfway stations between the north and the south, for population increases begin in the south in the early tenth century. The people were moving back southward again.

WHY MOVEMENT?

All these movements are entirely compatible with Pueblo values. The notion of movement, of adaptability to changing conditions and to drought, is deeply engrained in modern Pueblo society, and was clearly a central part of earlier thinking, too. Says scholar Tessie Naranjo, writing of her Tewa culture: "Movement, clouds, wind, and rain are one. Movement must be emulated by the people."[12] Part of this philosophy of movement and adaptability is a knowledge of one's destination, knowledge fostered by kin ties and trading relationships with distant communities. Ties of reciprocity, of social obligations, must have linked the people of the north with the south. Because of this, northerners moved south when drought desiccated their homeland.

Why did the northerners move? The ecological conditions of the northern and southern San Juan are very different.[13] It's no coincidence that most Pueblo I sites lie between 6,000 and 7,000 feet (1,829–2,134 m), where between 13 and 18 inches (330–457 mm) of rainfall can be counted on each year. This environment is cool, with early and late frosts, and close to the northern limits of maize, which grew best on carefully selected south-facing slopes. Agriculture involved considerable risk, but there were plenty of wild foods to fall back upon (figure 6.5).

Figure 6.5   A mano and metate from Chaco Canyon. *Courtesy NPS Museum Management Program and Chaco Culture National Historical Park. Image 7041b.*

Mountains also surround the southern San Juan, but the general environment is very different—much drier and warmer. Chaco Canyon has an average rainfall of only 9 inches (230 mm), but as much as three-quarters of it arrives between late spring and early fall. Chaco has about 60 percent of the northern rainfall but effectively the same amount of summer rain. While the canyon can have late spring and early fall frosts, and poor cold air drainage can keep temperatures low, the great cliff faces create locally warmer microenvironments that enjoy higher temperatures than the canyon bottom. This may be why most of the great houses are built close to the northern wall, where temperatures are warmer in winter. The same cliffs and mesa tops produce rainfall runoff vital for floodwater farming. All of this makes for an agriculturally diverse environment. However, wild plant foods and game are less plentiful than in the north.

These contrasting environments offer different challenges to the farmer. In the north, summer and winter conditions affect crop growth. In the south, the summers are all-important. Between the 880s and 890s, a series of intense droughts combined with shortened growing seasons played havoc with agriculture in the north by contracting potentially cultivable land. The areas favored by the villagers were especially vulnerable to drought and frost. In contrast, Chaco enjoyed above average rainfall during the same critical period and throughout the tenth century. So people with knowledge of the south moved there. This was precisely the time when the first great houses appeared in the canyon. During the late 900s and early 1000s, four more great houses rose in the canyon core as large additions were made to well-established communities.

The complicated histories and architecture of the northern and southern San Juan were closely intertwined throughout Chaco's florescence. By 875 the northern pueblo villages were at the height of their prosperity. The largest communities were never long lived, remaining in use for thirty to forty years. The northern climate was wetter in winter, with major temperature fluctuations, which could create havoc on perishable structures. Despite these limitations, some pueblos were substantial constructions.

Most northern villages had one or two large room blocks up to 650 feet (200 m) long with multiple fronting pit structures. Much smaller room blocks flank or surround the largest structure. For example, McPhee Village in the Mancos area near Mesa Verde was arc-shaped, with substantial masonry wall construction, and a ground plan that bears a remarkable resemblance to early Chaco building styles (see chapter 7).[14] Invariably, when the village was abandoned in the late ninth century, the blocks were burned down, each with their ritual paraphernalia in its proper place and with paired male and female human sacrificial victims buried in nearby pit structures.[15]

Chaco Canyon's contemporary settlements had no more than two to ten households, with ten to fourteen surface rooms and one or two pit structures. Such hamlets were commonplace in the northern San Juan between 750 and 850, but by 820–880, northern villages were much larger. In AD 875, only Pueblo Bonito and Una Vida could compare in size with the northern settlements, and construction began on them in the 860s, fully two decades after villages were commonplace in the north. There's some controversy over which part of Pueblo Bonito was constructed first, but most likely it was a central cluster of rooms in a large arched room block that mirrors the central block, a central arc that mirrors typical Pueblo buildings in the north at the time. By AD 875 Pueblo Bonito included one large pit structure and a pueblo of five to six household suites. The great house was much larger than anything else in the south but was still much smaller than any northern village.

By 925 the north was virtually empty—only five well-dated sites in southwestern Colorado date to 940–980. By then Chaco and the southern San Juan were booming. This was the period when northerners moved southward, first to the San Juan River, then farther south and into Chaco Canyon. By 920 Chaco was emerging as one of the major centers of Pueblo life. In the 1040s, much of the older portions of what is called Old Bonito, the central core of Pueblo Bonito, rose by the north canyon wall, perhaps to as many as three stories. Although the great houses of the day with their impressive architecture dwarfed the smaller settlements elsewhere in Chaco, they were many times smaller than the three largest villages of the northern San Juan in 860. The inspiration for them came from the north, but at the same time they became even rarer because they were multistory.

LEADERSHIP

How did these developing communities function? The early villages of the north were well spaced out, each controlling their own local areas. But even a superficial glance at individual sites reveals considerable differences in the kinds of resources they controlled. Some lay near soils that could sustain a community for many generations. Others were in environments with shorter growing seasons but with more nearby piñon groves. Each community faced different challenges, and, by the same token, required different forms of leadership. For all this diversity, as far as we can tell no village exercised any form of control over its neighbors.

At Chaco, the story appears very different. After 910 the climate was wetter, which reduced the risks involved in farming. Until about 900–920, impounded water behind the natural dam at the junction of the Escavada and Chaco Washes extended a short distance upstream. The dam prevented erosion of the Chaco Wash, keeping ground water at a fairly high level in the canyon bottom—essentially at a level where the maize could reach the subsurface water in fields on the floor. When the Wash breached the natural barrier at around AD 900, the lake vanished and the water table dropped abruptly. Chaco farmers had to change their crop watering strategies in short order. The dam breach adversely affected small-house communities on the south side of the canyon. Their owners simply resorted to old, proven—and never really abandoned—patterns of microniche farming.[16] Those who had taken advantage of high water tables in the central canyon now pulled back into the niches of the Chacra Mesa on the south side. Cultivators on the north side had mostly relied on high ground water for crop watering. When the water table dropped, they were faced with the need to use other options for crop watering such as irrigation canals and gridded fields. This period of adjustment coincides with a possible slowdown in great house construction in the canyon between about 940 and 1020.

Once new water-control methods came into play in the eleventh century, agricultural productivity increased dramatically. The new methods and their technologies required much more labor than the microniche farming on the south side. They may also have required new forms of leadership to adapt technologies for greater productivity, with all the potential for the manipulation of food supplies that entailed.

What form did this leadership take? In the north, village societies were generally egalitarian, even if there are signs that political and ritual power lay in the hands of a few people, or groups of individuals. At McPhee and elsewhere, these people may have occupied the largest, horseshoe-shaped blocks. We do know from burial discoveries that when they were abandoned, paired male and female victims were killed and their bodies deposited close to kivas in what could only be described as a ritual context. Their graves were pit structures in the village plaza, almost certainly controlled by kin groups. Gwinn Vivian believes that the northern populations had a form of social organization with a dual format that delegated specific functions to leaders, who made decisions in seasonal rotation.[17] Vivian is particularly impressed by the social organization of the modern-day Tewa people, which may offer an analogy for how society worked in the north. Tewa society has two halves, known as moieties. You inherit membership through your father, but this can change through marriage and other mechanisms. Each community has two moiety leaders who serve for half the year, roughly from solstice to solstice, the one more concerned with agriculture in summer, the other with hunting and plant gathering in winter. The moiety leaders organize all aspects of society, especially the ritual events that define the year and assure fertility of the fields. Thus, social control rotates between different halves of society, mediated by both human and supernatural groups. In this way, the Tewa achieve close coordination of all economic and religious activities, while, at the same time, no one can gain permanent power.[18]

During the ninth century, the ancestors of the Chacoans and the people of Mesa Verde may have lived alongside one another and interacted in the crucible of innovation that was the north. Thus, it's possible that

Chaco's great houses originated in northern pueblos, together with some of the rituals that unfolded in them. As Richard Wilshusen and Scott Ortman point out, some of the horseshoe-shaped room blocks of northern villages embrace an oversized pit structure with such features as a *sipapu*, the ritual conduit that separated the layers of the Pueblo cosmos.[19] There may have been community feasting as well—extensive middens lie close to the largest room blocks.

By 925 the largest Chaco room blocks were approaching the size of those in the north and were much more dramatic in appearance than their northern neighbors. They were two, sometimes three stories high and stood out among the small hamlets along the canyon floor. The rooms in the great houses were larger than those at smaller canyon settlements, requiring considerable amounts of labor to build them, far more than the household constructed rooms found in hamlets. Whether they were built at the behest of individual leaders, or powerful kin groups, remains an open question. But there can be little doubt that the social dynamics of Chaco's great houses originated in pueblo villages built generations earlier in the north.

Another expert, Lynne Sebastian, argues that the Chacoans could increase agricultural productivity in two ways.[20] They could cultivate gardens in different ecological zones to spread the risk of crop failure. Alternatively, they could develop water-control systems that captured and distributed runoff as efficiently as possible. At the basic level such decisions were for families or kin groups to make, but whatever strategy they followed had lasting consequences for future generations. Imagine, for example, families clearing gardens in different settings. As time went on and they were successful, the population would grow and the finite area for cultivation would be divided into smaller and smaller plots. Immediately, a serious issue arose. How did one allocate land equitably? There were many strategies, all of which required careful leadership—marriage alliances, inheritance rules, and increasingly careful management of the agricultural calendar. If people chose the water-delivery option, they would need to organize teams of people to dig and maintain water channels. Sebastian believes that the consensus agreement of earlier times now gave way to decisions made by those in positions of authority, with still further consequences, among them increasingly sharply defined roles in society and centralization of authority. Kin ties and social obligations were the glue that held everything together.

Herein may lie the importance of the fundamental changes in Pueblo I society. Each of these general agricultural strategies required labor and organization; both had productive potential. Inevitably the nascent pueblo society became less egalitarian and more socially differentiated. With the more labor intensive agriculture came larger food surpluses, and the ability to organize lavish rituals that commemorated this success—to both influence supernatural forces and to demonstrate success and social status. Inevitably, the ancient customs of reciprocity and mutual aid became strained under the new order, which led to the emergence of leaders, each with their own followers.

GREAT HOUSES IN THE SOUTH

We associate Chaco with great houses, but it's important to realize that they were not unique at the time of their founding. During the early 900s, Chaco was definitely not the center of the southern San Juan world. Great houses, with large kivas and six to twelve households, rose elsewhere, on the uplands north of the San Juan River, along the Chuska Slope, and in the Red Mesa Valley. They were centers of much larger communities comprising residences of one to three households clustered around the great house and dispersed over an area of a mile (1.6 km). The architecture was less formal than the later styles in the canyon, which nevertheless served much the same purpose. These were, perhaps, settings for ritual events, places where important ceremonies unfolded and feasting took place, where the functions of leadership unfolded in dispersed communities. Perhaps these backdrops were a temporary expedient, serving to help people reimagine what a community looked like, now the villages of the north were abandoned. Most of these endured only one or two generations. These sites flourished in areas with plentiful lumber, raw materials for making stone tools and pottery, game and wild plant foods in far more abundance than at Chaco (figure 6.6). These elements were the very raw materials that Chaco depended upon during its rapid growth and was to import from afar. Chaco's beginnings lay as much in the uplands of the north as they did within the canyon itself. So herein lies the solution to one of the mysteries of Chaco Canyon.

Figure 6.6   Chacoan granite axe head. *Courtesy NPS Museum Management Program and Chaco Culture National Historical Park. Image 29281.*

In its early stages Chaco was a place where immigrants were assimilating themselves into existing, ancient communities, bringing with them ritual practices and shared history from north of the San Juan. Since the communities of the north had themselves absorbed immigrants from the south and west, it's clear that they were aware of a much wider southern San Juan world.

But why was this southern world so much more attractive than the north? Why did Chaco's great houses flourish when the villages of the north failed? Why was Chaco such a magnet?

Perhaps the immigrants who moved into the north came from the southern San Juan during late Basketmaker III and Pueblo I. Then, a century or so later, they moved back south to a place that was warmer, with a longer growing season, a place with now more abundant rainfall. This was a familiar landscape of social memory, a place where ancestors had lived and died, where oral traditions commemorated mythic events. Northerners on the move returned to places that still had profound significance, where kin ties still endured, and memories were still alive. The immigrants returned to known landscapes, camping on the margins of Shabik'eshchee and 29SJ423 in Chaco, in places that survived in oral memory. Many early Pueblo II sites throughout the southern San Juan lie in the shadow of much earlier communities. Ancestors had lived and died here. This is where it was safe to return.

The landscape reverberated with memory, but, at the same time, Chaco was a special location and a central place. The canyon, with its diverse, if irregular, water supplies, was at the center of the San Juan Basin, a place with distinctive topography and distant views, a veritable center of the world for the people who lived there. It was, in the memorable words of the great scholar of religions, Mircea Eliade, an *axis mundi*, a center of the world.[21] And it was here that during the eleventh century, one of the great centers of the Pueblo world rose to prominence.

A REORGANIZED LANDSCAPE?

Something happened when the northerners moved south. The early great houses of the south seem to have reorganized the social landscape of earlier times in the north. The ways in which people organized their lives, their rituals, even their way of life, changed dramatically as they moved south. It was a fundamental change. Now major communities centered around a great house with a larger concentration of rooms. By

1050 the focus of community ritual performance had changed from an oversized pit structure up to 800 square feet (74.3 sq m) and a nearby plaza to a great kiva, some of them covering over 2,600 square feet (242 sq m) in some of the great southern communities. Great kivas did not become popular in Chaco until the mid-eleventh century.

Something new was going on—a scale of operation that began to transcend the individual community, where people needed to know what was going on as much as 40 miles (64 km) away to survive and flourish. No single group could live in isolation because of historical ties with much older communities, where ancestors had once lived. As a result, people "imagined" their communities as something much larger than the immediate vicinity of the settlement. This was one of the powerful forces that came into play as Chaco became the *axis mundi* of a much larger landscape, far larger than that imagined by even the largest Pueblo II great house.

Chaco Canyon rose to prominence in a highly competitive social landscape, something far more complex than we would have imagined even a generation ago.[22]

In the final analysis, everything resulted from the realities of an arid environment that acted like a vast pump—sucking people in when rainfall was more abundant, pushing them out to the margins, to other areas, when drought settled over the land. Even during the remarkable heyday of Chaco Canyon and its great houses, movement and flexibility never deserted the psyche of the Ancestral Pueblo.

∴ PART 3

APOGEE

The construction of the monumental and exquisite Chacoan architecture in such an inhospitable setting is a paradox that for decades has caused Southwestern archaeologists to scratch their heads.

Stephen Plog (1997)[1]

7 ∴ OLD BONITO

> In the beginning there was only Tokpella, endless space. . . . Only the Tawa, the Sun spirit, existed, along with some lesser gods. There were no people then, merely insect-like creatures who lived in a dark cave deep in the earth.
>
> Hopi creation story[2]

At Chaco, I feel as if I've entered a world of well-ordered layers. The great arc of sky ranges high over the land of the living on the canyon floor, where the Chaco Wash cuts into the brown strata of the earth, the underworld. The feeling is reinforced any time I gaze down into the depths of the great kiva at Casa Rinconada on the south side of the canyon. In the middle, a hidden passage from an entry room on the north side of the kiva passes below the floor to emerge in a circular enclosure probably screened by wooden slats, poles, or branches. Here was the symbolic place where the first people emerged from earlier worlds beneath the earth. The place of emergence, the *sipapu* in Hopi parlance, was the spot where the first inhabitants of the present world climbed up a hollow reed into a hole in the sky. *Sipapu* took many forms, often a hole in the floor of a kiva, sometimes a specific place. Many Hopi believe that the original *sipapu* lies near the confluence of the Little Colorado River with the Grand Canyon.

Few places bring you into such close association with the Pueblo cosmos. Therein lies one of Chaco's great fascinations.

For all its inherent spirituality, Chaco Canyon is frustrating for an archaeologist, who works with the tangible remains of human behavior.

111

We can never hope to talk to an inhabitant of Pueblo Bonito, or to understand the subtle nuances of Ancestral Pueblo human belief. All that survive are the material relics of human behavior—potsherds, abandoned ruins, and occasionally, thanks to the dry environment, well-preserved basketry, sandals, and textiles, or other organic remains. The long-abandoned great houses and small hamlets are monotone ruins, a far cry from the vibrant communities of ten centuries or more ago. The dancers and the drummers are gone, the rituals and chants that unfolded among them long vanished on the evanescent currents of history. We forget that Pueblo Bonito and Peñasco Blanco were once vibrant with bright colors, alive with human voices and the seductive scent of fresh wood smoke, at night aglow with flickering hearths and shadowy figures flitting among dark shadows. We can sense the cosmos that surrounded the Chacoans on every side, but never hope to reconstruct it in all its brilliant subtlety.

We're searching for a will-o'-the-wisp, for reflections of the intangible. Only rarely can we glance in such a mirror. The Australian historian Inga Clendinnon, an expert on the Aztec civilization of Mexico, aptly likened our quest for the intangible to Ahab's quest for the great white whale. "We will never catch him . . . it is our limitations of thought, of understandings, of imagination we test as we quarter these strange waters. And then we think we see a darkening in the deeper water, a sudden surge, the roll of a fluke—and then the heart-lifting glimpse of the great white shape, its whiteness throwing back its own particular light, there on the glimmering horizon."[3]

∴ ∴ ∴

By AD 800 Chacoans lived in small structures that housed one to four households, permanent settlements of small-room suites, mostly on the south side of the canyon. They farmed the most fertile soils with simple methods refined over many centuries of experiment and experience. As we have seen, the ensuing decades were times of movement when people from the north moved into the canyon and settled there. I found mention in the literature of one founding community at Pueblo Pintado that used clay vessels with clear northern ties, which tends to confirm that at least some of the immigrants came from the north, others from the south.[4] The process was probably amicable, involving arrangements with fellow kin who already lived at Chaco. During the next century, the canyon emerged as a major center of Pueblo society.

This was also the time when the first great houses rose along the north wall and south side.

The immigrants brought new architectural ideas with them. We've seen how arc-shaped structures already flourished in the northern and southern San Juan by the ninth century. The prototypes of what we may safely call "great houses" existed elsewhere by the early 900s, in places where Chacoan outliers later came into being. Chaco itself was not yet the center of the San Juan world, its nascent great houses still relatively insignificant structures. Over the next two centuries, the canyon became an *axis mundi*, a major hub of the northern Southwest. Its great houses assumed a great complexity and prominence.

The great French historian Le Roy Ladurie once remarked that there were two kinds of historians, parachutists and truffle hunters.[5] The parachutist observes the past from afar, on a grand scale, while the truffle hunter, fascinated by treasures in the soil, keeps a nose close to the ground. How right he is, and how well his comment also applies to archaeologists! Some of us are by temperament parachutists in everyday life. Many others are truffle hunters, with a fine mind for detail. I'm very much a parachutist, with a profound admiration for people who spend their careers studying the minute details of the past. I could never carry off the meticulous, time-consuming research involved with deciphering Chaco's great houses and the lives of the people who built them. This is some of the most complicated archaeology in the world. Archaeologists like Dabney Ford and Tom Windes spend their days in intricate detective work, poring over generations-old field notes, navigating through a maze of demolished and remodeled kivas, rooms, terraces, and plazas, sifting through the ruins of structures that were never the same one year to the next.[6]

For all their constant state of change, there was some overall plan. Great house or small farming community alike may have begun as architectural visions of a single individual, followed for centuries, but their execution involved massive rebuilding and repair in communities where spaces were occupied or otherwise used, then abandoned, or put to some other use. If my experience with African farming villages is any guide, then living in, or visiting Pueblo Bonito, Una Vida, or any other great house was to be in a partial ruin, in a structure always in a state of transformation. Residents of great houses—or of small sites—lived cheek-by-jowl with others, in communities riven by factionalism and not infrequent social tension, and never in an orderly, completely stable environment. Such communities could not have existed in any other way. To think of the great houses as tidy, sparkly clean towns is to do them historical injustice. I was struck with how the incidence of helminth parasitism in human feces found at Pueblo Bonito is near universal. These parasites result from communal living at close quarters, poor sanitation, contaminated food and drinking water.[7] These were not idyllic communities.

It's very easy to be seduced by great houses. As Steve Lekson has remarked aptly: "Chaco *today* is all about Great Houses. There would be no Chaco Culture National Historical Park . . . without Great Houses."[8] It would be a great mistake to limit ourselves to the dozen or so large great houses built between 850 and 1150. They were an important part of a larger architectural landscape, parts of which developed centuries earlier, others with the first construction of great houses in about 860. Lekson goes as far as to call this a "cityscape." I think this is a misnomer. Most archaeologists define cities as having at least five thousand inhabitants. No Chaco great house, let alone the population of the entire canyon during its heyday, ever achieved such numbers. A relatively dense population in Chaco's heart by San Juan Basin standards is certain, but certainly not an urban environment in the classic sense. Estimates vary from below one thousand inhabitants to as many as five thousand, but a figure of between two and three thousand seems a good compromise.[9]

Chaco's great houses began as very different structures from the massive, multistoried structures that survive today. They were by no means the first substantial settlements in the canyon. That distinction belongs to Shabik'eshchee and 29SJ423, which were settled in the fifth and sixth centuries. Both were part of linear clusters of pithouses and storage cists; both had great kivas. So at least some tradition of living at close quarters goes back centuries before the first room complexes appeared at Chaco.

The South Fork Community, the Pueblo I settlement of AD 800 on the South Fork of the Fajada Wash, which we visited in chapter 6, offers some precedents for later great houses.[10] This short-lived community was a cluster of small dwellings associated with a great kiva and a short road segment joining two room complexes. These two complexes were built using Type I masonry (see page 119), which made them taller and more conspicuous than other structures of the day. Furthermore, all the dwellings had sight lines to locally conspicuous landmarks, as if they were sacred topographic features. Interestingly, between 15 and 45 percent of the exotic toolmaking stone in the houses was a distinctive yellow, black-spotted chert that came from the Zuni Mountains, at least 100 miles (161 km) to the southwest. At the same time, the excavator and surveyor of the South Fork Community, Tom Windes, unearthed tools, raw materials, and ornaments in various stages of manufacture—signs of a nascent industry that assumed great importance in Chaco during later centuries.

Windes believes that there were other structures built with this Type I masonry at Pueblo Pintado, and on a much larger scale at Kin Bineola, whose chipped stone and ceramics seem to point to a southern origin (plate 15). This may mean that the early wave of groups out of the McPhee area in southwestern Colorado that moved down the Chaco Wash and into the canyon (see chapter 6) may well have branched out into major drainages along the way— into the Kin Bineola Wash, the Kin Klizhin Wash, and the South Fork of the Fajada Wash (figure 7.1). It's almost as if the canyon became the refuge for the inhabitants of all branch wash great houses sometime in the early tenth century.[11] These movements tell us that the Chacoans were well connected with distant communities, many of them in the Chuska region, in a web of interconnectedness that was to persist for four centuries. These connections were all part of the dynamic that had people constantly moving in and out of the canyon, sometimes in considerable numbers.

Figure 7.1   Tower kiva at Kin Klizhin. *Photograph by Gwinn Vivian. Courtesy NPS Chaco Culture National Historical Park. Negative 100255.*

Casa del Rio on the western approaches to Chaco is largely unexcavated, but boasts of a Pueblo I room block nearly 370 feet (113 m) long, later overbuilt with a great house in the 900s. There may have been a gap in occupation between the two structures, but we can guess, in the absence of excavations, that there must have been at least some cultural continuity between them. Casa del Rio has yielded large quantities of ground stone; it lay in a strategic position for different agricultural strategies, among them dune cultivation, farming on the floodplain of the Chaco Wash, and also the use of gardens nourished by runoff.[12]

Within the canyon itself, Pueblo Bonito and Una Vida began life as small hamlets, probably similar to that in the Fajada Wash, during the late 800s. The early stone houses were not demolished to make room for later ones but simply incorporated into the later construction. Una Vida's early houses must have assumed considerable importance in the minds of later generations, for they attached new construction to them rather than overbuilding, despite the asymmetry involved. Pueblo Pintado, at the eastern end of the canyon and 16 miles (25.7 km) east of Pueblo Bonito, may have been founded between (an estimated) 875 and 925, just as many villages north of the San Juan were abandoned, but so far the earliest rooms there have not been discovered.[13]

As we saw in chapter 6, construction of the first great houses coincided with the arrival of new groups in the canyon from the north and west, perhaps from southwestern Colorado and the Chuska. Until now, our historical binoculars have ranged widely over the San Juan and Chaco Canyon as a whole. Now we must work on a small scale, because almost all of what we know about Chacoan great houses comes from Pueblo Bonito in the heart of the canyon. People lived and worked at this famous site, and moved in and out of it, for at least 500 years, from the ninth to the late thirteenth centuries. During this long period Pueblo Bonito, like any great structure, was expanded in spurts, remodeled, and eventually abandoned. Untangling this architectural palimpsest taxes the skill of the most expert archaeologists. Only now, more than a century since the first excavations, do we have some understanding of Pueblo Bonito's history deciphered from changing architectural styles, pottery, tree-ring dated beams, and myriad other clues.

DECIPHERING PUEBLO BONITO

Every time I visit Pueblo Bonito I feel overwhelmed by its complexity. Almost invariably, I begin my tour by walking along the outside of the back wall, between the stacked rooms and the north canyon wall. Even in a ruined state, the massive structure is something special, a place built with vast labor according to a traditional vision deeply ingrained in its makers' minds. I always enter through the east wing, where the rooms are carefully preserved, the veneered masonry seemingly as fresh as the day it was laid. Last time I was there, it was a quiet fall day with few visitors, and I had the rooms to myself. They were quiet, serene spaces, isolated from the open plazas just outside. I imagined them occupied—stacks of maize cobs along the walls, women weaving in the shade, the constant murmur of voices from the terraces and plazas, a strong undercurrent of scents and odors, of sagebrush, human sweat, and rotting food. The archaeologist in me tries to sort out the confusion of crumbling walls and abandoned rooms, the jigsaw of kivas large and small open to the broad sky above, but with little success. Pueblo Bonito is the ultimate in archaeological puzzles.

In its heyday, Pueblo Bonito was an enormous and imposing structure in the center of downtown Chaco, with four stories and about seven hundred rooms, three great kivas, and thirty-three kivas (plates 1 to 3 and figure 1.3).[14] At its greatest extent, the site covered at least 3 acres (1.2 ha) at the center of a 3-square-mile (7.77 sq km) zone near the South Gap in Chacra Mesa, sometimes called "downtown Chaco." Fertile archaeological imaginations have labeled this area a "ceremonial precinct," a "cityscape," or an *axis mundi*, a central place of the Ancestral Pueblo world. There may be some validity in the notion of a sacred zone, since there are signs of a low masonry wall that once enclosed Pueblo Bonito, Pueblo del Arroyo, and Chetro Ketl, as if to separate them from the wider canyon landscape. The precinct may also have included Pueblo Alto, where traces of enclosure walls can be seen, thereby bringing both the mesa tops and the canyon floor into the central area.[15]

The original builders chose their construction site with care, under the north wall in the heart of the canyon, near a break in the mesas on the south side and beneath the sheer canyon wall dominated by Threatening Rock, a fractured portion of the sandstone cliff that seemed about to fall. Close by stood a solitary ponderosa pine, identified by excavators centuries later, on a site already occupied by earlier farmers. Pueblo Bonito is an archaeological icon, as famous as England's Stonehenge, Mexico's Teotihuacan, or Peru's Machu Picchu.[16] Here, we can trace the entire architectural and cultural history of Chaco Canyon from the 860s until the thirteenth century.

Building the great house close to the distinctive outcrop, perhaps a sacred landmark, may have enhanced Bonito's reputation as a sacred place. Not that the rock was always threatening. In its earliest stages, the great house lay to the west. As Bonito grew, it extended ever closer to the outcrop. The inhabitants tried to stabilize the sacred rock with pine timbers and a massive revetment wall built at its base. Neil Judd found numerous prayer sticks stuffed under the undercut portion of the rock, spiritual weapons used to soothe the tottering rock. The strategy worked. The prayer sticks and the wall warded off the slab until 1941 when it fell, crushing or damaging about sixty-five rooms. The location close to Threatening Rock may be no coincidence. Several other

great houses, among them Casa Chiquita and Hungo Pavi, also lie close
to striking rock formations (figure 7.2).

The great house also lay opposite South Gap, which steered runoff into
the canyon and tunneled summer storms into Chaco's heart. Maize gardens probably lay along both banks of the Wash, nourished by water from
South Gap and the canyons in the north wall. Neil Judd discovered several canals running alongside the mounds that lie before Pueblo Bonito.
These may have carried water from drainages around Chetro Ketl.

Figure 7.2   Threatening Rock in 1929, Pueblo Bonito to the left. *Photograph by
George A. Grant. Courtesy NPS Chaco Culture National Historical Park. Negative
77432.*

CHACO MASONRY

Chaco architects used adobe, masonry, and timber to build small homesteads and great houses. The investment was enormous, involving thousands of work hours and millions of carefully dressed stones, quite apart from the labor of felling, trimming, and transporting beams and other timber. As many as forty tons of stone may have gone into the construction of a single room.

The study of Chaco architecture has generated an enormous literature, of which Steven Lekson's classic study, referred to in the notes, is the most important. Readers interested in the details of Chaco architecture and masonry styles are referred to this admirable publication. We can only summarize the principal masonry styles here.

Reconstructing Chaco architecture involves both observation of surviving structures and what is sometimes called "reverse engineering." This analytical process of dismantling a mechanical device applies to Pueblo architecture in the sense that one can examine complex structures like Pueblo Bonito in terms of their various components, which were built in planned chronological sequences over many generations. As we see in chapters 7 and 8, this approach has worked well.

Chaco builders used three different techniques for building stone walls. They were also masters at sophisticated veneers.

Simple walls consisted of a single row of masonry, often set with an adobe mortar. If more strength was desired, the masons would build two parallel walls close to one another. However, they did not bond them together with interlocking blocks, nor did they fill the gap between them with earth or rubble. On occasion, they would "chink" the wall with small stones pressed into the surface of the mortar to create a smoother finish.

Compound walls (figure 7.3a) were constructed like the simple double wall, but the two walls were bonded together with interlinking stones. This interlocking created a much stabler and stronger wall. Once again, the outer surfaces of the resulting wall were carefully finished for appearance's sake.

Core-and-veneer walls (figure 7.3b, c) were the most common technique used in Chaco's great houses. Core-and-veneer developed at Chaco as early as the ninth century and does not appear

a.

b.

c.

Figure 7.3   Chaco masonry: (a) A door in Type II masonry in the North Wall at Pueblo Bonito; (b) Type III masonry at Pueblo Bonito; (c) Type IV masonry. *Photographs by George A. Grant, 1929. Courtesy NPS Chaco Culture National Historical Park. Negatives 80046, 80047, and 77440.*

elsewhere in the San Juan Basin. Here the builders erected a double wall, then filled the gap with a solid core of packed rubble or small stones and earth. Both the walls were carefully finished with rows of nicely trimmed building stones and clay mortar. An outer layer of hundreds of small sandstone fragments was pressed into a thick mud backing layer, forming a veneer so that no mortar was visible on the surface. Veneering protected the walls from erosion. This type of masonry appears to have developed uniquely at Chaco, perhaps as a result of a need to build multistory buildings.

After about 1020, the core-and-veneer became part of the load-bearing structure of the wall and technically is no longer a veneer. Here the load-bearing wall core comprised rough flat stones set in thick clay mortar. Each stone was oriented to only one wall face, overlapping or abutting the stone on the reverse side. This created a structurally sound wall. Then the masons covered the wall on both sides with sandstone ashlar, often in alternating bands of thick and thin stones, forming a variety of patterns. Finally, they covered the decorative veneers with fine clay plaster or matting. The builders continued to use small sandstone spalls not only as a form of veneer in the walls but also as chinking between larger blocks.

Core-and-veneer masonry was confined to great houses, while simple and compound walls were the rule for small houses and hamlets.

Archaeology at Pueblo Bonito began with Wetherill and Pepper, whose excavations cleared much of the ruins. Neil Judd followed in the 1920s and identified four construction stages, based on differences in the veneered masonry. He was the first to collect tree-ring samples and to date the site using Andrew Douglass's master chronology. Steve Lekson published a definitive study of Chaco architecture in 1984, in which he identified seven major building stages in the canyon based on analysis of the architecture and on tree-ring dates.[17] In recent years Dabney Ford and Tom Windes have led a systematic effort to obtain datable timbers from Ancestral Pueblo sites, many of them from smaller wood fragments such as door lintels and secondary roof beams, thereby reducing the chances of dating beams that have been reused at a later date.[18] As of this writing, they have obtained over four hundred new dates for Pueblo Bonito, from 1,454 cored wood fragments. Altogether, they have sampled an estimated 6 percent of the more than fifty thousand timbers used in the site's construction. Their work has hardly begun; even a sample this large leaves many chronological questions unanswered. Our understanding of Chaco architecture and masonry is still very incomplete.

The Ford and Windes research confirmed the essential validity of Lekson's seven-stage construction sequence, which gives a general framework for Pueblo Bonito and for great house construction in the canyon generally. This story began in the mid-ninth century.

OLD BONITO (AD 860–935)

Neil Judd unearthed two pit structures deep under Pueblo Bonito's West Court during the 1920s but did not investigate them thoroughly. His discovery established that there was a Pueblo I settlement on the Bonito site, but when it was abandoned remains a mystery. The earliest dated rooms of the great house cluster to between 860 and 862. Construction may have commenced decades earlier, but this is just a guess.[19]

Pueblo Bonito, like Una Vida 3 miles (4.8 km) to the east, began as a small community of stone houses, like those at the South Fork Community. These early houses soon formed part of later construction. Old Bonito was a crescent of multistory rooms built of Type I masonry facing inward toward a group of kivas, one of above-average size. Three wedge-shaped buildings made up the arc, with rooms four to six times the size of those of contemporary Chaco households in the western portion (figure 7.4).

Type I masonry walls were constructed of very wide and fairly thin slabs of dark, hard, and tabular sandstone that was brought from quarries above the canyon, located on the bench between the two cliff formations on the north side. Bonito masons didn't use sandstone from the cliff behind Bonito, which was softer and much less tabular—less

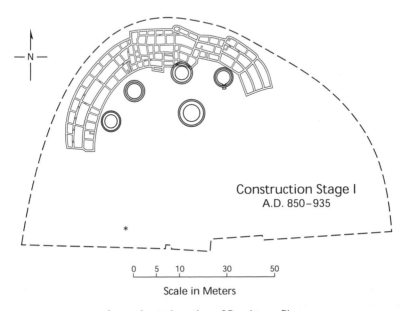

Construction Stage I
A.D. 850–935

0   5   10   30   50

Scale in Meters

*Approximate Location of Ponderosa Pine

Figure 7.4   The first stage of Pueblo Bonito. *After Stein, Ford, and Friedman, 2003.*

effective for wide walls with slabs of sandstone. The use of wide, hard slabs allowed the builders to erect multistory structures. The resulting wall surfaces were quite rough, so they were heavily plastered to create a smooth surface. The masons then pressed very small fragments of the softer sandstone into the plaster to create a surface of closely spaced spalls. Neil Judd called this effect *mosaic work* and thought that all of Old Bonito was covered with this spall veneer, which protected the walls from erosion. Type I stone walls didn't bear the weight or provide the height of later Bonito masonry. Despite this, the architecture allowed the building of a two-story complex, but one considerably lower than later construction.

In its very early stages, Old Bonito was a modest place, a larger settlement than its neighbors, perhaps with sacred associations. The arc-shaped structure was a residential community for many generations as much as it was a sacred place. As far as we can tell, the system of governance, of decision making, remained much the same as it had for centuries—basically egalitarian.[20]

Thus, Old Bonito was no casual building, erected and remodeled by generations of architects by haphazard whim. It lay on a north-south orientation from the beginning, the arc-shape defined at this early time. This was a revered edifice, preserved carefully throughout Pueblo Bonito's entire lifetime.[21] The central structure had the appearance of a sunken court, bounded on either side by room blocks that were 3.6 feet (1.1 m) higher, something quite different from the towering structure of later times. When the site grew after 1040 (see chapter 8), the wedge-shaped court became even more secluded, intimate, perhaps an intensely sacred place.

Old Bonito had modest beginnings, at a time when rainfall was generally below average, except for a brief period during the 960s and again in the late 980s. There were years of seeming architectural inactivity that coincide in part with below average rainfall. Year after year, the canyon's farmers, still mainly on the south side, lived through persistent drought.

Vulnerable farmers

The first time I visited Chaco, I was fresh from years of fieldwork in tropical Africa, from excavations carried out in the heart of landscapes farmed by people living from harvest to harvest. Their rhythm of planting and harvest had changed little from ancient times, a routine of passing years and seasons where everything depended on the first rains. I remember a savagely hot October day in northern Zambia, where the sun shone from a dust-filled, pale blue sky. Each afternoon, we gasped in the shade as huge thunderclouds mounted on the horizon, just as they do at Chaco. Day after day, the clouds dissipated with the setting sun, so we waited yet again. Then came the magical day when the first heavy raindrops pelted on the parched gardens, cleared and ready for the maize. The drops became a downpour. The women watched silently from the doors of their huts, wondering if the time for planting had arrived, whether their crops would grow or wither in the gardens as the rains failed to return.

The silent waiting, the sense of quiet fatalism, has lingered with me over the years. I sensed that the same thing happened at Chaco in the past. Like the Zambian farmers, I realized that Chaco households had lived from year to year, harvest to harvest, minimizing risk by planting on different soil types, growing a variety of crops. But the specter of hunger was always present in the background, complicated in the Chaco case by an arid environment where water control was all-important, and by a growing number of great houses.

Three great houses—Peñasco Blanco, Pueblo Bonito, and Una Vida—lay opposite major breaks in the Chacra Mesa, at spots where the inhabitants could exploit the precious summer runoff from these drainages.[22] Their siting was no coincidence in a time of uncertain rainfall. The farmers may have experimented with simple water-control devices, mainly to spread water over their gardens rather than to channel it.

Tree-ring records and geomorphological studies tell us that the early 900s were times of below average rainfall and also of major hydrological changes in the canyon that helped set the stage for the dramatic construction boom of the next century. In about 900, the Chaco Wash broke through the natural dune dam at the end of the canyon and cut below the canyon floor. The side arroyos adjusted to the new regime by similar downcutting. Entrenchment of the Wash caused side tributaries to erode to the base of the main channel, thereby lowering the water table. As the downcutting worked its way gradually upstream, the pattern of drainage runoff was affected, perhaps delaying further experimentation with water-control devices. This may be why great house building slowed between AD 900 and 1020 at great houses like Una Vida and Kin Bineola. Meanwhile, both the hydrology and geomorphology of the south side of the canyon lessened the effects of the downcutting, so that the communities there could continue to use the highly flexible farming methods of earlier times. Their cultivation depended on the exploitation of small patches of ground in favorable locations often some distance from one another.

These sixty years were precarious ones for Chaco farmers. The best farming opportunities may have lain downstream and outside the canyon. Then, in 1040, at the beginning of what is called the Classic Bonito phase (1040–1100), the climate stabilized. There were more good rainfall years and water tables rose once more. The Wash channel began to fill again, perhaps aided by the construction of a masonry barrier in the breached dune dam below Peñasco Blanco. Such a dam would have created a small lake, but the real purpose would have been to restore the canyon bottomlands to their former state. An investment in water-control structures of all kinds would have been a wise move, even if the now-restored flatlands were subject to occasional floods that would destroy canals and their control gates.

Any investment in major agricultural works, wherever it occurs, requires a high level of standardization, simply because of the amount of labor involved. The Chacoans constructed water-control systems on the north side of the canyon that committed them to a single method of crop watering, using canals that distributed water evenly through carefully maintained fields laid out in standardized grids. The system itself was simple in technological terms, involving canals, on an average, about 4 feet (1.2 m) wide. Simple control gates of core and veneer masonry channeled the water flow from one gridded field to another (figure 7.5).

By using earthen and masonry dams, head gates, canal networks, and gridded fields, the farmers on the north and parts of the south side of the canyon increased agricultural production dramatically, but at a cost of increased vulnerability to prolonged drought, for their agricultural systems were less diversified. Between 1080 and 1100, twenty dry years signaled the beginning of a period of marked oscillations in rainfall that, in the end, were to prove too much for Chaco farmers. At first the continued aggradation of the Wash and still-high water tables softened the impact of less rainfall. Between 1098 and 1118, rainfall again increased, thirty good years that saw a surge in great house construction, only to be followed by a fifty-year drought from 1130 to 1180, when aggradation slowed and water tables fell dramatically. This time, the people farming the north side paid the price for investing heavily in agriculture nourished by summer rainfall and flood waters. There was little room to maneuver. Fine tuning water-control systems would work only if there was enough rainfall to fill the canals and irrigate the field grids. And, most years, there was not.

The situation was much better on the south side, and in the Escavada Wash, where no one had put all his or her agricultural eggs into a single basket. Here, each community had many options, its fields dispersed

Figure 7.5 Irrigation channel in the floor of Chaco Canyon. *Courtesy NPS Chaco Culture National Historical Park. Slide 833.*

over considerable distances and placed at strategic points like dunes or arroyo floodplains where local conditions allowed the planting of crops in different microenvironments. The effect was just like investing in a mutual fund: the risk was spread, not concentrated in a single stock— the gridded fields on the north bank of the Wash. Even in the wettest years, there were only two zones of gridded fields on the south bank.

We gain an impression of how these flexible strategies worked from studies of the agricultural practices of the twelfth-century Bis sa'ani great house on the Escavada Wash (figure 7.6). The investigators learned how soil textures and drainage were all-important, that loamy-to-sandy soils were preferred. Bis sa'ani farmers relied on runoff from nearby impermeable badlands, placing their fields at their base and in nearby watersheds. An estimated 380–470 acres (154–190 ha) of cultivable soils would have supported between 120 and 150 people, a figure close to the population estimate from the rooms in the structure—about 100 people. Even a slight drop in rainfall would have had drastic consequences on crop yields; longer term droughts would have been disastrous without outside support.[23]

The expansion of Chaco's great houses, between 1050 and 1100, when the canyon was center of the Ancestral Pueblo world, depended in large part on a highly vulnerable agricultural system based on a single

Figure 7.6   Bis sa'ani. *Photographer unknown. Courtesy NPS Chaco Culture National Historical Park. Slide 3497.*

method of watering crops planted in gridded fields instead of diverse farming strategies. The Chacoans were playing with agricultural fire but were somehow lulled into a sense of false security that eventually came to haunt them. It's a familiar scenario, played out again and again in different ancient societies that were vulnerable to drought cycles. Everywhere, people paid a high price for their vulnerability. Some of these societies, like the Moche of coastal Peru, or the Sumerians of Ur in Iraq, collapsed. Others, like the Ancestral Pueblo, survived, because their strongest weapon against crop failure was mobility. But as we shall see, they paid a high price for their survival—their agricultural practices took them across a subtle threshold of vulnerability.

The spiritual realm

Every subsistence farmer lives from harvest to harvest, at the mercy of the capricious forces of the environment. These forces cajole and threaten, provide bounty or unleash famine. Invariably, they are seen as the benign or malevolent forces of the supernatural world, involved and propitiated with ritual. Medieval European farmers considered crop failure the wrath of God. Penitents processed through town squares; rogation services in great cathedrals interceded for rain. Like subsistence farmers everywhere, the Chacoans who built Old Bonito lived in a world where ritual was essential to human survival.

We have no idea what these rituals were, but they must have linked the people with the continued fertility of the land—as such rituals commonly do in subsistence farming societies. I learned this many years ago during my months among Zambezi Valley subsistence farmers in Central Africa. The villagers farmed a hot, dry, and dangerously unpredictable environment. They lived in the midst of a symbolic landscape, where the world of day-to-day existence passed seamlessly into the spiritual realm. Human life revolved around the cycles of planting, growth, and harvest—birth, life, and death. Life had always been this way, and it would never change. The living inherited the world of their ancestors and passed it on to future generations, knowing that in the fullness of time they would became ancestors themselves, guardians of the land. Ancestors were *varidizi vepasi,* "owners of the land." They were the disembodied spirits of people, men and women who had provided for, and protected, their families, in life, and continued to do so from the otherworld. The ancestors had no material form. They were ubiquitous, were generous providers, and enhanced human life. The dead, with all their strengths and weaknesses, were the intermediaries between the living and the forces of the spiritual world.[24]

When a person died, his spirit left the body and hid in the remote bush. The descendants danced on the grave at the funeral. A year later, they danced once again, to lead the ancestor back to the household to become a protector of the living. Many times, we would hear the drums beating all night, summoning an ancestor, an owner of the land, to live alongside its descendants. The people believed that human existence thrived in the fullest sense when one lived alongside the home of the dead, near the places where the ancestors once lived. Every year, heads of households participated in rituals that brought rain, offered the first grain from the harvest to a prominent ancestor (figure 7.7).

Figure 7.7   Yucca sandal from Gallo Cliff Dwelling. Chacoan clothing and technology was effective but simple, making use of local materials such as yucca for sandals. *Courtesy NPS Museum Management Program and Chaco Culture National Historical Park. Image 33288.*

These humble Zambezi farmers had a vision of the past that incorporated both myth and oral histories. These cherished tales drew together different kin groups and traditions into common historical narratives that changed from generation to generation. Some individuals enjoyed enhanced status as heads of senior lineages; but none of them could claim greater power than that of the ancestors, the source of the fertility of the lands that fed everyone.

I believe that we cannot understand what happened at Chaco after 900 without some basic perceptions of the Pueblo spiritual world. To understand Pueblo Bonito and its great house neighbors requires envisioning an Ancestral Pueblo world of layers and directions, questing for the elusive but ever-present intangible of the past. Ultimately, we're searching for a landscape profoundly grounded in ancient Pueblo religious beliefs.

In the 1870s the pioneer anthropologist Frank Cushing made some of the first studies of Pueblo religion.[25] Since then, a vast body of research has surrounded the subject, without necessarily the cooperation of its modern-day practitioners. Much of Pueblo religion flourishes out of sight, in the privacy of kivas, in the minds of the few individuals who are the repositories of sacred knowledge, who pass it from one generation to the next. We know enough, however, to detect some common features of Pueblo religion, found in all Southwestern societies. Of course, we can never hope to reconstruct the subtleties of ancient

Pueblo belief from the material remains of the past found in archaeological sites. But we can be certain that many of the commonalities that link Pueblo beliefs across the Southwest have very ancient roots. Such beliefs are very relevant to Chaco's remote past, for they already governed daily life well over a thousand years ago. So we start in the present and hope that the near-universal features of Pueblo religion, including the well-known kachina cult, discussed in chapter 13, inform our understanding of Chacoan society.

We know that Pueblo society at a general level had a long and homogeneous history. Puebloan worldview varied little from one society to the next and extended back into the past. The Pueblo lived in a world bounded by sacred mountains, a world ordered by well-defined directions. Their universe had three layers: the sky, the earth, and the underworld. The underworld and its subdivisions are the most important realm, the village being the point of emergence, the *sipapu*, or the earth's navel. In Puebloan belief, the earth as we know it is the most recent of four worlds in which humans have lived. If humans live harmoniously, then the forces of the supernatural world will honor their requests, provided they follow the proper rituals and ritual procedures. If the ritual fails, then disaster ensues because the cosmic order has been disturbed.

Time is unimportant, measured as it is by the endless cycle of the seasons, the passages of the sun and moon, and of the solstices. As the anthropologist Alfonso Ortiz once remarked: "the grand dualities of the cosmos also serve to unify space and time."[26] The sun father and the earth mother continually interact. The summer and winter solstices provide the winter and summer divisions that have always defined the Pueblo year. Individuals are born into this world from the underworld and return to it when they die. The Pueblo world has always been one of harmony and order, the basic values of this life often reenacted in dramatic performances. This is a world where the group matters more than the individual. There is a preoccupation with maintaining a human existence that has always remained the same, and will remain the same in the future. Herein lies the fundamental tenet of Pueblo existence, and a basic principle behind Chaco Canyon—a world of unchanging harmony, but of flexibility and movement, where independence, kin ties, and a larger vision of the world were the keys to survival.

Direction is intensely significant, too, reflecting the duality between summer and winter, the agricultural cycle and the quiet months. While duality is important to all Puebloan peoples, it is a stronger organizational force among the Eastern Pueblo societies of the Rio Grande Valley, where pueblo villages are divided into moieties, halves, which can reflect these two seasons, and east and west. This may be why Old Bonito and other great houses began with, and maintained, a symmetry between east and west in their buildings and kivas. Perhaps they reflect the existence of two equal social groups in society, who divided ceremonial, social, and political activities between them as part of the balance inherent in Pueblo existence. North and south were in opposition and asymmetrical. North was the realm of the spiritual; south that of the living, physical world. In many respects, Chaco Canyon and its great houses was an artifact of these beliefs, a prism for the wider San Juan world.

The archaeologist John Fritz has taken these concepts still further; he argued that Pueblo Bonito and Chetro Ketl lie equidistant from a north–south line that bisects the canyon from Pueblo Alto to Tsin Kletsin on Chaco Mesa.[27] This north–south axis is represented by a wall (built late in the canyon's history) that bisects Pueblo Bonito into two halves through the center of the plaza. This same wall is aligned with the great kiva at Casa Rinconada on the south side of the canyon. Fritz identifies an east–west alignment, too, with the great houses on the north side of the canyon, smaller communities on the south. He believes this reflects the opposition between the sacred and the profane, and the spiritual importance of the great houses on one side of Chaco.

We do not know if Chacoan society was organized on principles of duality that characterize the modern Eastern Pueblos of the Rio Grande or on an organizational structure more typical of the Western Pueblo groups, including Zuni Pueblo and the Hopi villages. Western Pueblo peoples place more emphasis on individual households, organized socially through clans that have important ritual responsibilities for the village. Recent research by John Ware suggests that both Eastern and Western organizational systems are quite old and were probably present in some form during the growth of Chacoan culture.[28]

Whatever the organizational details, there were Pueblo "livings"— agriculture and religion—an existence where the realities of an arid, harsh environment framed human experience. As we shall see, the same two partners governed Chacoan life one thousand years ago.

8 ∴ A TIME OF GREAT HOUSES

> He [the Sun] sat down alone by the fire pit and
> smoked over the yellow fox pelt, just sitting there
> for a while after finishing. At the proper time he
> gathered up the yellow pelt, went outside, and re-
> placed the gray pelt with the yellow one. This time
> the yellow dawn appeared and brought light to the
> world.
>
> From a Hopi story by Ekkehart Malotki,
> "The Boy Who Went in Search of His Father." [1]

I run my hand over the fitted masonry in the southeastern rooms of Pueblo
Bonito. My fingers massage the carefully shaped stone blocks, the intricate veneers made up of different shapes. I imagine a few men sitting in the winter sunlight surrounded by stone slabs. The masons
examine each piece carefully, rejecting many, trimming some deftly
with stone hammers to form a rectangular, flattish shape. In midafter-
noon, these men carry them over to the incomplete wall, where they
eye the jigsaw of shapes. Without a word, they set to work, each fitting
stone slabs into the patterned wall, chipping, shaping, stepping back
to check the fit. They work fast, with the skill of long experience, gen-
tly tapping stones into place, course after course. One of the men picks
up a weathered ponderosa beam, rescued from a collapsed room on
the other side of the plaza. He places it across a growing doorway,
then walls it into position with barely a moment's hesitation.

The rapid building seems like magic, until you realize that the builders have generations of experience behind them and a knowledge of
the qualities of the stone honed from years of room construction. . . .

133

∴ ∴ ∴

960–1020: a period of unpredictable rainfall and, apparently, a time of quiet consolidation at Chaco. There was little building, or even remodeling, at Pueblo Bonito. The original arc-shaped structure remained in use, still a residential pueblo as much as a sacred place. Chaco Wash was downcutting, following the breaching of the dune dam at the western end of the canyon. Then, by 1040, rainfall increased. The Wash filled in once more, and people began cultivating the canyon bottomlands with plots of carefully gridded fields.

For the next forty-five years, Chaco entered a time of extraordinary growth and outreach, when the canyon became a center of gravity for people living over a large area of the northern Southwest.

PUEBLO BONITO AD 1040–1105

We begin the story at ground zero, in downtown Chaco, where Old Bonito nestled under the canyon's north wall. Once again, the most thoroughly investigated great house provides us with a narrowly focused portrait of what happened in the heart of Chaco during these years. These decades witnessed an explosion in great house construction, notably at Chetro Ketl, Pueblo Alto, and Pueblo del Arroyo, as well as major social change in the canyon (figure 8.1).[2]

As we saw in chapter 7, the first two centuries of Pueblo Bonito's history centered round the original, arc-shaped building that remained in use with remarkably little change. By 1020 (the date is uncertain), the structure apparently had powerful supernatural associations. Pueblo Bonito may not have changed much during the late tenth century, but it's entirely possible that there was great house building underway elsewhere in the canyon. Some time during these two centuries, Chaco's masons developed the characteristic core-and-veneer masonry that was far more sophisticated than Type I construction, capable of supporting much heavier ceiling weights, and carrying the loads of two or more stories.[3]

Between 1040 and 1050, building resumed at Old Bonito. By this time, some parts of the original structures may have been in disuse. The builders now constructed a massive structure that wrapped around the old building. One room in width, over thirty rooms long, and up to three stories high, the extension enlarged and buttressed Old Bonito while remaining faithful to the form of the now two-centuries-old building.[4]

Figure 8.1   Chetro Ketl, showing the great kiva. *Photography by Jerry Livingstone, 1987. Courtesy NPS Chaco Culture National Historical Park. Negative 25261.*

Meanwhile, a linear north-south block of twelve to sixteen rooms rose in the southeastern area of the pueblo, erected in the 1040s, a break from the curvilinear architecture of earlier structures.[5] The two ends of the crescent-shaped pueblo were now connected with low stone walls that served to delineate the space within. Additionally, the remodelers changed the axis of the entire building from cardinal north–south to 9° east of west of north and 4.6° north of east.

These ten years of remodeling were just the beginning. Between AD 1050 and 1070, Pueblo Bonito became labyrinthine in its complexity. An elongated parallelogram of kivas and rooms rose on the eastern side, only to be razed to its foundations after 1077 and replaced by the most ambitious construction project in the site's history in 1081 (figure 8.2c). This involved demolishing the southeastern section of Old Bonito, then erecting an entirely new room block that joined the eastern end of the arc with the original building.[6] The number of stories required to achieve a constant height on the east side varied from four to three, but we cannot be sure of the reason because the lower levels are deep below debris from the fall of Threatening Rock in 1941.

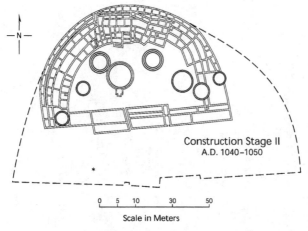

Construction Stage II
A.D. 1040–1050

0 5 10 30 50

Scale in Meters

a.

*Approximate Location of Ponderosa Pine

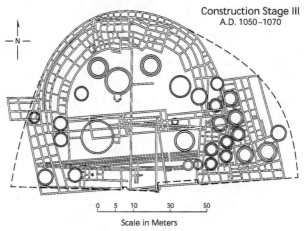

Construction Stage III
A.D. 1050–1070

0 5 10 30 50

Scale in Meters

b.

*Approximate Location of Ponderosa Pine

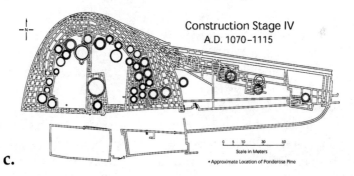

Construction Stage IV
A.D. 1070–1115

0 5 10 30 50

Scale in Meters

*Approximate Location of Ponderosa Pine

c.

Figure 8.2   Plans of Pueblo Bonito, stages II to IV (a to c). *After Stein, Ford, and Friedman, 2003.*

The years 1071–1073 saw activity at the southwestern end of the arc, where a two-story building rose to the same roof height as Old Bonito's western structure. Sometime after 1085, the builders formalized the north–south/east–west axes with rows of single-story rooms. The north–south room axis may have formed a causeway that connected Old Bonito with the newest areas. A room row that ran from east to west closed off the enclosed courts within to form the classic D-shape of a Chaco great house.

By this time, the great house would have been a confusing jigsaw puzzle of new rooms alongside buildings falling into decay. The southern wall lay adjacent to two rectangular mounds built between about 1075 and 1105. They are in fact paved platforms with retaining walls that were then covered with 18 inches (46 cm) or more of overburden, whose significance escapes us. A defile separates the two mounds, which runs along a north–south axis that aligns with the great kiva, Casa Rinconada, on the south side of the canyon (figure 8.3).[7]

A network of low walls, known as the Northeast Foundation Complex, now extended east from the main pueblo, built directly on a clay

Figure 8.3   Casa Rinconada. *Photograph from Fred Mang, 1979. Courtesy NPS Chaco Culture National Historical Park. Negative 30583.*

pavement laid in Old Bonito times (see figure 8.4). Tom Windes, who has excavated the "foundations," showed they were actually partially built walls, capped in about 1050 for anticipated, but never completed, later construction. Similar structures occur at other great houses. To complete the walls would have required an enormous expenditure of time and labor—and abundant food surpluses produced by ample rainfall.

RESIDENCE OR SACRED PLACE?

Pueblo Bonito beggars the imagination with its scale, its many rooms, and its setting hard against Chaco's north wall. Archaeologists find it mesmerizing in its complexity and have tried to decipher its meaning for generations. Was the great house a residence, a place where a few people lived who supervised ritual activities, or simply a vast storage place?

Early investigators like Richard Wetherill, George Pepper, and Neil Judd assumed that all of Chaco's great houses were classic pueblos, that is to say, dwelling places that were "communal towns." In recent years, Chacoan archaeologists have abandoned the term "pueblo," which implies dwellings, in favor of "great house." Not that the new label is without its critics, for it also implies residency as much as other functions. Wendy Bustard defined the problem succinctly when she subtitled an article on Pueblo Bonito's functions "When a House is not a Home."[8]

From the archaeologist's point of view, everything depends on the analysis of artifacts, food remains, and other remains of human activity found in household contexts. I stress the word "household," for that's about the smallest social unit that an archaeologist can study. In the case of Pueblo Bonito, a household is an architectural formulation, a set of interconnected rooms where at least one was used for domestic activities such as cooking or preparing food, and where there are such built-ins as mealing bins, firepits, and slab-lined storage bins or pits. Researcher Wendy Bustard has used a form of spatial analysis called *space syntax* to study activities at Pueblo Bonito. Space syntax is based on a body of social theory that assumes that architecture reflects the social strategies that prompted it. She has shown that the uses of space within large and small Chaco sites followed distinctive patterns, that smaller settlements were predominantly domestic spaces, while great houses witnessed much more diverse activities.[9]

Bustard found that Old Bonito's earliest structures were typical of the time—an arc of rooms, two deep, with a pit structure in front for every four or five rooms. As time went on, the construction of kivas and room blocks became progressively more formalized, like the well-known standardized unit pueblos of the northern San Juan, but with one important difference. Pueblo Bonito and other early great houses had larger, multistory rooms. Two hundred years later, when building resumed, the builders erected large, rectangular room blocks with kivas inside them. A stairway led to the second story. Unlike the earlier room blocks, there were plenty of ways to gain access to different spaces, an unusual feature of pueblo architecture. Between 1075 and 1085, the two wings were extended to enclose the hemispherical plaza, but their spatial organization was quite different. The western wing with its two stories of parallel room suites allowed people to move east–west, but north–south access was virtually impossible. On the east side, a two- to three-story block of rectangular rooms and two kivas allowed access from all directions. Bustard believes that these changing access patterns reflect a change over many generations from more integrated spaces toward one where rooms were more segregated.

Bustard's analysis makes a convincing case for Pueblo Bonito having begun life as a residential site, for the room architecture mirrors that at known small house units elsewhere, although the spaces are somewhat larger and without domestic features such as mealing bins. As one might expect in household areas, the rooms are more integrated. These early room complexes contrast dramatically with later spaces, only a very few of which have such domestic features as firepits. It is as if only a few people lived in the arcs of the pueblo, while most of the rooms were used for other, as yet unknown, purposes. Bustard suggests they were used by large kin groups for specific, but unknown, functions. By 1075 featureless rooms that were even less integrated predominated, with no interior access between floors. There was constant construction, perhaps attuned to rapidly changing social needs.

Bustard's argument has weight. Pueblo Bonito began life as a place where people lived, then became a great house with few inhabitants, plenty of storage space, and strong ritual associations. Here we skate on thin scholarly ice. Pueblo Bonito is a ruin, abandoned for nearly nine centuries. We have but a fraction of the original structure to work with, albeit a completely excavated one. In historic pueblos such as Acoma and Hopi, the ground floor rooms served for storage, while people lived in the upper stories. Perhaps the same was true of Pueblo Bonito, where but a fraction of the original upper stories survive. But those higher level rooms that have been excavated were all from the later stages of the pueblo. They were virtually devoid of firepits, bins, or other built-ins so characteristic of domestic space. They also lack the partitions that separate households at Acoma and Hopi. Furthermore, the large number of interconnecting rooms at Pueblo Bonito are unique in the canyon.

People who live in a place for some time leave artifacts behind them when they leave. Pueblo Bonito was no exception, but the headlines have gone to the spectacular objects found with the burials in Old Bonito. Enormous quantities of humbler artifacts also came from the Wetherill and Judd excavations, which emptied the site in the days before today's fine-grained excavation methods. These included large quantities of domestic artifacts, identical to those from other great houses and smaller settlements. Stone tools, cooking pots, and serving bowls abound in the Pueblo Bonito collections. Between one thousand and two thousand restorable, whole vessels came from Pueblo Bonito, giving a ratio of under one vessel per room (ceremonial pots and incomplete vessels were excluded). This compares with a figure of 1.36 domestic vessels per room from the small site 29SJ627, in Marcia's Rincon west of the Visitor's Center, studied by Wolcott Toll and Peter McKenna. This twenty-five-room house site was occupied between the late 800s and early 1100s, a period about the same as Pueblo Bonito.[10]

The residence question is still unresolved, even if most people believe the site was predominantly a ceremonial center. But, regardless of function, how many people lived at Pueblo Bonito in its heyday? The absence of burials, even in the mounds in front of the pueblo, surprised early investigators. Those that did come to light were concentrated in Old Bonito and lay in fully extended or disturbed positions, in contrast to those from smaller house sites that were buried in tightly flexed positions. One archaeologist, Wesley Bernardini, believes that Pueblo Bonito was occupied by a mere seventy people, while more than two hundred rooms were used for storage.[11] Another authority, Tom Windes, points out that Pueblo Bonito had a long history of construction and reconstruction, which was far from orderly in its progression. In this respect, it's just like a modern pueblo, with complex patterns of use, abandonment, and dilapidation. No question that Pueblo Bonito served as a residence, but there is no architectural evidence that there was ever a large resident population. The largest number of inhabitants may have been in the early 1100s, when the pueblo was at its largest extent. Even then, we have no idea how many rooms were in use at one time. Windes estimates the population never rose above one hundred people at peak residential periods in the early years or after 1100.[12]

The AD 1000s are marked by little habitation debris, as if the character of the site changed profoundly, at a time when ritual was all-important, a development marked by intensive small kiva construction, by the great kivas, and by the lavishly decorated burials in Old Bonito. Tom Windes notes that the greatest construction activity came by the 1070s, when beams were more standardized and more timber was harvested. It is as if managerial supervision of construction were tauter. By the 1100s, the kivas were smaller, as the ritual functions of the site changed once again. Construction activities faltered, were less supervised, as people engaged in much more diverse activities. Undoubtedly, many of the same ritual activities continued, but everything seems less centralized. To what extent all of this represents cultural continuity is uncertain, for the maze of construction events masks what may have been major changes in the role of the pueblo, as Chaco ceased to be the center of the San Juan world after 1100.

WHY BUILD GREAT HOUSES?

The Egyptian pharaoh Khufu's great pyramid at Giza near Cairo reaches toward the heavens in a massive architectural statement of royal power. The pyramid was a symbolic ladder for the king to ascend to his rightful place alongside the sun god in the heavens. Four hundred and eighty one feet (146 m) high, Khufu's pyramid covers 13 acres (5.3 ha), part of a mortuary complex that was built as one vast construction project involving thousands of villagers. If ever there was a purpose-built architectural project, the great pyramid was one, erected during the pharaoh's reign as a single, carefully designed project.

Pueblo Bonito is a quite different architectural phenomenon, also an important sacred place, and, for a few, a mortuary. But, unlike Giza, it was built in fits and starts—Old Bonito first, then the frenzy of building activity after 1020 and a constant process of remodel, repair, and recycling of rooms and room blocks. There is no sense of a finite construction project here. Pueblo Bonito was what one might call purpose-built architecture, where construction ebbed and flowed according to changing needs, different ritual practices, and shifting political and social currents. Great house architecture reflected changes in Chacoan society. This notion of purpose building bears directly on another fundamental question: how were the great houses built, by how many people, and who organized the work?

Like the Giza pyramids, Chaco's great houses were a different kind of construction project, on a scale, however sporadic, far greater than the labor investment required to build a suite of rooms in a farming community. Pueblo Bonito and its contemporaries were construction projects that required considerably more people than a few households, careful organization, and sufficient food surpluses to support the workers as they labored on site. Great house construction required individuals who were expert builders, who knew the properties of veneer architecture and wooden beams used in roofs and lintels.

But why would people go to the effort of building such imposing structures anyway? Public architecture can have many meanings and is a reflection of society's priorities. Gothic cathedrals like Chartres in northern France rose during late medieval times to glorify God and to give thanks for His bountiful harvests. The Aztec capital, Tenochtitlán in the Valley of Mexico, was a depiction of the center of the world, designed to impress the visitor with the power of the sun god Huitzilopochtli. Chaco's great houses were mere villages by Aztec standards, but we can only assume that there were compelling political, social, or spiritual reasons to erect such large structures in an arid high-risk environment. Great houses make little sense in a world where dispersed villages had flourished for centuries—unless they served an important part in society, however intangible the role.

How much work was involved?

It's almost impossible to produce accurate estimates of the amount of labor required to erect, say, an Egyptian pyramid, or, for that matter, a Chacoan great house. Attempts to calculate the effort involved in building with living subjects makes for entertaining television, but rarely produce authoritative estimates on the time needed to fill a wall core with rubble or to lay a course of veneered stone. Steve Lekson made some informed calculations using both Park Service data and calculations made by anthropologist Charles Erasmus on Central American sites.[13] He calculated the number of person-hours required to build each stage of Pueblo Bonito. Labor requirements peaked in about AD 1050, remained high, and peaked again in the early 1100s. But these peaks were relatively modest. For instance, during a peak between 1095 and 1100 the person-hour figure was 55,645 a year, the equivalent of sixteen hardworking people working ten-hour days, three hundred sixty-five days a year. His figures are modest by ancient Egyptian or Aztec standards, and reflect a far smaller investment by society as a whole.

One clue comes from the core and veneer construction, which is an extremely efficient way of constructing room complexes with a relatively modest labor expenditure. The walls go up quickly and are structurally sound. The genius of Ancestral Pueblo builders lay in their profound knowledge of masonry construction in a style perfectly suited to pueblo architecture. Almost certainly, they sought to minimize time and effort in construction.

Mary Metcalf has modified Lekson's calculations by measuring the amount of time to build walls and roofs, which she regards as a "rough measure of the scale of construction."[14] She also broke down the construction activity into the building of kivas and rooms as separate projects, and differentiated between different roof styles. For instance, the construction of cribbed (timber-lined) roofs required much heavier beams, which involved much higher construction costs.

Metcalf estimates that 805,000 person-hours were needed to build Pueblo Bonito, excluding the Northeast Foundation Complex and the two mounds in front, which would raise the figures even higher. A quarter of this figure went into the construction of Old Bonito, with a total of 2,736 person-hours annually, this over about seventy-five years, but constructing simpler masonry. After a one-hundred-seventy-five-year lull,

Figure 8.4   Computer-generated reconstruction of Pueblo Bonito at its apogee. *After Stein, Ford, and Friedman, 2003.*

the remaining three-quarters of the site's labor costs fell during a sixty- to seventy-five-year period after 1040. Construction figures during this time varied dramatically, with no less than 29 percent of the entire effort coming between 1075 and 1085, a decade that saw an expenditure of 23,428 hours a year.

Metcalf then refined her calculations even further to compare the labor invested on what she calls civic construction (kivas and like structures) and domestic areas. Old Bonito kiva construction represented only about 5 percent of construction investment, but this figure later rose to about 40 percent during two short periods, between 1050 and 1060, and between 1075 and 1085. The basic configuration of Pueblo Bonito changed little, but civic space became infinitely more important.

All of Chaco's great houses involved major labor investment. Metcalf's estimates range from over 130,000 hours at Kin Kletso to well over 500,000 at Chetro Ketl. These figures are impressive by any standards, even when one remembers that much of this construction took place sequentially. The amount of effort for civic construction varied considerably, from a high of 149,000 for Pueblo Bonito and a low of 3,000 hours at Wijiji. The highest investment in such activity was at Pueblo Alto, Pueblo del Arroyo, and Pueblo Bonito, all more than 18 percent. All the others had a figure of less than 10 percent, indicating higher residential populations.

Contrast these figures with those for small sites and you gain an impression of focused construction. Between the eleventh and twelfth centuries, the average small site required about 9,000 hours, some more, some less, about one ninth of the amount of effort required for construction at Pueblo Bonito between 1060 and 1075, when there was a lull in building activity.

How, then, were these buildings erected? Did people work for months on end, perhaps during the quiet agricultural periods of the year? Or was construction a fulltime activity, supported by food surpluses gained from carefully managed water-control and gridded fields on the floodplain? Mary Metcalf argues that thirty people could have completed the eleventh-century construction at Pueblo Bonito by working forty hours a week for ten years, distributed over a forty-five-year period. If she is right, then the burden of building Pueblo Bonito was not that large. But many variables remain unaccounted for. Did the builders work every day for regular hours throughout the year, or at a more leisurely pace? What construction was going on elsewhere at the same time? And how was the labor organized? The answer comes from a study of Chacoan households.

1. An aerial view of the central-western portion of Chaco Canyon with Chetro Ketl at bottom right. Pueblo Bonito is along the bright cliff line toward the center of the picture. The view is to the west with the Chuska Mountains showing as a thin, dark line on the horizon. *Courtesy Adriel Heisey.*

2. The heart of Chaco Canyon, showing Pueblo Bonito, Chetro Ketl to the right, and Pueblo Alto above the Canyon at upper center. Traces of ancient roads emanate from the latter. *Courtesy Adriel Heisey.*

3. Pueblo Bonito after a snowstorm. *Courtesy Adriel Heisey.*

4. Pueblo Alto. *Courtesy Adriel Heisey.*

5. Casa Rinconada at sunrise. *Courtesy Adriel Heisey.*

6. Pueblo del Arroyo at sunrise. *Courtesy Adriel Heisey.*

7.   Hungo Pavi. *Courtesy Adriel Heisey.*

8.   Peñasco Blanco looking east-southeast down Chaco Canyon.
Courtesy Adriel Heisey.

9. Kin Kletso. *Photograph by Al Hayes. Courtesy NPS Chaco Culture National Historical Park. Slide 39.*

10. Pueblo Pintado. *Photograph NPS Chaco Project. Courtesy NPS Chaco Culture National Historical Park. Slide 269.*

11. Turquoise-encrusted cylinder jar, bone scraper with inlaid turquoise and jet from Room 38, and a ceramic mug from Pepper's 1920 excavations at Pueblo Bonito. *Courtesy Deborah Flynn Post.*

12. Aztec West. "Rooms at the corner of the great house." *Courtesy Adriel Heisey.*

13. Salmon Ruins.
Courtesy Adriel Heisey.

14. Paquimé (Casas Grandes), Mexico. *Courtesy Adriel Heisey.*

15.   Kin Bineola. *Courtesy Adriel Heisey.*

16.   Cliff Palace at Mesa Verde. *David Muench/Corbis.*

The power of the household

Melissa Hagstrum, author of a memorable study on the subject, puts it well: "Chaco operated through the idiom of the household and its functions were phrased in kinship terms."[15] She is right, for the household and the family were the foundation of Chacoan society, the structures that shaped everyday life and the work associated with it—just as they are in any subsistence farming society. Households farmed the land, gathered plant foods, and hunted. Their members prepared food, manufactured pots and weapons, built houses, and fashioned ornaments. Each family and household was an autonomous unit; each organized its annual work cycle. The household was a flexible component of Chacoan society, connected to neighbors, outsiders, and others by ever-changing kin ties, links of friendship, and ritual obligations (figure 8.5). Such relationships were crucial in a semiarid environment like that of

Figure 8.5   Small house communities Bc 50, 51, and 59, south side of Chaco Canyon. *Photograph by Fred Mang, 1979. Courtesy NPS Chaco Culture National Historical Park. Negative 30581.*

the San Juan Basin. But, ultimately, each household was self-sufficient, with complete autonomy over the labor needed to farm its own land, to create artifacts. If extra hands were needed for a particularly large task, such as small canal building or maintenance, a household simply called on members of their extended family in a quiet ebb and flow of reciprocity for all but the demanding jobs.

Such reciprocal exchanges placed important obligations on every household, for a request for help fulfilled an immediate need but also incurred a future obligation to reciprocate when called upon. Such reciprocity could be burdensome, especially when the request came at the height of the farming cycle. But the people responded, because they knew that they might need help themselves one day. Chaco was a difficult farming environment at the best of times, so each household spread itself thin to meet its obligations and to feed itself. There were, of course, many times when household would join household for essential communal tasks such as digging and maintaining irrigation canals, building houses, or ritual activities. But these chores were invariably scheduled at a time convenient to everyone, as much as possible during the quiet times of the agricultural cycle. In a society where the household was the basic economic unit, it could be no other way.

Agriculture and craft production of all kinds went hand-in-hand in Chacoan society. In such an unpredictable environment, a household had to be able to make rapid decisions, such as switching from farming when crops were poor to the production of artifacts, such as baskets, that could be exchanged for food staples. For this reason, each household maintained trading relationships with families from other settlements with whom they exchanged products for food, usually after the harvest.

In each household, people moved effortlessly from farming to craft production and other activities, for their activities dovetailed into one another like pieces of a jigsaw puzzle. For instance, a family might make pottery during the heat of the day, so that the clay dried readily. Basketry or weaving were tasks that could be taken up at any time, so, in a sense, the two activities complemented one another. The basically simple technologies used by the Chacoans required long experience and a close knowledge of the properties of such materials as clay, fibers, and stones for toolmaking. The technological knowledge acquired by both men and women overlapped and was highly flexible in the sense that everyone knew something of each craft, even if some individuals or households became known for their expertise in, say, potmaking or weaving. For instance, turquoise workshops are known from some Chaco settlements, a craft easily mastered by individuals with knowledge of stone implement manufacture, a common craft at Chaco.

The adaptable Chaco household with its technological skills was the core of society, its food surpluses and products the way that people provided goods and labor for fellow kin, and to society as a whole, while maintaining the viability of daily existence. Their flexible, and ingenious, household craft technology meant that both men and women could turn themselves to a wide variety of tasks for the common good. Everyone who labored on the stone walling of the great houses had learned their basic skills at home, erecting and repairing their own dwellings, even if the work at, say, Pueblo Bonito, was supervised by an expert. We can be certain that both men and women were heavily involved in great house construction. The weaving of burden baskets to carry stone slabs alone was a time-consuming task for every household. Quite how this work was organized remains a mystery, but it may have involved different kin groups and obligations placed on extended families and households.

Chaco's households were part of a society governed by obligations for the common good, notably for ceremonial life that placed demands for goods and labor on each of them. Those who presided over these obligations were well aware of the ebb and flow of the agricultural year, of the rhythms of household farming and craft production.[16] There was a marked seasonality in such activities as great house building, which could only be carried out in the quiet agricultural months. In this sense, the supervisors of Chaco ceremonial were similar to the pharaohs who built Egypt's Pyramids of Giza. All the Egyptian large-scale work unfolded during the flood season when the fields were idle.

Chaco reached its apogee during a period of more plentiful rainfall, which led to larger food surpluses at the household level and less of a struggle to make both ends meet. Thus, assessments for material contributions, for labor, could more readily be added to the annual obligations of a household. These obligations took many forms. One of them was basketry, which must have consumed large amounts of time, making woven containers for carrying building slabs, for transporting food and other staples from elsewhere. Such activities could be completed any time, as could the weaving of rabbit fur and turkey-feather blankets, perhaps used in public ceremonies. Men made thousands of turquoise and shell ornaments, using stone drills and abrading stones. Apart from food, households in the canyon contributed most of the staples that were the underpinnings of ceremonial life.

Clearly, the relationship between household, small community, and great house lay at the center of Chacoan society, something that we have tended to forget with our near-obsession with larger structures and the growing complexity of canyon life. Despite much work on smaller communities, we still do not know much about the relationships between the populations of small settlements and great houses.

While artifact production was an all-year activity, any organization of labor for the common good was a seasonal matter, dictated by the agricultural cycle. The skills needed for building great houses or roads, for cutting beams, were not different from those used at home, as part of the simple intersecting technologies that were in use every day. There were other labor obligations, too, especially for the preparation of food for major ceremonies, which involved women, perhaps working at home, cooking foods that were contributed to the Ancestral Pueblo equivalent of a potluck.[17]

Nearly everyone at Chaco, whether religious specialist, ceremonial officer holder, expert stone toolmaker, or potter, was a farmer and a father, or a mother and a cook—roles that every household performed in their daily lives as part of their subsistence. Each was autonomous, but none could be entirely self-sufficient in an environment so unpredictable as that of the San Juan Basin. In the final analysis, what made Chacoan society tick were the flexible autonomy of the household and the complex obligations of kin, reciprocity, and labor for the common good that fostered it.

9 ⋮ TENTACLES OF
INTERCONNECTION

The underlying rhythms of nature govern their
whole existence, from the timing and order of ritual
dramas to the planning of economic activities.

Alfonso Ortiz[1]

Early morning, spring AD 1085: The men had left their camp at dawn,
high in the Chuska Mountains, warmly wrapped against the cold. They
walk from pine to pine, quietly assessing the trunks. The forest is a
shadow of its former self, a thicket of young trees and shoots. Only a
few mature trees still stand, most of them with bent trunks rejected by
the generations of woodcutters who have passed this way.

By midday, the lumbermen have walked a long way, with only a
few new beams to show for their efforts. Mature trees are more plentiful now, in more inaccessible terrain. The men clamber up hillsides,
stare expertly up the trunks, assessing their potential as roof beams,
lintels, or lesser timbers. The oldest woodcutter nods silently. The
younger men deftly fell the pine with their ground stone axes, then
trim off the branches, throwing them in piles. The trunk is long enough
for a roof beam. They stack the lumber in a pile to season and dry out,
leaving the rest on the ground, knowing that the women will soon
arrive to collect huge bunches of firewood to fire their pottery kilns.

∴ ∴ ∴

STAPLES FROM AFAR

Maize was Chaco's staple, but it is not known whether the canyon was completely self-supporting during the apogee of eleventh-century great house construction. Certainly, the Chacoans were expert farmers, who were past masters at conserving and managing water, also at soil selection, so much so that it seems likely that most of their corn came from within the confines of the canyon and its immediate environs. But did the Chacoans also import maize from other great house communities at the periphery of the San Juan Basin? Until recently, this question was unanswerable, but we now know that the chemistry of maize cobs reflects the chemistry of the waters in the soils where they were grown.[2] Trace elements in modern corns grown by Native American communities in the region show significant differences from one location to the next. A team of archaeologists and geologists have begun a project to examine the chemistry of ancient maize cobs, using Hopi Blue corncobs from experimental gardens at the Crow Canyon Archaeological Center, at Cortez, Colorado. As part of the project, they have sampled known cultivated soils at Chaco Canyon and also at Aztec and Salmon Ruins to the north, as well as from the Newcomb region of the Chuska region to the west and other locations.

With this background comparative data, the research team then examined seven cobs excavated by George Pepper from Pueblo Bonito and ten from Aztec, the corn covering a broad spectrum of Chaco occupation. The Chaco strontium ratios showed that at least some of the Pueblo Bonito corn came from the Newcomb area. The Aztec maize was grown on the nearby Animas River floodplain.

This innovative research shows convincingly that at least some of Chaco's maize was imported from elsewhere, but it does not answer the question of questions—did the Chacoans subsist almost entirely on imported corn? One suspects that they did not, for no farming society in its right mind would settle at a location where they did not have at least a reasonable chance of supporting themselves year-in, year-out. We can be certain, however, that visitors to the canyon brought gifts of maize to major ceremonies. Rations brought by visitors may also have helped support major ceremonies and the building of great houses. But this is a far cry from a scenario that has Chaco supported entirely by imported maize from prosperous outliers. Hundreds, if not thousands, more samples will be needed before we can assess the role of imported maize in Chacoan life.

Maize and beans were the staff of life at Chaco, but firewood and wooden beams ranked a close second. For centuries, the Chacoans had relied on local trees from the woodlands of Chacra Mesa for their roof beams and door lintels. By the late tenth century, such timber was in short supply. The growing population of the canyon was stripping the landscape of both trees and firewood. Chaco households had always exchanged food and other materials with people living at a distance, usually within the framework of kin ties and mutual obligation. Such ties were wise insurance in environments where rainfall was unpredictable and the risk of crop failure high. Now the Chacoans turned to the outside world for timber and for pottery they could no longer produce in large quantities, because their production depended on ample supplies of firewood. The web of interconnectedness that linked Chaco communities with other groups tightened and intensified as demand for construction lumber and firewood increased.

Timber

Every Chaco settlement, large or small, required substantial lumber: roofing beams and door lintels, secondary supports of all kinds (figure 9.1).[3] The construction of Pueblo Bonito alone consumed over fifty thousand

Figure 9.1   Sagging Type IV masonry at Chetro Ketl, eloquent testimony to the importance of timber in Chaco architecture. *Photograph by George A. Grant, 1929. Courtesy of NPS Chaco Culture Historical Park. Negative 77443.*

pieces of timber by one recent estimate. That was just a start. As many as two hundred thousand trees, mainly ponderosa, provided the ceiling beams of ten great houses over a period of three centuries or so. One conservative estimate has it that five of the larger great houses would have required twenty-six thousand beams each, the five smaller ones, among them Pueblo Alto, fifteen thousand apiece. But Chaco is a treeless environment. Where, then, did the lumber come from? Whatever the source, the environmental effects, especially in terms of deforestation, must have been devastating—this before you factor in the enormous quantities of timber and brush required for firewood and for pottery making.

Timber is a barometer of Chaco's growing dependency on the world without. During the 800s and 900s, the builders of both large and small sites used mostly piñon, juniper, and cottonwood, trees that grew relatively close by. Three early great houses—Peñasco Blanco, Pueblo Bonito, and Una Vida—had access to ponderosa pines and limited Douglas fir from the mountains, for their beams.

Then the pattern changes. By 950, nonlocal ponderosa is the dominant beam timber, while spruce and fir increase as time goes on. Chetro Ketl consumed as many as six thousand of the forty-five thousand or so such trees used in Chaco's great houses. By 1030, the founding of new great houses appears to have finally decimated local supplies of long, straight logs. Ponderosa was still favored, but more and more fir and spruce came into the canyon from higher elevations. By the mid-eleventh century, 92 percent of all the construction lumber at Pueblo Bonito was imported, 93 percent at Chetro Ketl, 71 percent at Una Vida. In contrast, Pueblo Pintado, outside downtown Chaco and closer to surviving tree stands on Chacra Mesa, obtained only 20 percent of its timbers from nonlocal sources. Even with imported timber, the demand began to outstrip supply. We know this because, after 1030 and when great house construction was at its height, Pueblo Bonito's builders used more and more beams from younger trees instead of the older timber favored earlier.

A major ponderosa source was the Chuska Mountains and Piedmont, more than 50 miles (80 km) west. These are the most drought-resistant of conifers, which probably flourished in groves closer to Chaco, with the nearest dense stands at least 25 miles (40 km) away. Ponderosa is the most common beam timber through great house history, probably because it was closest and the most abundant of the long, straight conifers. The available stands, however, were soon depleted. We know this because the woodsmen harvested few trees with trunks more than 13 inches (35 cm) in diameter. Many were smaller than 5 inches (12 cm). Ponderosa is a relatively fast-growing tree, but the reservoir of trees never kept pace with selective harvesting. By 1030 the Chacoans were seeking trees at higher altitudes, in subalpine forests. The nearest stands of fir and spruce today are at elevations between 6,500 and 8,000 feet (1,981–2,450 m) in mountains more than 47 miles (75 km) from the canyon, and these were the altitudes at which Chacoans were forced to obtain much of their construction lumber. The Dutton Plateau and San Mateo Mountains to the south were also rich in ponderosa stands, but research on these sources is at an early stage.

Just how much damage the Chacoans wrought on tree communities is a matter of debate. They were selective in their felling, so much so that they thinned rather than wiped out entire forests, leaving the larger mature and very young trees alone. The effect may have been the same as modern-day thinning.

Such was the demand for timber that during the period of major construction from 1030 to 1100, Chaco society had a strong orientation toward the south and west, a semicircle defined by the Chuska Mountains 60 miles (100 km) to the west and Mount Taylor, 50 miles (80 km) to the south. These mountains support extensive stands of fir, pine, and spruce, and were certainly major sources for Chacoan lumber. Furthermore, the Chacoan road system, described in chapter 10, oriented the canyon to outlying communities both near the Chuskas and Mount Taylor. After 1100, timbers came from the La Plata and San Juan Mountains to the north, as new outliers came into being along the San Juan River.

Judging from the tree-ring counts at Chetro Ketl, tree felling occurred virtually every year, sometimes to help with piecemeal reconstruction and remodeling, sometimes to fuel large-scale construction. The same rings show interrupted growth patterns, as if most of the felling took place in spring. Tom Windes tells me that most other great houses show signs of more episodic cutting.

Few stone axes have come from Chaco itself, which suggests that the beams were debarked, trimmed, and cut to a more-or-less standardized size in the forests, then transported to the canyon. The actual felling and transportation may have been in the hands of relatively few people, whose leaders skillfully balanced the exploitation of closer, depleted growth with that on more distant higher ground.

Felling trees and trimming beams was a laborious task, but it paled alongside the logistics of transporting the lumber from forest to canyon. The beams display no telltale signs of scarring from being dragged or rolled, so they were carried long distances, presumably by organized work parties. The Chacoans had no wheeled carts or draft animals, no

Figure 9.2   Transporting a large timber the traditional way, as reconstructed by Neil Judd for *National Geographic Magazine. Courtesy Department of Library Services, American Museum of Natural History, New York.*

convenient waterways or sledges. Everything traveled on human backs. Cutting and transporting timber may have been the most labor-intensive part of building great houses, requiring careful organization to ensure a constant supply of new beams. No one knows what drove the people of Chaco to undertake this enormous labor. The transportation alone must have involved hundreds of people every year. Whether they were driven by compelling ritual beliefs, or coerced by powerful leaders, we don't know. Nor do we know whether the canyon sent out organized work parties to the mountains, or whether the felling was carried out by people living in outliers with social and ritual ties to Chaco (figure 9.2).

Pottery

Timber was a staple. So was pottery. Clay vessels were essential to the fabric of Chacoan, and indeed all, Southwestern society.[4] The vessels carried water, stored food and possessions, served as cooking pots, and had many ritual functions. It's thought that each household made its own pottery, using simple techniques passed down from mother to daughter and through the generations. But there were specialists, too, women who were famed for their ceramic skills, just as there are today. Most potters built up their vessels with clay coils, pressing and molding the vessel into shape, smoothing the coils into thin, even walls, then either coating them with a clay and water mixture known as "slip" before drying and painting them or giving them a corrugated surface with their fingers. Potting is a cherished skill, at which few people truly excel. Potters working without wheels, as Pueblo potters do, need a steady hand and an expert eye, sensitive fingers to gauge the thickness of a pot

Figure 9.3 A Hopi woman making pottery with the coiled method. Oraibi Pueblo, 1903. *Photographer unknown. Corbis.*

wall. Every vessel was different, every one made individually, dried carefully in the shade before painting and firing (figure 9.3).

Firing a clay pot requires a fine appreciation for the properties of firing clay and, above all, copious amounts of firewood to maintain high firing temperatures and to produce the hot ash that insured an even hardening. And herein lay the crunch for Chaco's potters: their predecessors had stripped the landscape of its readily available firewood.

Pottery is the archaeologist's barometer of cultural change, which makes for mind-bogglingly dull technical literature, but for a mass of important information about changing trade patterns (see Box, pages 156–158). The insights come not only from painted designs and pot forms but from the characteristics of temper mixed with the clay to bond it, which varies from one region to another. For instance, vessels from the Chuska region to the west were often tempered with sanidine basalt (trachyte), a rock of volcanic origin characteristic of that area.

Enormous numbers of clay vessels entered Chaco from afar. Between 1000 and the twelfth century, no less than 50.4 percent of all pottery in the canyon was imported. Almost certainly this was a consequence of local firewood shortages, which inhibited convenient production of local wares. The distinctive tempers in Chaco pot clays tell us that San Juan Basin tempers were sometimes used early in the canyon's history, which is hardly surprising, given the origin of its communities. During the 900s, pottery came from the Red Mesa Valley to the south. By the mid-to-late 1000s, trachyte tempers from the Chaco core identify Chuska to the west as the primary source. After that, the main source was the San Juan River area in the north. The Chacoans even received pots from as far away as the Mogollon and Kayenta regions.

CHACO CERAMICS

Pottery is the life blood of archaeologists everywhere; Chaco Canyon is no exception. Potsherds and complete vessels provide vital chronological information in the Southwest, epitomized by Alfred Kidder's work at Pecos three-quarters of a century ago, when he used changing ceramic styles to trace Southwestern society back from the present into the remote past. Fortunately for Chacoan archaeologists, tree-ring chronologies provide an increasingly accurate timescale for developments in the canyon, but pottery still provides valuable information on such topics as trade and the dates of unexcavated sites. Pottery classifications do not make for exciting archaeological literature; the detail is often mind-numbing, and much of it relevant only to specialists. There are passing references to pottery styles in these pages, so here is a much simplified primer to Chaco Canyon wares.

Cibola White Ware was manufactured over a large area from Chaco south into the Zuni Pueblo area and is the most common of all Chacoan ceramics. Constant debate surrounds the subclassification of Cibola White, whose design motifs and forms changed through time. The sequence of change styles is based on stratified excavations and tree-ring chronologies. The situation is complicated by the ebb-and-flow of contacts between Chaco and outliers, and with other regions. Here is a commonly used (simplified) sequence:

AD   **Ceramic Type**
600–800   *La Plata Black-on-White*
   (The earliest form of Cibola White, made throughout the San Juan Basin. Simpler geometric designs executed in mineral paints. Open bowls are common, usually decorated with triangle sand linear designs that are similar to those on basketry, even sandals. Simple cooking pots, known as Lino Gray were the precursors of later corrugated cooking pots.)

875–1040   *Red Mesa Black-on-White* (Figure 9.4)
   (Characteristic of Pueblo I sites in the San Juan Basin. Black geometric designs, mainly bowls, but other vessel types as well. Cooking wares were made with clay coils around the neck, flattened, not smoothed [so-called Kana'a Neckbanded ware].)

Figure 9.4 Chaco Red Mesa Black-on-White vessel from site 29SJ 1360, AD 875–1040. Height: 4.1 inches (10.5 cm). *Courtesy NPS Museum Management Program and Chaco Culture National Historical Park. Image CHCU 7230.*

1000–1140   *Escavada Black-on-White*
(Manufactured throughout most of the San Juan Basin. Features geometric designs on gray or white. Mostly bowls with a few jars and pitchers. Many design motifs are solid triangles paired or attached to solid farming lines.)

1030–1150   *Gallup Black-on-White*
(Found throughout the San Juan Basin. Numerous pitchers and jars, also hatched designs combing parallel lines and solid designs, including triangles and Vs.)

1075–1150   *Chaco Black-on-White*
(Pitchers and bowls, hatched designs with elaborate designs. Cooking wares were often made with a corrugated surface made by pressing the moist clay with a stick or finger. Many corrugated vessels came from the Chuska region.)

1100–1150   *Chaco-McElmo Black-on-White* (frontispiece)
(Includes elements from Cibola, Mesa Verde, Chuska, and the Little Colorado region. Mugs like those made at Mesa Verde occur. Use of hatching declines, carbon paints are used.)

The distinctions between these various forms need not concern us here but are based on surface finish, the fine clay slip applied to the vessel, surface polish, the use of different clay tempers, such as trachyte from Chuska, vessel forms, and different decorative motifs. The diversity of the latter increased through time. Generally, motifs became more diverse through time, but the designs became more stylized. For instance, the Classic Bonito phase of the eleventh century saw geometric hachured designs painted with mineral-based paints more common in Chaco Canyon than in surrounding areas. Economic and political considerations affected pottery styles, among them the cost effectiveness of producing numerous vessels with more-or-less standardized designs. For instance, in the early twelfth century the classic Chaco hachure design declines as Chaco-McElmo vessels appear, these without hachure and decorated with carbon paint derived from plants such as Rocky Mountain beeweed that was more economical to obtain and use.

The most unusual Chaco vessels are Cylinder Jars, found in caches at Pueblo Bonito, and rarely at other Chacoan sites (plate 11). Room 28, in Old Bonito, yielded no less than sixty-three Cylinder Jars in a single such cache. A total of one hundred nineteen Cylinder Jars came from this general precinct, as opposed to only eighteen from other great houses and small sites in Chaco and the northern San Juan. Clearly, these jars, often with small knobs and handles, had unusual ritual significance.

Toolmaking stone

Good quality toolmaking stone was essential for societies that depended heavily on sharp-edged stone tools for hunting, woodworking, and other day-to-day tasks, such as agriculture (figures 9.5 and 9.6).[5] Of all

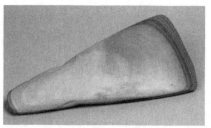

Figure 9.5   Stone knife from unknown Chaco Canyon site. *Courtesy NPS Museum Management Program and Chaco Culture National Historical Park. Image CHCU 1279.*

Figure 9.6   Stone hoe, made of slate, notched on the sides for hafting. Length: 7.5 inches (19.1 cm). *Courtesy NPS Museum Management Program and Chaco Culture National Historical Park. Image 4372.*

such rocks, obsidian—lustrous volcanic glass—was the most desirable, especially for making small artifacts like arrowheads. Before 920, obsidian was imported occasionally, with imported stone accounting for about 10 percent of all such tool material in Chaco sites. Then Narbona Pass chert from the Chuska Mountains superceded it, accounting for 21 percent of all the chipped stone found in the Chaco core after 1020.

A question of relationships

Clay vessels, timber, and toolmaking stone: Chaco could not survive without these essential commodities, most of which came from the Chuska region between 1050 and 1100. This linkage between the canyon and the mountains was far more than a long-term commercial transaction, involving the exchange of staples. The relationship was a complex soup, involving kin links and mutual obligations, ritual ties and ceremonial roles, ancient ideas of mobility, and, of course, straightforward trade. There was a duality at work here, between highlands rich in essential resources and a canyon at lower elevation that supported a relatively dense population and had strong ritual drawing power.

The relationship between Chaco and Chuska went back centuries, to long before the first great houses rose in the canyon. Generations of hunter-gatherers and farmers had moved back and forth between highlands and lowlands, their movements dictated in part by agricultural conditions and the passage of the seasons. This was the fundamental mechanism behind the back-and-forth of later centuries, when canyon and highlands were linked by a close and economically vital web of connections tied, ultimately, to an intensely sacred place.

"Chaco interaction" has become somewhat of an archaeological buzzword in recent years, as people try to define the full extent of Chaco's relationship with the wider world outside the canyon. The same web of interconnections that linked Chaco and Chuska also tied the communities in the canyon with areas in other directions—to many locations in the San Juan Basin, to the Zuni Mountains, the Red Mesa Valley, and to the Mount Taylor area to the southeast, where timber was abundant.

A TASTE FOR THE EXOTIC

Chaco's external connections thrived off unspectacular staple commodities, an exchange system as old as history itself. But the same trading networks carried exotics, too—seashells and bright turquoise, copper bells and tropical birds and their feathers, the currency of ritual, status, and public ceremony.[6]

The burials in Old Bonito, described in chapter 11, were drowned in shell and turquoise beads and pendants fabricated in raw materials from afar. Such ornaments proclaimed unusual social status but not necessarily wealth. George Pepper recovered one burial with a cactus stalk fragment wrapped in cloth, a badge of office for both Hopi and Zuni priests in historic times. Many ceremonial sticks and other ritual objects come from the burial areas, too, so social status and political power may have depended on secret knowledge and religious powers. Judging from the lavish ornaments buried with young interments in Old Bonito, such powers were inherited.

These unusual finds have prompted a spate of theorizing about their meaning. Was Chaco the center of a huge regional system, its leaders responsible for redistributing goods through different communities as a way of compensating for food and other shortages in a harsh environment prone to drought? Was the canyon the hub of an elaborate turquoise production and distribution center? Or was Chaco a place where groups from a wide area regularly came together for elaborate ceremonial observances? Some earlier researchers even argued that Chaco was a place where traders from the south, from Mesoamerica, came to acquire exotic goods such as turquoise.

Let's took more closely at the exotica themselves.[7]

Shells

Freshwater, marine, and even fossil shells from local formations, arrived in the canyon from as early as Basketmaker times. The marine varieties came from the Pacific Coast and from the Gulf of California, freshwater shells from as far away as Arkansas, Texas, and perhaps California. Pueblo Bonito yielded more than twenty shell species. At least twenty additional forms have come from other Chaco great houses. Most of the Pueblo Bonito shells formed part of necklaces and pendants buried with the dead, some from kiva offerings (figure 9.7). The most common forms are *Glycy-*

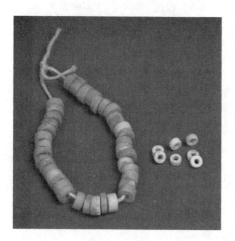

Figure 9.7   Shell beads from Kin Kletso. *Courtesy NPS Museum Management Program and Chaco Culture National Historical Park. Image CHCU 727.*

meris gigantea and *Olivella dama*, both found in the Gulf of California. Many imported shells became mosaic inlay. Room 40 at Pueblo Bonito may have functioned as a shell workshop, just as there were turquoise work areas in several great houses. Some exotic shells such as *Murex* and *Strombus* served as ritual trumpets until they broke, when the owners recycled them for other purposes, for they were hard to procure. Complete fossil shells had ceremonial associations and were coated with red and yellow ochre.

Turquoise

Shiny turquoise was, above all, an ornamental material. The Basketmakers prized turquoise. So did their immediate successors, but this much prized commodity did not become commonplace until Old Bonito times. Almost all turquoise became beads, pendants, or mosaic inlay, processed in workshops found in both great houses and small sites. The best-known workshop comes from a small site, 29SJ629, where the excavators recovered thousands of miniscule chips.[8]

No question, turquoise was a mark of social status; the two most elaborately decorated burials at Pueblo Bonito bear this out. They were buried with more turquoise than all the twelve burials in the room above them combined, while these in turn lay with more than all the people in the western burial cluster. Very few turquoise ornaments come from burials at other great houses or in small sites.

Turquoise was also an important kiva offering, buried in caches during kiva construction as early as Basketmaker III times. Caches appear in the great kivas at Chetro Ketl and Casa Rinconada and in those at other great houses (see plate 11).

Every fragment of this exotic material came from outside the canyon. The closest source is at Cerrillos, New Mexico, to the east, but there were many other outcrops throughout the Southwest. Thanks to neutron activation analysis of elements in Chaco turquoise, we know that Chacoans were active in two turquoise exchange networks that were active between 900 and 1200. One linked the Cerrillos area with the Tucson Basin and the Zacatecas area of Mexico, the other Chaco, the Tucson Basin, and areas far to the south in Mesoamerica. Perhaps the contemporary Hohokam farmers of the Tucson region acted as intermediaries in a trade that flourished from Chaco's earliest days.

The turquoise trade extended far beyond the San Juan Basin, even into modern-day Mexico. This is one of the reasons why some earlier archaeologists believed that Chaco received both traders and important ideas from Mesoamerican civilizations to the south. They also based their reasoning on two other exotics—copper bells and macaws.

Copper bells and macaws

Forty-one copper bells have come from Chaco Canyon, most of them from Pueblo Bonito (figure 9.8). They first appear around 1050, but the source of the ores from which they were made remains a matter of debate. For years, it was thought that they originated in Mexico, a reflection of new trade routes from the south, perhaps through Hohokam communities in Arizona. Bells date to as early as AD 800 in western Mexico and Central Arizona, but analyses of the trace elements in their metal show too much variability to give conclusive proof of their place of origin. According to J. W. Palmer, who analyzed a series of bells, bell casting began, perhaps in the Anasazi and Hayataya regions, in about AD 1000, using copper-cuprite and malachite sources present in the Southwest but not in Mexico.[9] There's a possibility that Chaco's bells come from Hohokam sources rather than Mexico, but, pending further analyses, the jury is still out. By 1220 workshops at Casas Grandes in Chihuahua, Mexico, were producing numerous copper bells, but by that time Chaco was deserted.

Figure 9.8   Chacoan copper bell. *Courtesy NPS Museum Management Program and Chaco Culture National Historical Park. Image CHCU 31204.*

Macaws (*Ara macaw*) are colorful tropical birds with bright red, yellow, and blue feathers, native to the Mexican lowlands south of Tamaulipas (figure 9.9).[10] The Chacoans imported adult birds, so they cannot have been bred within the canyon. One possible source may have been the Mimbres region, where there are pictures on clay vessels showing macaws being carried in baskets. Few macaws reached Chaco. Thirty-seven skeletons come from Pueblo Bonito, small numbers of skeletons and birds from other canyon sites. Room 38 in the north-central block of Pueblo Bonito contained twelve macaw skeletons and may have been a repository for birds that played an important role in major ceremonies. On the basis of Zuni practices, both George Pepper and Neil

Figure 9.9 Military macaw. *Guy Motil/Corbis.*

Judd suspected that there had been a Macaw clan at Pueblo Bonito, which used the bird's feathers ceremonially.

The trade in shell and turquoise expanded greatly between 900 and 1000, just as demand for Chuska timber increased. After 1050, copper bells, macaws, and additional exotic shell species joined the list of imports. The small range of truly exotic objects hints at trade that focused on essentials and on raw materials, and only on relatively rare artifacts and materials that had highly specific ritual significance. As a result, few people now believe that there was direct trade between Chaco and Mexican societies.

A partnership of staples and ritually powered objects flowed into the canyon, but we don't know what went out in exchange. There cannot have been large enough food surpluses to provide full reciprocity for more than two hundred thousand timbers. Perhaps Chaco's most important asset was the rituals that unfolded inside the canyon, and specifically at Pueblo Bonito. Most of the exotic objects at Chaco come from Pueblo Bonito, as if the largest of the great houses had a special role in canyon life. We cannot be completely sure of this, for only Kin Kletso has been fully excavated and there were few exotics there. Nor have many come from partially excavated houses such as Chetro Ketl, Pueblo del Arroyo, or Pueblo Alto.

Agriculture and religion: the realities of a harsh farming environment and a carefully regulated ritual calendar were the mechanisms that drove Chacoan life on well-ordered wheels. As we shall see in chapter 10, the ticking of this same ritual clock extended far from the canyon, communicated by road, and by ideas shared over a large area of a semiarid world.

10 ∴ "DISCONNECTED HETEROGENEITY"

> In the beginning was the Black World, where the
> Holy People, First Man and First Woman, began.
> They came up through the four worlds, and Coy-
> ote accompanied them from the first to the present,
> it is said. . . .
>
> Navajo tale about Coyote[1]

The heavily laden men walk slowly along the narrow path in pairs, a team
carrying a carefully trimmed ponderosa trunk on cross timbers. They've
picked up the large tree from a large, carefully stacked pile near the
village, where they've been seasoning for several years. The men pick
their way carefully along the winding path, keeping a safe distance
from another laden team ahead of them. Their eyes cast ahead on the
dusty track, looking for loose stones or erosion gullies where they might
trip. They wind downhill to the floor of the San Juan Basin, which
shimmers ahead of them in the morning heat.

A party of women carry laden baskets on their heads, piled high with
maize cobs and beans, kept in place with tied cloths. Their children heft
water pots and bundles of dried venison, walking upright, carefully,
behind their mothers. Each household plods along together. The journey is slow, deliberate, the destination the sacred canyon beyond the far
horizon. . . .

∴ ∴ ∴

The English humorist P. G. Wodehouse set down a classic stereotype
of the archaeologist, when he wrote of "a mere hole in the ground which

of all sights is perhaps the least vivid and dramatic, is enough to grip their attention for hours at a time."[2] Wodehouse was writing about spectators at a construction site, but, until recently, his remarks could well have applied to archaeologists at Chaco, indeed anywhere. Today's researchers live with the consequences of wholesale excavation at Pueblo Bonito in the late nineteenth and early twentieth centuries. Today, any form of digging is strictly controlled and carried out for specific purposes, and even then on the smallest possible scale.

Since the 1970s much of the focus of Chaco archaeology has changed, away from excavation and site-oriented research to a much greater concern with the entire Chacoan landscape. The wider perspective resulted from changing interests among archaeologists generally, also from an explosion of new data acquired from cultural resource management projects that made use of aerial photography and other advanced survey devices. This is not to say, of course, that there is no site-centered research, quite the contrary. Dabney Ford and Tom Windes's research into the chronology of Pueblo Bonito is only one example of such work. We now know that the story of Chaco cannot be told simply by studying its great houses and small settlements. Much of the story lies far beyond the canyon walls, buried in a hard-to-decipher ancient Chacoan landscape, once dissected by roads and innumerable paths—tentacles that linked communities and households over hundreds of square miles.

THE CHACO SYSTEM

In 1901 a federal land agent named Samuel J. Holsinger observed traces of roads emanating from Chaco Canyon. Holsinger was more concerned with Wetherill's land claims than archaeology. His report describing the roads was never published and languished forgotten in government archives until the 1970s.[3] This was the decade when systematic aerial infrared photography and satellite imagery came to Chaco, at a time when archaeologists like Gwinn Vivian were turning their attention to such issues as the nature of Chacoan water-control systems. Vivian and his colleagues were searching for irrigation canals when they came across what appeared to be roads near the great houses. Their discoveries came just as space technology revealed what appeared to be a road network in the San Juan Basin with Chaco at its hub. Subsequently, many less conspicuous road segments have come to light on Soil Conservation Service photographs of the 1930s.

The roads caused a considerable stir in archaeological circles. They confirmed what many researchers already suspected—that Chaco Canyon had interacted with a far wider world.[4] They reappeared at a time when archaeologists had become much entranced with *general systems* theory, a popular theoretical concept of the 1960s. It made sense to extend systems theory to ancient human cultures, now termed *cultural systems*, made up of many interacting subsystems: economic, religious, social, and so on. Such systems models had immediate appeal as a way of interpreting what appeared to be a sophisticated road network centered on Chaco. Inevitably, researchers began to talk of a *Chaco System*, a vast cultural network that spread its tentacles across the San Juan Basin and beyond. The term is still commonly used a quarter-century later. But we need to sharpen its meaning.

The Chaco System is, at best, an imprecise label, which in strict dictionary terms refers to a group of interacting entities that formed a unified whole. But what were these entities? In Chaco's case, they were communities, loose aggregations of Pueblo households that flourished long before great houses rose in the canyon. If you accept this point, then you can view the Chaco System as a way of developing lasting contacts that extend beyond community boundaries. But how can we define these communities as having relationships with Chaco? A number of criteria for identifying such relationships come into play—large great houses, core-veneer masonry, blocked-in kivas, and formal great kivas, also roadways and distinctive Dogoszhi-style ceramics (figure 10.1). There are other features, too, such as enclosed plazas, earthworks and berms, and tower kivas.[5]

Figure 10.1   Three Black-on-White cylinder vessels in the Dogoszhi style from George Pepper's excavations at Pueblo Bonito. *Courtesy Deborah Flynn Post.*

Cultural research management projects of every size imaginable have provided a mountain of new data on great houses outside the canyon in recent years. There is now so much information that a group of ten archaeologists, each with regional expertise, got together in 1999 to assemble a comprehensive database of what was known about great houses and the communities associated with them. The Chaco World Database is founded on a set of standardized variables, which rarely occur at every great house, but do occur in clusters through time and across the landscape where a set of communities share them—but neighbors do not. For instance, core-veneer masonry and low kiva/room ratios at great houses characterize communities with clear associations with Chaco Canyon itself, such as those in the San Juan Basin.[6] The intense research of recent years is adding more and more great houses to the database, giving us a comprehensive look at the outlying communities unimaginable even a generation ago. But how do we know whether these many communities interacted with Chaco's great houses and households? One clue comes from Chaco's roads.

A QUESTION OF ROADS

From the moment of their rediscovery, Chaco's roads were an enigma. At first, the canyon seemed to be the hub of a vast network, even if the pathways on aerial images were incomplete. When people began to trace them on the ground, they had considerable difficulty identifying them in many places. But the idea of a network persisted, with a "Great North Road" and a South Road aligned on the cardinal directions and significant east–west branches. In 1982 archaeologist Robert Powers argued that "the roads enter Chaco Canyon near the locations of several of the large- and medium-sized Chacoan structures."[7] He thought that they converged on a zone circumscribed by Pueblo Bonito, Chetro Ketl, and Casa Rinconada. These sites represented the apex of Chacoan power and, through the roads converging on them, controlled distant, outlying communities.

Even the most superficial surveys proved that Chacoan roads were deliberately built, with a depth of between 4 and 20 inches (10–50 cm), cut down to some kind of solid substratum. Some segments run across bare rock without modification; others are excavated quite deeply into the subsoil, sometimes planned cuts through low ridges. The main concourses averaged about 26 to 39 feet (8–12 m) wide, sometimes considerably wider. Lesser branch roads average about 15 feet (4.5 m) across. Edging stones, masonry walls, sometimes grooves, and most often low earthen berms, delineate the sides. Rockcut stairways and ramps for log ladders, notably in Chaco Canyon's walls, carried the roads down steep terrain (figure 10.2).

Wherever they appear, the Chaco roads are of standardized design and construction, right down to the dimensions and edging. They are invariably associated with such features as great houses and great kivas,

Figure 10.2   Jackson
Stairway, Chaco Canyon.
Courtesy of NPS Chaco Culture
National Historical Park. Slide
5311.

and with low, horseshoe-shaped masonry structures, often called *her-*
raduras, which lie close to roads, invariably in places where the topography allows a view of the roadway ahead. A *herradura* often marks a
subtle change in the direction of the road. Earthen mounds (berms)
also stand close to roads, especially south of the canyon, and may have
had a sacred meaning.[8]

Almost every known segment in some way articulates with a great
house in a general way. But there are more specific associations as well.
During the second stage of Pueblo Bonito, the builders erected an arc
of multistory rooms as a backing wall to Old Bonito but did not knock
doorways through into the existing pueblo. The same feature also rose
at Chetro Ketl, where rooms at the back face a road, and at Pueblo Alto
above the canyon, where they are part of the west wing, facing a passing road. These complexes did not face the plaza. Rather, they fronted
roads and had connecting doors between each room as well as external doorways. Everyone agrees that these room complexes served for
storage. Steve Lekson makes a distinction between the typical domestic storage use of rooms facing the plaza and the outer rooms. He be-

Figure 10.3   Pueblo Alto. *Courtesy of NPS Chaco Culture National Historical Park. Slide 5311.*

lieves that the complexes were for longer-term storage for the community as a whole. Tom Windes, who excavated Pueblo Alto, with its strong road associations, believes the complexes were used on a short-term basis by travelers on the nearby roads. Still another authority, Gwinn Vivian, argues that the reason there were no doorways was because the builders had not yet mastered an economic and safe way of cutting doors into existing rooms. His conservative explanation suggests that additional rooms were storage areas, used by the inhabitants of the pueblo on a daily basis.[9]

Pueblo Alto, at the intersection of several roads, lies on the mesa above Chaco, about a half mile (0.8 km) north of Pueblo Bonito (figure 10.3). It's sometimes called Old Alto, to distinguish it from New Alto, a McElmo-style great house about a quarter mile (0.4 km) to the west. A low wall connects the two sites. Tim Windes and other Chaco project archaeologists excavated Pueblo Alto from 1976 to 1978, investigating not only the pueblo rooms but a huge midden at the southeastern corner of the site. Tree rings tell us that construction of the one-story, D-shaped pueblo began in about AD 1020 and continued throughout the century. In the early 1100s the builders added an arc of rooms to the front, filling in a central plaza surrounded by the three original wings.

The pueblo stands at a windy mesa-top location that commands an impressive view of the canyon and its great houses, among them Una

Vida, Tsin Kletsin, and Peñasco Blanco. You can see the pueblo atop
the mesa from several canyon-bottom great houses. This commanding
position also lies at the focal point of a number of Chacoan roads, among
them the Great North Road. Several of them converge on a narrow
opening in a wall extending from the northeast corner of the great
house. Another passes just to the west of the pueblo.

Signs are that Pueblo Alto had a somewhat different function than
other great houses. Tom Windes has shown convincingly that a residential population used only about five of the pueblo's nearly one
hundred rooms. More than 150,000 potsherds and numerous food remains have come from its vast midden, far more than from other Chaco
trash dumps with their day-to-day domestic activities. It may be that
Pueblo Alto was a staging point for canyon visitors, or a place where
feasting took place.[10]

We know that several roads converged in the canyon as a whole
(see plate 2). But there are no signs of a road system centered on Pueblo
Bonito and downtown Chaco. At some great houses like Pueblo Alto,
above the canyon, roads abut or enter the great house. At others, like
Peñasco Blanco, the road passes by the site and has no structural relationship with it. Every road seems to link directly with some destination, but they rarely, if ever, connect them to one another. They may
have had the same overall general purpose, but there are no signs that
they were part of a comprehensive, functional network.

If the roads were indeed a network, how large an area did they encompass? Here opinions differ widely. Steve Lekson and others carry
the roads well beyond the San Juan Basin, perhaps to the San Juan
Range in the Rocky Mountains and south to the Mogollon Mountains,
and from the Rio Grande in the east to the Little Colorado River in the
west.[11] The road network has shrunk and expanded promiscuously,
not so much on the basis of ground observation but by joining great-
house dots on a map (figure 10.4). One estimate talked of no less than
1,500 miles (932 km) of roads.

Reality is more modest. In 1992, Bureau of Land Management archaeologist John Roney produced a meticulously researched map of
known and ground-observed roads that was strikingly different from
the ambitious networks espoused by others.[12] No road, not even the

---

Facing page
Figure 10.4   Chacoan roads: (a) The extent of known roads. The map is an
incomplete depiction of a complex lattice of roads across the San Juan Basin
and beyond; (b) Roads approaching, and within, Chaco Canyon.

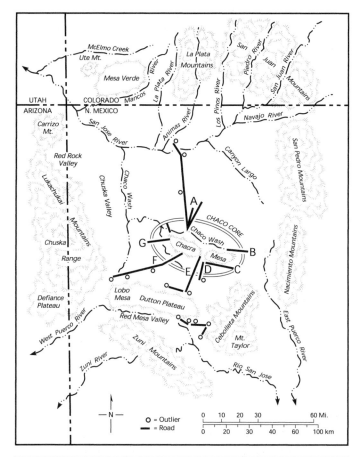

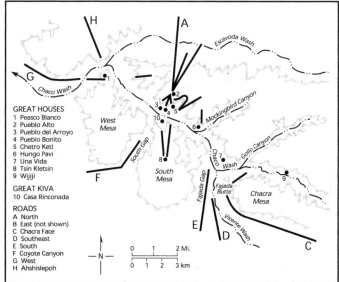

Great North Road that headed from Chaco toward Salmon on the San Juan River, was a complete link between individual great houses or even the canyon and a specific house. (The North Road seems to terminate at Kunz Canyon but almost certainly angles down the canyon to its confluence with the San Juan River, where the Salmon Ruins lie on the north bank. This extension requires turning to the west along a logical and convenient route, which goes against the common assumption that the road only headed north—an important cosmological consideration when considering such issues as the so-called Chaco Meridian [see chapter 12].)

Roney produced a carefully researched estimate of known road distances, to a total of 129.3 miles (208.1 km), a far smaller total. He noted that most roads were site-specific short segments, some of them "floating" without visible links.

Roney's conservative figure is probably closer to reality, but it does not allow for the difficulties of identifying ancient roads across the landscape. In Chaco itself, alluvial flooding may have obscured many critical road segments, while wind erosion and other factors may have contributed to the erasure of roads elsewhere. (It should also be noted that road studies have focused on the San Juan Basin, largely because the surveys were carried out for Bureau of Land Management purposes, as part of the task of managing resources during oil and gas development. There are definitely roads beyond the confines of the Basin, but we haven't looked intensively for them yet.)

Nevertheless, it's almost certain that Chaco's roads were never a network that connected different communities. While a few do link larger villages to neighboring hamlets, most seem to have directed attention toward nearby landmarks that had a presumed religious meaning. Two, or perhaps three, roadways do indeed emanate from Chaco Canyon and extend to the edges of the San Juan Basin. But even the destinations of these roadways are a mystery, although they pass through or near major Chacoan communities (figure 10.5). They seem to point toward major landmarks. The linear North Road seems to terminate at Kutz Canyon (although most experts extend it farther north to Salmon Ruin), the South Road goes directly to Kin Ya'a, where it passes to the east of the great house and moves toward the conspicuous Hosta Butte. No road extends to Narbona or Washington Pass, where chert and so much fine trachyte-tempered Chaco pottery originated. No road extends into Red Mesa, where chert, obsidian, and petrified wood originated. What is known as the Coyote Canyon Road is said to run to the general area of the southern Chuska Valley, near where most Chaco

Figure 10.5 New Alto. No roads lead to this site, but they do to nearby Pueblo Alto. *Courtesy of NPS Chaco Culture National Historical Park. Slide 5311.*

beams came from—but it is poorly documented. Furthermore, so few stone tools or pot fragments occur along the roads that it's possible that few people traveled along them—although they could have passed along without dropping anything![13]

The Chaco roads are deeply intriguing because they provide unequivocal evidence that the canyon was the hub of a much larger world, but they defy interpretation because many of them seem to lead nowhere.

WHY BUILD ROADS?

Why, then, did the Chacoans build roads? What did they use them for? Here we enter a realm of intelligent speculation based on an incompletely mapped jigsaw of road segments, associated with great houses and kivas, with blocks of rooms adjacent to roadways. Did these roadways have a purely economic function—to transport lumber, clay vessels, and people? Or were they of purely symbolic significance, even if they were sometimes used by people wending their way to Chaco? Interpretations have ranged over the entire gamut, from sophisticated economic networks to pilgrimage roads.[14]

Westerners think of roads going from A to B, engineered to move armies, commodities, goods, and people from place to place as conveniently as possible. Anyone who has traveled along a dead-straight Roman road in Europe, like Britain's Watling Street, knows where these ideas came from. The well-engineered highway runs for mile after mile across the landscape, deviating neither left nor right, construction standardized, designed with one purpose alone—to administer and safeguard the state and enhance its commerce. The Inca rulers of Peru also used roads in this way, making them wide enough to accommodate llama caravans or armies on the march, zigzagging them up mountain sides, across deserts, sometimes with thousands of steps carved into steep slopes. The Inca system revolved around central administrative control, the imposition of government by force if necessary, and an efficient message system. In the early days of the Spanish occupation of Peru, a team of Inca messengers could carry a message from Cuzco to Quito in Ecuador and back in ten to eleven days, faster than Spanish emissaries on horses or mules.

Under this rubric, it's hardly surprising that people thought of the roads as the way by which people made their way to Chaco Canyon for communal ceremonies, bearing tribute in the form of ceramics and exotic goods to a canyon that was both ritual center and a great marketplace.[15] Such theories argued that all kinds of commodities came to the canyon from afar. There they were consumed or stored for a while before being redistributed to outlying communities, again along the road system. This interpretation saw Chaco as the hub of an economic system that functioned as a whole of its constituent parts. In this way, every community shared evenly in the resources available in an environment of uncertain rainfall and patchy food supplies. This was a fine theoretical scenario, but one that had a fatal flaw. The roads did not form a complete network, they formed a mosaic of short segments. Furthermore, none of them ended at a known spot where valuable resources like timber came from. The only major investment in roads appeared to be near great houses, great kivas, and *herraduras*.

Constructing and maintaining roads requires massive labor. But even the longer roads such as the South Road are most developed along segments located in or near communities. Most disappear altogether away from populated areas. Most roadways have barely discernible berms, despite the ramps and stairways discussed so regularly in the literature. In addition, the roads were never consistently maintained after they were built. In fact, few of the crosswise roads display signs of any maintenance at all. Thus, road construction is more consistent not with regular interaction but with sporadic contact between local communities, who constructed the routes closest to their villages in response to leaders who suggested longer roads to distant features of the sacred landscape.

John Roney's work prompted a reexamination of simple economic theories. Another archaeologist, John Kantner, took an area in the southern Basin, then used a method from geography that involved Geographic Information Systems (GIS) and a computer-generated topographic grid to calculate the amount of time needed to walk each grid square of his research area. Kantner assumed that people using roads for economic purposes would take the shortest, most economic route in terms of topography, what he called a *cost-path*, generated by GIS data. He found that only two road segments, including a portion of the South Road, coincided with the predicted cost-path. Wrote Kantner: "Chacoan roads do not fit well with economic explanations based on regional interaction."[16]

Did people even travel on the roads at all? After all, who needs a road 40 feet (12 m) wide to transport beams? Many years ago, Neil Judd photographed Zuni workers in Chaco Canyon transporting a log "after the style of the ancient people" (see figure 9.2).[17] They carried it lengthwise, not crosswise, supporting it on cross-timbers. Two hundred thousand logs could easily travel to Chaco by people walking alongside, and not on, the roads. In his study of Pueblo Alto, Tom Windes studied the roads nearby, where he found numerous fragments of what appeared to be storage jars, probably used to carry water for travelers. He and others have never found traces of camps or hearths along the roads, as if the journeys along, or by, them did not involve any overnight camping.[18] Most likely the people used ancient footpaths for many if not all of their journeys. Throughout North America, foodstuffs, exotic raw materials, and essentials of every kind traveled enormous distances—from village to village, up and down rivers and streams, and, above all, along footpaths. These paths twisted and turned, across deserts, through woodlands and dense forests, along river banks and lake shores, carrying people and their loads, and ideas as well. Intervillage paths were vital to survival and to maintaining the ties of kin, the collective and individual relationships that were the foundations of all exchange and of the ancient obligations of reciprocity, which kept these spiderwebs of interconnection alive from one generation to the next. The presence of obsidian and exotic shells in numerous sites tells us that such paths, such linkages, crisscrossed the San Juan Basin thousands of years before Ancestral Pueblo culture developed in the north. From the economic perspective, there was no need to construct wide highways when narrow paths did the job just as well, even when hundreds of people were involved.

In a variant of the economic theory, David Wilcox of the Museum of Northern Arizona has proposed that Chaco was a tribute state, which used its roads to control a vast network of tribute gathering from outlying communities and also to move the armed forces needed to enforce the collection.[19] Wilcox believes that Chaco needed such a network to reprovision itself with maize and other foodstuffs. Apart from logistic considerations for an armed force of an estimated one thousand men, were the roads an economic way to transport foodstuffs? A military and tribute explanation holds little water.

Were the roads part of a closely integrated communication system?[20] For generations, Chaco experts have pointed to the tower kivas as facilities in elevated positions that were used for communication between great houses and the Chaco core. Tower kivas are defined as multistory kivalike structures (or elevated kivas) that project one or more stories above the rest of a great house structure (see figure 7.1). The Chaco World Database reveals that nine out of the ten tower kivas in its archives are about 25 miles (40 km) apart from one another, perhaps close enough for signaling. But a recent study of tower kivas at the southern great houses of Kin Ya'a and Haystack showed that, even if intermediate stations were built between them, they were not built to communicate with one another. Their elevated positions improved the view of the local community but did not increase long-distance visibility at all.[21]

We are left with the notion that the roads had a quite different function, one that was essentially nonutilitarian.

REDISTRIBUTION: THE FLOW OF GOODS AND COMMODITIES

As far as the flow of commodities into the canyon is concerned, we've seen how the sources of such items as tool-making stone changed over time. The mechanisms for this interaction are still unclear.[22] One theory has it that pilgrims brought large quantities of objects of all kinds into Chaco at the times of major ceremonies. Many clay vessels and other artifacts may even have been destroyed during these events. This theory has been challenged, but it's interesting to note that the highest frequencies of imported commodities and objects are found in the great houses and not in smaller settlements. The importation may have been in the hands of households, but it was oriented toward great houses.

Everyone agrees that large quantities of material commodities and goods flowed into the canyon, but almost nothing flowed out in return. Nor were outlying communities bypassing Chaco and importing, say, beams, in their own right. Here ceramics provide a clue. Mostly local pottery forms—not Chaco vessels—occur in the outliers, as if trade was one-directional, aimed toward the canyon, and was not all that frequent.

The utilitarian commodities that arrived in the canyon came almost entirely from the inside edges of the San Juan Basin, as if Chaco imported them from a fairly limited area of what is now northwestern New Mexico. When John Kantner and his colleagues examined the composition of pot clays from the Lobo Mesa area south of Chaco Canyon, they found that the mountainous boundaries of the San Juan Basin seem to have restricted interaction over a wider area. Most communities obtained their materials from local sources; only Chaco Canyon acquired large quantities of important staples from a distance.

Valuables such as turquoise and copper bells came from much farther away, but we don't know whether they arrived along direct routes or through many hands. Steve Lekson believes that these exotica stimulated sociopolitical developments in the Southwest, starting at Chaco Canyon. These rare objects, he says, were part of a "political-prestige economy" that was widespread over the northern Southwest during the eleventh and early twelfth centuries.[23] Lekson's theory suffers from a lack of exotic finds, except at Chaco itself, although, of course, there are some finds from outlying sites, notably some macaw feathers from a cave in southeastern Utah. The limited numbers of exotics hint that contact between Chaco Canyon and a very much wider world was irregular at best, if it occurred at all. We return to broader interpretations of Chaco in chapter 11.

Interdependence and redistribution have been catchwords in Chaco circles for a long time. Classic redistribution models would have commodities flowing into Chaco, being stored, then sent out again. Now that we know much more about outlying communities, especially in resource-rich areas, we know that there is no evidence for Chaco artifacts or commodities in them. Their needs were met from local sources. Undoubtedly, they interacted with their neighbors, but there was little need for a formal regional economy. Chaco had no resources needed by outlying communities, almost all of which lay in resource-rich areas.

An alternative on the redistribution model argues for Chaco acting as a "regional exchange facilitator."[24] Under this scenario, people from outlying areas brought food and other items for exchange to places like Pueblo Alto's plaza. At best, such exchange would have had delayed gratification, for there is no evidence of materials moving between outlying areas of the San Juan Basin. And, for instance, if people did bring corn to Chaco, they would have carried out their empty vessels or baskets, for there is no evidence for the movement of pottery from area to area within the Chaco world. As far as we can tell, there was no advantage in redistributing food or other materials. There was no economic interdependence between Chaco and any outlying community other than those of kin ties.

A "NONSYSTEM" AND SHARED IDENTITY

Chaco was not part of a unified world. There was no single consolidated and integrated social or political unit. There was, as John Kantner puts it, a "disconnected heterogeneity."[25] The most striking characteristics of the region run to diversity rather than homogeneity. This is particularly true of great house architecture, even if ritual activities were an important part of life in them. Exotic bird bones, wooden artifacts with ceremonial associations, turquoise ornaments—such artifacts are most common at Pueblo Bonito—they do occur in lesser numbers at other great houses both in the canyon and elsewhere. These associations may mean that great houses were part of a shared cultural pattern, but one that varied considerably from one location to another. The so-called Dogoszhi pottery style is much more standardized than earlier ceramics, so much so that it's been taken to represent some form of symbolic unity (see figure 10.1). In fact, the variability from one community to another is sufficient to allow for individual symbolic identities among them, reflected in such features as different spacing and framing of painted decoration.[26]

There was, then, a very low but important degree of shared identity between many widespread communities. But this identity faded, the farther one traveled from the center.

Current opinion favors an interpretation of the Chaco world not as a unified, interacting whole, but as something very different, a "nonsystem." We know that the distinctive Chacoan features such as the forms of great houses, roads, and possibly the Dogoszhi style, developed in or immediately around Chaco Canyon. They appear to represent a developing ideology that was closely related to a nascent social differentiation within the canyon. These ideas and features spread to the southern San Juan Basin, an area that probably had historic ties to Chaco Canyon. These ties facilitated the spread of such ideas as great house architecture. (Some of the outlying great houses are about the same date as those for Chaco's earliest such structures.) The Chaco World Database reveals how these features appeared in the south. They also spread down the Rio Puerco and Rio San Jose drainages, west up the Chuska Slope, and north into the San Juan area.[27]

Chacoan culture became more elaborate as the canyon became increasingly important as a ceremonial center. However, despite what some authorities believe, I suspect that Chaco never became politically so important that its leaders could influence activity in distant communities. But something else happened. As outlying communities began to become less egalitarian, their emerging leaders began to emulate Chaco's increasingly elaborate communities. This provided vital, and sometimes much needed mutual legitimization, with the outlying communities providing material goods in exchange for the developed ideological infrastructure emanating from Chaco. This turned Chaco into a pilgrimage center, occasionally visited by people bearing gifts or offering services such as labor. Participating communities reaped the benefits of occasional large-scale social occasions, of an extended social network, and perhaps even enhanced observations of seasonal changes or farming schedules.

This is a return to earlier pilgrimage models, but with a difference. The strongest mutual relationships and closest ideologies lay between Chaco Canyon and communities within the San Juan Basin, especially those to the south and west. Outlying communities beyond the Basin do not seem to have been so closely tied to Chaco, although they were well aware of its existence. These communities acknowledged its reputation by adopting some of the Chacoan features to varying degrees and modifying them—and the associated ideology—to fit local social and political circumstances. There was factionalism, competitive emulation, and symbolic displays of obligation, which reflected the different goals of both canyon leaders and their counterparts in outlying communities.

As for the roads, they represented an attempt to connect Chaco Canyon's center with important religious points on the landscape. They were clearly elaborated at points close to participating communities, as if each contributed to the overall effort by expanding the pathway within its own boundaries, thereby symbolically tying themselves to

Chaco. Other roads outside the San Juan Basin may have been emula-
tions of the Chaco pattern that served local functions. As Kantner says:
"In a real sense, many outlying communities may have been trying to
emulate at a much smaller scale what Chaco Canyon was doing across
the San Juan Basin . . . as if they aspired to their own 'mini-Chacos.'"[28]

Under this scenario, the Great North Road may have been an attempt by Chaco to tie itself more closely to the San Juan area at a time
when the canyon's influence over the west and south was declining.
Without ties to the south and west, the religious leaders of the canyon
would have lost access to much needed utilitarian commodities as well
as to exotic objects that legitimized their ritual authority and were tied
to the great ceremonies in the canyon. When these ties ceased, it was a
clear sign that the communities in these areas no longer found it necessary, or it proved too costly, to sustain such a relationship.

All of this adds up to a fairly compelling scenario. Chaco Canyon
was not the center of an elaborate regional system. Rather it was the
center of a patchwork of independent communities whose leaders depended on one another for legitimacy and ideological support, a search
for legitimacy reflected in material terms by the flow of essential commodities and exotics into the Chaco core. It's clear, too, that the roads
had some deeper symbolic meaning, perhaps connected to the sacred
landscape, an issue that we explore in chapter 11. At this point, too, we
must also identify the mysterious leaders who presided over what
appears to have been an intensely sacred place.

11 ∴ THE CHACO ENIGMA

Over your field of growing corn
All day long hang the thunder-clouds;

Over your field of growing corn
All day shall come the rushing rain.

Hopi song-poem[1]

The masked dancers move backward and forward in serried lines, the men in one row, the women in another. They sing in rhythm, facing one another, keeping the pace with their feet, progressing along the sides of the plaza. Brightly colored headdresses and masks adorn the dancers, who follow ancient routines, passed from generation to generation. The dance has always been this way, witnessed by hundreds of people sitting on the terraces above, as much part of Chacoan life as planting and harvest, and the passage of the seasons. . . .

∴ ∴ ∴

Chaco Canyon flourished at the heart of a diverse world, not an economic network but a political, social, and spiritual world where life revolved around two ancient Pueblo imperatives—agriculture and religion. The roads that emanated from the canyon were no highways; they were a means of sharing identity, pointing toward important sacred landmarks, linking dispersed communities to common cosmological beliefs. This cosmology, with its emphasis on ancestors, the passing of the seasons, and the cardinal directions, was maintained by an elaborate ritual cycle, performed with sedulous care and precision,

181

year after year. The great ceremonies of the ritual cycle were the part-ners of agriculture, indivisible from them in a society where farming and religion were as one. What, then, do we know of this ritual cycle, and of the men and women who orchestrated ceremonial occasions so important that they drew in people from long distances, bearing gifts with them?

THE RITUAL CYCLE

We've called Chaco Canyon an *axis mundi*, a sacred place. Whether this axis coincided with Pueblo Bonito, Casa Rinconada, or another great house is unknown, but there seems little doubt that Chaco was a central place in local belief, a logical place for major religious ceremonies.

Harmony, flexibility, movement: I wrote earlier that the Chacoan world was founded on these principles. Today, and certainly in the past, Pueblo religion was a cosmological and philosophical system that per-vaded every aspect of life. The details vary infinitely from one group to another, but there are some universals, many of which must have operated in the recent and more remote past. Many important rituals unfolded with the passing of the seasons, the equinoxes and solstices, with planting and harvest. The gods controlled not only humans but also the cosmos. But they had obligations like people—to share their bounty with others. Thus the notion of reciprocity permeated through human existence, to the point that deities were, in a sense, family. The gods could bring illness, hunger, and other misfortunes—through a failure to make offerings, in order to purify oneself against the power of the dead and from violated taboos.

The broad outlines of the Pueblo worldview seem to differ but little from those of subsistence farming societies in many parts of the world living in similar environments and with an equivalent social complex-ity. Writes Alfonso Ortiz: "I get the distinct impression that by simply altering the terminology a bit for ancient Near Eastern religions the statements could apply just as well to the Pueblos."[2]

The Pueblos set careful limits to the boundaries of their world and ordered everything within it. If modern analogies are any guide, then the great houses and lesser settlements in Chaco Canyon were part of a world defined by mountains and bodies of water along the four car-dinal directions. Theirs was also a world of layers, their cosmos care-fully defined in terms of space. In Tewa society, for example, the Pueblo world had a center—but a center with many locations—because sacred space can be re-created again and again. The notion of the center was the point of intersection of as many as six directions, the seventh being the center itself. But the notion of the center was infinitely flexible, represented in many ways, for, symbolically, it was important to establish its importance in peoples' minds. Everything is defined and represented with reference to a center. Pueblo priests would set out sand paintings by defining the boundaries first, then work their way inward toward the center. Such painting was an intensely sacred act, intended to represent some aspect of the cosmos. Chaco was one of these centers.

Boundaries, detail, order, and a center: everything had its place in the Pueblo cosmos. Everything in the universe, animate and inanimate, had two aspects—essence and matter. Everything in the cosmos was knowable, and thus controllable. Such control came only from meticulous attention to detail and correct performance to the repetition of familiar formulas, rituals, and performances. If humanity's mental state is harmonious, the gods will provide what is asked of them. If it is not, then severe consequences will result. Humans, animals, and the supernatural world are a seemingly unbroken chain of existence.

The duality of the universe was the Sun, the father who dwelt in the cosmos, and Earth, the mother. Myth after myth seeks to unify these two separate entities, through dance and performance, through tales of sacred clowns who are thought of as children of the sun, through cosmic poles erected in plazas that represent the center, the link between the layers of the cosmos.

A reassuring cycle of public rituals unfolded at Pueblo Bonito and other great houses, certainly at the solstices but also at other times, days and nights when drums sounded and rows of masked and feathered dancers moved to and fro in meticulously choreographed performances. There was feasting, the distribution of gifts, burlesque and singing, mockery, parody, competition, performance supported by every household with gifts, labor, and spiritual belief. The ritual cycle *was* Chaco and defined Chaco's identity in the cosmos.

The responsibility for the ritual cycle lay with Chaco's leaders, who remain one of the great mysteries of the Chaco story.

THREE TIERS OF SOCIETY?

We've seen how Chaco life revolved at the daily level around the family and the household. So far, we've skirted the issue of leadership, in the belief that we can only hope to understand its nature with many of the historical facts and interpretations in place. Whoever governed Chaco sat at the center of a diverse and heterogeneous world made up of more-or-less self-sufficient communities—with the exception of Chaco itself, which depended heavily on imported staples.

Archaeologically speaking, our only insights into the structure of Chaco society and its leadership come from excavations into Old Bonito completed nearly a century ago. The records are incomplete, the excavations crude by today's standards. But they give us a tentative portrait of some of the most influential people in the Chaco world.

As we've seen, Old Bonito remained virtually unaltered for almost two centuries and then remained a revered place throughout its life. The reverence came from its antiquity, its orientation, and from the burials of hallowed ancestors interred in its rooms. Most of the 131 burials from Pueblo Bonito come from two-room clusters in Old Bonito, a select few deposited in the central block, most of the others excavated by Neil Judd from the western arc.[3] These striking interments provide us with some clues as to the nature of Chacoan society.

The burials from the north-central cluster, found and excavated by George Pepper, were of men and women who enjoyed a higher life expectancy and were somewhat taller than other known Chaco folk, a sign that they had a better diet than most canyon dwellers, but not that they escaped the parasites that afflicted everyone living in close quarters under unsanitary conditions. These individuals also enjoyed a lower rate of iron deficiency anemia than the inhabitants of nearby small houses, where the incidence was as high as 83 percent. Almost certainly, Pepper's burials were those of the few people at the pinnacle of a Chaco society of increasing complexity.

Looking at the known canyon population from large and small sites, biological anthropologist Nancy Akins identifies three tiers of Chacoans. The people who lived in small sites formed the lowest tier and most of the population. They were buried in middens and rooms with readily available artifacts, most commonly clay vessels. (Modern Pueblo people point out that burying people in trash heaps was not disrespectful, for these were sacred places for the spirits of animals and plants that were used by the people.) Akins is certain that the people buried in rooms at Pueblo Bonito were of a higher status than those interred in smaller canyon communities. They were taller and healthier, as if they had access to better food. They were buried more formally, placed in interconnected rooms designated as burial places. Above all, the grave goods associated with them were of far greater value and of much better workmanship.

The middle level of Chaco society lay in the western burial cluster at Old Bonito, people interred in four contiguous interior rooms with no outside access. In addition to clay vessels and more personal ornaments, people here were laid to rest with bowls and pitchers, baskets, ceremonial sticks, beads, and other ornaments (see plate 11). These rooms fell into disuse; drifting sand and trash smothered the burial chambers as the roofs collapsed.

The uppermost tier of Chaco society lay in the oldest part of the pueblo, at the center of the arc. The burial rooms were difficult to access and completely sealed. This area of the site was a repository for ceremonial items of all kinds, including sacred sticks, rare minerals, beads, bracelets, and pendants, cylinder vessels, and pipes. A magnificent turquoise-inlaid cylindrical basket came from the same area.

George Pepper excavated the northern burial cluster at Old Bonito, finding between twenty-four and twenty-eight burials in four, perhaps five, adjacent rooms. Room 32 contained a single adult burial associated with a cactus-stalk fragment covered with cloth, resembling the badges of office carried by Hopi and Zuni priests, numerous clay vessels and ceremonial sticks. Room 33, the smallest, yielded sixteen disarticulated skeletons lying on a floor of wooden planks. Seven were male, seven female, and two were of undetermined sex. All but three of them were middle aged. Thousands of fragments of imported turquoise and shell beads lay scattered in the room, along with inlaid ornaments, flutes and ceremonial sticks, and clay vessels. The burials had been disturbed, but sometimes rearranged, either by later interments or by looters.

Below the planks, Pepper unearthed a second floor, this time with the timbers lying east to west. Below this lay two male burials, by far the most lavishly adorned of all. Offerings of beads, pendants, and turquoise lay in the four corners of the room. The first male was awash in turquoise beads and pendants, while the second lay on a layer of clean sand covered with wood ash. He lay on his back, with his knees slightly flexed upward, head to the north, feet resting against the south wall. The man had died violently; his skull was gashed severely, his left leg badly cut and chopped. Once again, the body was covered with turquoise pendants, ornaments, and beads. A shell trumpet lay at his right knee, together with other shell ornaments. Under one of the shells lay a magnificent cylindrical basket inlaid with a turquoise mosaic of 1,214 pieces. Inside the basket lay thousands of beads and some turquoise pendants. Another mosaic once executed on basketwork lay near the body, together with a jumble of other precious objects. These two men were buried with much greater care than anyone else and lay with ceremonial sticks, rare minerals, and elaborate shell inlays.

When Nancy Akins examined the two clusters of skeletons, she noticed at once that they were, anatomically speaking, two different populations.[4] While they displayed significant anatomical differences, they were more closely related to one another than to people from any other of the great houses or small sites. Bonito's burials probably represent two closely related groups with unusually high social status, perhaps individuals from different moieties or clans. The distinction is a striking one. In a recent study Michael Schillaci has analyzed burials from Bonito and elsewhere in the canyon, as well as from outside locations. He believes that a diverse population lived in Chaco, an aggregation of regional populations, which is what one might expect, given the early history of movement into the canyon. As one also might expect, there was likely some gene flow with Rio Grande groups to the south. He writes: "The Chacoan culture might have been composed of multiple ethnolinguistic groups with separate biogeographical affinities, all sharing a largely similar material culture."[5]

People of unusual social status either acquire it during life or inherit their position. Some bones from children came from the northern room burial area with its lavish grave furniture. Akins believes that this is a sign that they inherited elevated social status at birth, thereby qualifying them for interment with the elite.

Here, then, are people buried apart from others, individuals who inherited their social position, buried in rooms that pottery tells us were in use from the tenth to twelfth centuries. One of the richest burials was of a man in his fifties, who could have been born as early as the 970s, during Old Bonito times. He lived during a time when good rainfall favored floodplain agriculture, when food surpluses were accumulated, and trade with distant communities expanded exponentially. There were numerous ways that power came to individuals—through the ownership of ceremonial artifacts and objects symbolic of authority, through control of major ceremonial events, from perceived supernatural powers, and from esoteric knowledge about the movements of the sun and moon, and the timing of the solstices. Intangible factors, like the order of creation of a kin group or date of arrival in the canyon, could also play a role.

With these empowered roles came the notion of secrecy, and, at the same time, the public display of symbols of power and leadership. Leadership was a heavy burden, which involved tight control of information, heavy ceremonial responsibilities, and much closely held knowledge. Chaco's leaders were a small, tightly knit elite, to which most people could never aspire. The hierarchy was maintained by ritual knowledge. And once the burial places were abandoned, Chaco's power in the San Juan world dissipated rapidly.

All these elements of a somewhat more hierarchical society appeared between 850 and 1050. In the mid-eleventh century, Chaco flowered rapidly, in a fast changing world where the canyon became a major ritual center of the San Juan world.

It appears that control over ritual activity, over the ceremonies that insured the proper operation of this world, lay in the hands of a few hereditary office holders with secret and extremely potent spiritual knowledge and power. Under these circumstances, their authority would have stemmed not from secular power, from wealth or political author-ity, but purely from religious acumen. It must also have resulted from exceptional diplomatic skills that mediated disputes, navigated through factionalism, and maintained carefully tended relationships with con-temporaries in outlying great houses with ambitions of their own.

We can never hope to fully understand the subtleties of the intricate relationships between Chaco and other great houses far from the can-yon. To what extent did their leaders desire to emulate Chaco's pre-eminence? How close were the ideological beliefs shared by the diverse communities of the San Juan Basin? Beyond a certainty that the ties were loose at best, we will probably never know.

CHIEFDOM OR STATE?

Generations of archaeologists have argued passionately about Chaco. Everyone agrees that it was a special place, a canyon with unusual agri-cultural potential, its topography redolent of powerful spiritual associa-tions. But did the Chacoans live in a basically egalitarian society, as had their predecessors and, indeed, as historic Pueblo societies did? Or was Chaco the center of a powerful chiefdom or even the focus of a great Southwestern civilization with close ties to a much wider world?

As we have seen, economic theories were fashionable in the 1970s. James Judge argued that the loose confederation of farmers in earlier times later became a more formal redistribution network centered on Chaco Canyon, a larger regional system. In 1989 he elaborated his scheme even further and suggested that Chaco Canyon was the focal point of a regional system that ran on scheduled rituals, founded originally around turquoise production.[6] Turquoise became a form of currency that was exchanged for foodstuffs in drought years, while also fulfilling an important ritual function. The system prospered, then expanded during the good rainfall years of 1045–1080. After that, new centers formed to the north, eventually eclipsing Chaco itself.

The trouble with Judge's scenario is that turquoise may not have played the key role in Chacoan life that he assumed. The stone was indeed used in ritual, but there is no good reason to believe Chaco's inhabitants controlled production, nor was the stone stockpiled, as it would have been if it was a staple that "financed" the system. Another scholar, Lynne Sebastian, argued along somewhat similar lines.[7] Chaco, with its unique ecology, was supported by staple foodstuffs. During periods of good rainfall, the system could expand. During this period, elaborate water-control systems on the north side of the canyon allowed the inhabitants to produce larger crop yields, and thus produced the surpluses that supported local leaders and eventually allowed for a hereditary succession.

Sebastian's economic and political model argues for substantial food production, so much so that David Stuart believes that the leaders focused less on farming and more on displays of power, through construction of great houses, roads, and other large works.[8] This was fine, as long as they had enough food, firewood, and other economic resources to maintain the superstructure they had created. Around 1090, droughts disrupted Chacoan society profoundly, to the point where it reorganized and farming communities moved out to the better-watered highlands.

These scenarios do not necessarily call for a particularly elaborate society to support them. Judging from the Pueblo Bonito burials, there was some limited social ranking in Chaco society, with a small elite with supernatural and economic powers and a large farming population living in smaller settlements. A three-tier society perhaps, but a tiered society known only from one great house, so it's difficult to know how the other, largely unexcavated structures fit into this pattern.

Clearly, Pueblo Bonito and other great houses with their large kivas were places where important ceremonies unfolded. In modern Pueblo society the exchange of goods of all kinds is an integral part of ceremony, to the point that it's often difficult to draw boundaries between what is sacred and what secular. Wolcott Toll has argued, and I agree, that the key to Chaco society lay in a number of common features of modern Pueblo ceremonial, such as seasonal commemorations, which probably apply with equal relevance to earlier institutions.[9]

Historic Pueblo society was governed by the endless cycles of the changing seasons, by the solstices, equinoxes, and the routine of the agricultural year.[10] Corn pervaded every aspect of Pueblo and Chaco life—from birth to death, from the past into the future. As historic groups did, they must have danced and sung to corn—at planting, as the crop grew, and when it was ripe. The beliefs about corn extended back many centuries. Corn was formed with the first humans, was associated with legendary Corn Maidens and with the ancestors. These societies lived in a harsh, unpredictable environment, where crops could fail in one area and grow well in another, when in the next year the situation was reversed. Like their successors, the Chacoans must have nurtured corn with management, prayer, and song. Many ceremonies involved the exchange and distribution of food and other necessities brought to the occasion from some distance. These were public occasions, involving society as a whole, consciously or unconsciously designed to bring a sense of cohesion, of common identity, while allowing people from far-flung communities to attend in safety. There was no central control, no coercion to attend. But such regularly scheduled ceremonies, of commemoration, perhaps involving the changing seasons, harvest, and other occasions, were catalysts for societies that were fundamentally egalitarian, where office holding, even if hereditary, involved guardianship of ritual knowledge, political acumen, and the acquisition not of wealth but of social recognition acquired through redistributing food and other commodities to people near and far.

If, however, the Pueblo Bonito burials are any guide, Chaco society may have been somewhat more elaborate. Were the leaders of this society clan leaders who wielded great authority, most of it intangible and unrecognizable in archaeological sites? Or were they religious specialists in a society where ritual served to integrate a society of competing groups? Unfortunately, we don't know.

A CHACO HEGEMONY?

Was Chaco Canyon something perhaps much more elaborate, even a small civilization? One scholar, David Wilcox, believes Chaco was a small state administered from Pueblo Bonito, with territorial chiefs living in outlying communities who paid tribute to Chaco's leading families.[11] To enforce their authority, they maintained a standing army of about five hundred to one thousand soldiers to maintain central authority. Since, at most, Chaco Canyon supported some three thousand people, at least half women, children, and the elderly, it's unlikely that there was enough manpower to support a small band of full-time soldiers, let alone an army. That there was violence is unquestionable— the Old Bonito burials with their injuries prove that—but this is very far from documenting the existence of a repressive state.

If the evidence from Old Bonito is to be believed, then a relatively few people directed the labor of numerous households. They were buried with turquoise and shell, with regalia of religious authority. But were they secular chiefs who presided over a far-flung civilization? To the south lies Mexico, with its long tradition of civilization. Could the inspiration for Chaco Canyon have come from the south, from Mesoamerica? Under this scenario, Pueblo Bonito was a terminus of an ancient trade network based on central Mexico, perhaps even a place where Mexican traders once lived so they could manage the Chaco end of the network. This hypothesis is long discredited. The anatomy of the Pueblo Bonito burials links them closely to ancestral and historic Pueblo populations. Furthermore, the number of Mesoamerican and northern Mexican objects imported into Chaco, such as macaws, are so small that they cannot possibly support the idea of a flourishing trade network. Most of them are late in date and may represent occasional rare objects that were passed over long distances, along with useful information, their functions adapted to local needs.[12]

The second, and most widely held, school of thought argues that Chacoan society was an entirely indigenous development, shaped in part by the harsh realities of the local environment. Chaco society developed from preexisting social and political institutions, developed in times when people were tied to their gardens for the first time. At the same time, the ancient need to acquire intelligence about food and other matters linked groups with one another, as did obligations of reciprocity that evened out differences in crop yields in widely separated areas from year to year. I wrote earlier about a web of interconnectedness, a tentative spiderweb of connections and obligations that passed information, also food and exotics in small numbers over considerable distances.

But was this a closely controlled society, centered on Chaco, whose leaders ruled over, and dominated dozens of outlying communities? Steve Lekson believes that the periphery of this world allows us to understand the center.[13] He identifies more than 150 outlying communities, scattered as far away as Chimney Rock in the northeast, westward along the base of the Rocky Mountains, then southward through southeastern Utah and into northeastern Arizona and to the Mogollon

Rim and Quemado. This is a huge area of the Southwest, with Chaco at its center, unequalled in size and prestige in its heyday. Lekson identifies three zones: a circle some 2.4–3.7 miles (3.8–6 km) around "downtown Chaco," a "Chaco Halo," with a radius of some 3 miles (4.8 km) around the canyon, and the "Chaco Basin," extending some 62 miles (100 km) from the center. Within the Basin, redistribution of goods was a reality. Beyond this circle, it vanishes. Lekson calls the outer ring of his vast world the "Chaco Hegemony," a zone where great houses with what he calls uniform architecture flourished, where the organization of labor, of space, and trade in exotic objects resulted from "Chacoan political influence or authority."[14]

In large part, Lekson bases his argument for this hegemony on standardized architecture, created space, and building for permanence. The great houses were powerful messages about how the Chacoan world worked, and what its cosmology was. He refers to his hegemony as "low octane," as a region where architecture spoke, and where exotic symbols like brightly colored macaw feathers, copper bells, and turquoise denoted ritual power. "When macaws reached the Southwest, they were hotter than Hula Hoops," proclaims Lekson, who is fond of flamboyant phraseology. He calls the political structure of the greater Southwest a "case of macaws and effects."[15] To Lekson, Chaco's hegemony was marked by a "political-prestige economy," where exotic objects like macaw feathers traveled widely as meaningful political gifts. These artifacts circulated quite independently of more prosaic commodities such as beams or pots.

From this, Lekson constructs a political history, with Chaco starting off as a local phenomenon. In the early eleventh century, social and economic rivalries expanded outward beyond the canyon, a process marked by the construction of Pueblo Alto above it. "In the search for allies and confederates, Chaco discovered its centrality. Geography and climatic shifts set the stage for redistribution. These led, in turn, to the accumulation of food surpluses that brought about some form of political hierarchy." Beyond the Chaco Basin there was what he calls "an economy of fluff, political-prestige economy: rare, costly, symbolic, and above all portable."[16] Lekson argues that in our concern with commodities like timber, we have ignored prestige artifacts.

Lekson's hypothesis is based on the assumption that Chaco brokered a redistribution network, a modification of James Judge's redistribution theory we discussed in chapter 10. He writes of a "scalar threshold of 2,500 people in the canyon, a point at which almost invariably leads to more elaborate political structures."[17] He also writes of a *Pax Chaco*, where families lived under the protection of their great house. Chaco became a "node and a magnet," a place where people in-migrated and swelled the existing population. The central authority controlled violence throughout the Chaco world. The hegemony endured until 1125, when Chaco's great houses fell into disuse.

A great deal of Lekson's argument depends on architecture and the distribution of often fragile and poorly preserved exotica such as bird feathers. Confronted with the impressive array of archaeological evidence not only from Chaco but from outlying communities, the Chaco hegemony stands on shifting sands. As we saw in chapter 10, there is no evidence whatsoever that Chaco's great houses did anything but receive commodities and exotica. There is no evidence from pottery or other artifacts that they redistributed anything, even to nearby communities. Nor did the roads serve as a trading network. The evidence for a "prestige-power economy" based on exotic objects is based on a mere handful of finds, most of them from Pueblo Bonito in the heart of the canyon, and almost no such artifacts from any outlier whatsoever. We now have the advantage of the Chaco World Database, which records dozens of outlying communities and their characteristics. What is remarkable is not the uniformity of their features, but the great diversity within them. These were independent entities dispersed over an enormous region of great environmental variation, impossible for any center, however powerful, to control closely.

Lekson's ingenious model stumbles on the realities of the evidence, on data assembled from field surveys and meticulous studies of surviving artifacts from more than a century of research.

Nevertheless, for all their independence, these communities must have had some way of communicating at the political level. Some years ago, British archaeologist Colin Renfrew wrote about relationships between different communities. He talked of "peer-polity interaction," the notion that societies without elaborate social hierarchies dealt with one another as equals, as peers.[18] In so doing, their leaders used various well-proven mechanisms, among them common religious beliefs, ceremonial gifts, and validation by public ritual. Such interactions never ceased, were sometimes competitive, and deeply symbolic, a way by which ideas spread, and leaders developed relationships between each other and their communities. These relationships might ebb and flow, but they were a constant reality, a way of communicating over distance without any redistribution or need for rigid political dominance or tribute.

Chaco Canyon was indeed an important center, a sacred place of great spiritual power known to communities for hundreds of miles around. The rituals that unfolded in its great houses attracted people from within the rim of the San Juan Basin, who contributed food and other commodities as offerings to the canyon. It appears that all Chaco exported was its ritual power, which, in societies where agriculture and religion went hand in hand, was no mean export. Its economic and political influence on anyone except its closest neighbors was small, at best.

THE GOVERNORS

Who, then, presided over Chaco Canyon? There are many scenarios—powerful chiefs with inherited political, religious, and economic power, or putative "big men," who retained the loyalty of their followers by redistributing goods and food, or religious leaders are common scenarios. Our only solid clues come from the Old Bonito burials with their religious regalia and lavish costumes, and from ethnographic accounts. Frank Cushing described the Zuni as being governed by a council of the principal priests of the six cardinal directions, which he called "Masters of the Great House," their place of meeting over the center of the world. They were policy makers, did no manual work, never farmed, never engaged in warfare or routine governance. The people supported them and their secret religious knowledge with food and labor. Cushing's characterization has been criticized, but Chaco's supreme leaders may have presided over society in a somewhat similar way.[19] These governors, an arbitrary term but probably appropriate, were guardians of the arcane religious knowledge that sustained a society where agriculture and religion went hand in hand, and where the meticulous performance of public and private ritual were crucial to human survival.

∴ PART 4

MOVEMENT

So these, too, are the People of Chaco. They are very much with us now. God and the Pueblo deities willing, they will be always, for as long as there is a world and people on it.

Kendrick Frazier[1]

12 .·. READJUSTMENT

They didn't abandon this place. It is still occupied.
We can still pray to the spirits living in these places
from as far away as our pueblo. The spirits are
everywhere. Not just the spirits of our ancestors,
but tree spirits and rock spirits. If you believe that
everything has spirit, you will think twice before
harming anything.

Pueblo oral tradition[2]

Late summer, AD 1140: The sun shines from a washed-out, brazen sky.
The heat shimmers against the canyon walls, weighing heavily on the
family sitting in the shade. Generations of their ancestors have lived in
this small farming community under the rugged south wall at Chaco,
but they never experienced heat and aridity like this. Husband and
wife gaze listlessly across their parched fields, where the young corn
stalks wither in the heat. No dark thunderclouds are building on the
western horizon; the sky is cloudless, as it has been for weeks. The
family's grain bins are empty. Even the precious seed for the next planting is dwindling.

The children lie in the shade, so weak that they can barely move.
The youngest is four years old, lying on a blanket, eyes closed, face
skeletally wasted. Mother and father fear that she will not last the night.
They will be almost too weak to bury her the next day. . . .

.·. .·. .·.

Now that we have an accurate picture of Chaco's rainfall, we can see that the waves of great house construction in the canyon coincided with periods of more plentiful rainfall (see figure 3.6). There was a wave of building between 1020 and 1050, and another one from 1050 to 1075, a third between 1090 and 1116. Road construction began after 1050, at first, apparently, to the south, then to the north, as great house construction along the San Juan surged.

The Chacoans had lived through droughts of short duration on many occasions. Between 1040 and 1100, when great house construction was at its height, they witnessed three periods of increased rainfall, separated by short dry spells. More rain and higher water tables made Chaco Canyon one of the more secure places to live in the heart of a San Juan Basin that was a precarious environment for farmers at the best of times. Between 1080 and 1100, there was a two-decade dry spell that was cushioned somewhat by the high water table and filling of the Chaco Wash. Then followed thirty years of much more abundant rainfall that may have lulled the Chaco farmers into a sense of complacency. There was a great surge in great house construction, but primarily in the smaller, more compact McElmo style associated with the north. This was the time when outliers like Salmon and Aztec came into being in the north, along the San Juan and Animas Rivers.

But Chaco was in trouble. A major drought began around 1130 and lasted for fifty years with only a minor break. Maize yields plummeted after 1130. Traditionally, the strategy was to revert to wild plants as a substitute for domestic crops, but by this time the farmers had become so dependent on domesticated foods that the switchover was much harder, especially when the dry conditions drastically affected plant growth of all kinds. Nor were wild animals like rabbits readily available. After 1100 the people had imported turkeys, probably from the northern San Juan, as a substitute, then probably raised them for food as a replacement for lagomorphs. Had the dry spell lasted but a couple of years, both great houses and smaller communities might have survived. As it was, there was no reprieve and after 1130, Chaco emptied fast. Within a generation or so, both great houses and smaller settlements on the south side of the canyon lay empty (figure 12.1).[3]

There was no one moment of readjustment, nor did hundreds, if not thousands, of people perish in a harrowing famine. The Chacoans did what they had always done in times of drought. They moved away—to areas with more plentiful rainfall, to communities where they had nurtured ties of kinship and exchange for generations. The movements came, as nearly everything else at Chaco, household by household, a

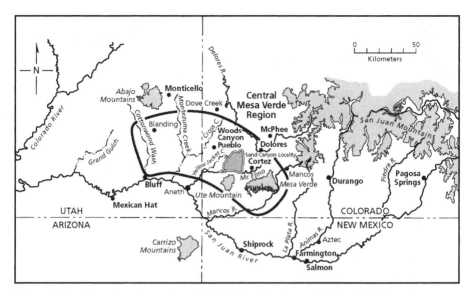

Figure 12.1   Map showing archaeological sites in chapters 12 and 13. *Data from Varien and Wilshusen (2002).*

steady-but-rapid erosion of population in the canyon, but still not enough to ease the pressure on farming land parched by years of drought. People moved to the better-watered lands to the west, where Chaco's timbers came from; to the south and where they had kin ties; and to the north, the place of origin of many of their ancestors over two centuries earlier. By 1140 Chaco was finished.

Household mobility was always a fact of life at Chaco, with a constant flow of families in and out of the canyon. They would leave for a season, decide to dwell with kin in the highlands for a while, or perhaps a quarrel would cause people to move away. But the community of which they were a part remained in place for centuries, each with their own gardens and water supplies, and rights over other foods and resources. Long-established communities defined Chaco's cultural landscape. Each had a history: each was the social context for the households that formed part of it. Emigration from Chaco during the twelfth century began as part of the constant household movements that were a routine part of life. As conditions worsened, food became scarcer, and efforts to grow more crops failed in the face of drought; the small-scale movements became what one might call migration streams, rivulets of households that led to growing communities elsewhere. These growing streams could have structured the growing depopulation of Chaco, to the point that entire communities, not just households, moved away. The canyon population shrank and shrank, with only the most persistent hamlets hanging on, until even they were no longer viable.

The centuries have drawn a veil over the suffering that must have accompanied the drought and the emigration. Infant mortality was always high. Now it must have increased in the face of food shortages and increasingly contaminated water supplies. About 26 percent of all Chaco's burials in better times were of children under five years of age, a figure that rose to 45 percent in outlying areas. Judging from a study of twelfth-century Pueblo burials near Gallup, New Mexico, which is admittedly no more than a rough yardstick, 50 percent of the population was dead by age eighteen.[4] This same study tells us that Gallup women had to average four births each just to maintain the farming population in that area, with 60 percent of all adults dead by age thirty-five, many of them women in their child-bearing years. And poorly nourished women are often unable to reproduce frequently enough to sustain their households. The same must have been true of Chaco, even if food was a little more plentiful. Few burials have been studied, but everyone from a smaller settlement showed signs of malnutrition and constant hard work, including pathological conditions resulting from grinding grain, and numerous broken and poorly set bones. By the eleventh century, 83 percent of Chaco's children suffered from severe iron deficiency anemia, which increases the risk of dysentery and respiratory disorders.[5] By the time of the two- to three-decade drought of 1010–1030, Chaco was crowded, diminished water supplies were contaminated, and life expectancy was falling (figure 12.2).

Throughout the years of abundance, the great ceremonies unfolded according to ancient custom and meticulous protocol, ceremonies that appeased the gods and brought rain. Sometimes rainfall faltered, summer thunderstorms passed elsewhere or never materialized, and crops

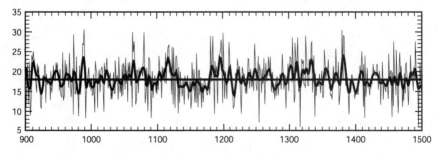

Figure 12.2   Chronicle of the great droughts in the northern San Juan from tree rings. *Data from Varien and Wilshusen (2002).*

withered in the fields. But the rains had always returned a year or two later—chants and prayers were answered. The Chacoans were used to such dry years from ancient times. They diversified the locations of their gardens, made use of every drop of water, cleared new land where the soils were fresh and not exhausted from generations of planting. People moved out of the canyon to live with relatives, just as they had done for centuries.

Then came a more serious drought in 1090, an intense dryness that lasted for five years. Soon storerooms were empty, precious seed for the next year's planting exhausted. Considerable numbers of people moved northward, later to help found great houses at Salmon, Aztec, and other locations where fertile soils, water, and timber were to be found. To the people who lived stoically through the drought, it must have seemed as if the forces of the supernatural had deserted them, that their leaders were ineffective intermediaries with gods and the ancestors. David Stuart believes that the drought of 1090–95 was a defining moment, when emigration began, when great house construction accelerated outside the canyon, and Chaco's leaders were powerless in the face of drought.[6]

The rains returned, great house building and remodeling resumed, the years when Pueblo Bonito's plaza was fully enclosed, and the major center at Aztec rose north of the San Juan River. At some point, the canyon's leaders must have lost control of the apparatus of ritual that brought timbers and other commodities, also exotica, to their great houses. No longer did they orchestrate the meticulously performed ceremonies that were the barometer and calendar of the farming year for more than eight generations at Chaco. As emigration continued, the beating heart of Ancestral Pueblo life moved northward—to the San Juan River, to southwestern Colorado, and the Mesa Verde region. Soon, Chaco Canyon was only a memory but a powerful one, incised into the oral traditions of dozens of Pueblo communities in the San Juan Basin and to the north.

As long as the rains continued, new gardens could be planted, new settlements constructed for their owners. But when the rains faltered in about 1080, then failed, a half-century later, this growth caught up with the Chacoans and their leaders. No matter how hard they worked, building canals, kivas, and still more great houses, it was to no avail. In spiritual terms, the intangible social contract between the gods and humans must have appeared to be in tatters. But expansion continued outside the canyon. After 1100, growth came in the form of more great houses, especially in the north, and in remodeling within Chaco itself.

After a generation of what must have been frenzied building and ritual activity, the system readjusted and the people dispersed. Chaco changed not because of violence, although there is some evidence for this, or because of leadership failures, but, in the final analysis, simply because of drought. In this most unpredictable of environments, rainfall is the drummer of all society, impervious to elaborate ritual and formulaic recitations, to sacrificial offerings and elaborate dances.

Archaeologists have rightly had a long and well-founded suspicion of what they call "environmental determinism," the notion that climate "caused" the rise and fall of civilizations. Climatic determinism dates back to the 1920s and was popularized by geographer Elsworth Huntington, then discredited. Huntington's climatic theories came at a time when almost nothing was known of ancient climate change, whereas today we have an infinitely more fine-grained understanding of climates in the past. The Southwest in particular is exceptionally well served by tree-ring research, now so refined that we can track the progress of major droughts from northwest to southeast across the region. And it's clear from this research that the correlations between surging great house construction and more abundant rainfall at Chaco are indeed precise. No question, climate was a major player in Chaco's history and its readjustment—to the point that we can safely say that drought, combined, of course, with all manner of cultural factors, played the dominant role in its implosion. In a marginal farming environment like that of the San Juan Basin, climate *was* Chaco.

In the end, the rainfall that brought farmers to Chaco caused them to move out.

CHACO SHIFTS TO THE NORTH

By about 1100, several great house communities flourished north of the San Juan River, inhabited at least in part by people who had moved northward from the canyon in times of drought. We shouldn't be surprised, for Chaco's history always revolved around relationships with others, with people, fellow kin, and communities outside the narrow confines of the canyon. Some experts call Chaco a "supracommunity," a regional development, and there is no question that they are correct.

Life in the canyon revolved around the family, the household, and the community, the latter defined for our purposes as a cluster of dwellings separated as a group from neighboring clusters. As we saw in chapter 11, Chacoan outliers share a constellation of architectural and other characteristics, including great houses and kivas, core-veneer masonry, and other features, which don't occur universally but rather in regional and chronological clusters. For instance, core-veneer masonry and low kiva-to-room ratios occur in San Juan Basin communities that are obviously associated with the canyon. What these features tell us about the degree of integration of the Chaco world is still debated. One convenient way of defining such integration is by identifying communities sharing Chacoan architectural features (figure 12.3).

There's talk of a Chaco System, of a Chaco Hegemony, of a Chaco World, or of a "disconnected heterogeneity." Such labels give a false impression of reality. We've seen that there's no reason to believe that this "world" was a unified and integrated social or political unit.[7] For

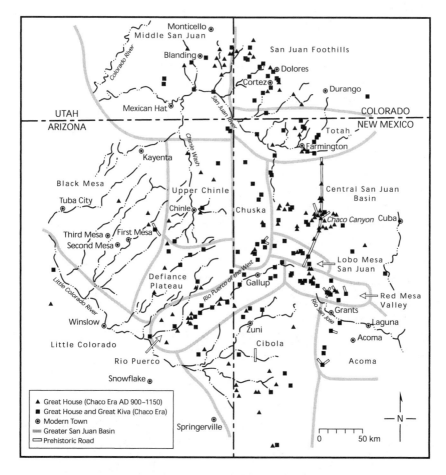

Figure 12.3   Map showing Chaco outliers. This map is incomplete and omits many sites. *Data from Kantner (2003).*

all this heterogeneity, there were some points of connection. All great houses apparently had ceremonial functions, reflected in the ceremonial artifacts and common material culture found in them. Painted wooden artifacts, turquoise ornaments, exotic bird remains—these occur, albeit sparingly, in great houses rather than smaller, domestic settlements. Most such known artifacts occur, however, at Pueblo Bonito and in Chaco's great houses—at places where there have been substantial excavations. The general cultural pattern may have been shared, but the distribution of ceremonial artifacts suggests highly variable ceremonial activity. Even the widely distributed Dogoszhi pottery, remarkable for its standardization over a large area, displays minor local variations that may reflect local or regional symbolic expression.[8]

Chaco may have inspired great house architecture and other cultural traits, but their occurrence over a large region reflects no more than a low but important degree of shared identity, just like that found in other areas where people share common religious beliefs and even political allegiance, which is diluted the farther one moves from the center. It's in this context that we must describe the apparent northward movement of Chacoan culture and ritual after 1100.

There's historical perspective to the northward move. Chacoan architecture and other traits developed in the canyon as early as the mid- to late tenth century. Such features occur in the southern San Juan Basin by late 920s to 940. The south, and especially the west, had long had close ties to Chaco, so it's hardly surprising to see great houses founded there during a period of less rainfall in the canyon, following the better rains of the early tenth century. One response to drought was always to move, and such movements southward into friendly communities may well have carried the new architecture, and presumably the religious beliefs associated with them.[9]

By the late 940s, Chacoan features appear in communities down the Rio Puerco and Rio San Jose drainages (see figure 12.3). They appear on the Chuska slope by the 900s, perhaps earlier. By the middle of the tenth century, communities on the inner edge of the San Juan had adopted Chacoan traits. An explosion in great house construction occurred in outlying areas during the higher rainfall years of the later eleventh century following the construction of earlier ones in the late 800s and 900s. These increases in construction coincide in general terms with rises in imported shell and turquoise at Chaco, and with sharp rises in labor expenditure in the canyon.

Some great houses lay empty as early as the eleventh century, but many more in the first half of the twelfth, probably as a consequence of persistent drought. This drought was short lived but much more severe than earlier ones, occurring at a time when Chaco Canyon's need for timber and other materials, and labor, were at their height.

After a century of research, we can finally trace a consistent picture of a Chaco world based on a canyon that had become an increasingly important religious center. Chaco's leaders never controlled outlying communities, but their great houses engaged with their powerful neighbor in ways that benefited both sides. Members of these communities may have visited Chaco on occasion, bearing gifts or offering labor, especially those to the south and west. But the extent of any even slightly close relationships was within the San Juan Basin itself. Different parts of the Chaco world tied themselves to the canyon in distinctive ways, to achieve widely differing objectives, both for themselves and Chaco's leaders.

The wider Chaco world emerged not so much to contend with a marginal farming environment—that had always been a reality—but with a new, more politicized era where emerging leaders aspired to power and religious authority, to a legitimacy that could be sustained only by legitimization by others. And when Chaco itself faltered, the center of the canyon's world moved north.

AZTEC AND SALMON

After 1100, large-scale construction within Chaco Canyon slowed somewhat. Large-scale construction had accelerated along the San Juan River, at the Aztec and Salmon sites in 1080. With the drought, the center of gravity of ritual activity seems to have shifted northward, away from the canyon to a new center—Aztec. There's a tendency to assume that Aztec was a place of refuge for people fleeing Chaco, but it was much more, a complex of as many as three to four great houses, many of them unidentified until recent years.

Aztec lies near the confluence of the Animas and San Juan Rivers near the modern town of Aztec, 50 miles (80 km) north of Chaco (figure 12.4; plate 12).[10] The pioneer Southwestern archaeologist, Earl Morris, excavated the conspicuous West Ruin, "Aztec West," between 1916 and 1927, uncovering four hundred rooms and domestic artifacts, also ritual items, including macaw bones. He revealed Aztec West as a classic Chaco great house, a D-shaped structure with twelve kivas and an enclosed plaza. Aztec West is the third largest such building: its great kiva is among the largest in the north.

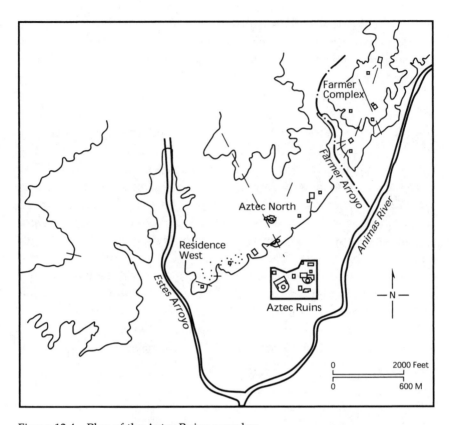

Figure 12.4   Plan of the Aztec Ruins complex.

The Aztec Ruins are far more than just one great house. A series of buildings (Aztec North) associated with the Aztec West complex extends for some 2 miles (3.2 km) along a terrace above the Animas River immediately to the north. Chacoan Aztec was a large and important place. Pottery samples and tree-ring dates are unraveling the complex history of the site. They tell us that people settled at Aztec North as early as 1050, at the beginning of a period of higher rainfall. The settlements there thrived until 1140. Sometime before 1110, the inhabitants cut and stockpiled large numbers of wooden beams. Construction of Aztec West began in that year (figure 12.5). The builders completed the first stage in a mere decade or less, between 1110 and 1120. More timber stockpiling took place between 1113 and 1119, before the second stage rose between 1118–1125 and 1130. Aztec West was an astounding feat of great house building by any standard.

Aztec East, the second great house, was built continuously over a period of one hundred fifty years. The layout, with its similarity to the

Figure 12.5 Aztec West. *Photograph by Robert Powers, 1979. Courtesy NPS Chaco Culture National Historical Park. Negative 18009.*

West Ruin, hints at a formal plan, laid out when some construction began, perhaps as early as 1110 to 1115. Then it slowed, continuing sporadically during the great drought of 1130 to 1180, accelerating rapidly once ample rainfall resumed in the 1190s, most building taking place in the McElmo style during the good times of the thirteenth century. Through times of plenty, and those of hardship, Aztec's people maintained and struggled to complete an ancient community design on the local landscape. Completion came long after its designers had passed on. The patterns of timber usage reflect skilful adjustment to changed circumstances. Exotic ponderosa pines formed the roofs of Aztec East rooms before 1140. Thirteenth-century beams tend to be of local juniper.

The Chacoans built a magnificent great house at Aztec West, then strove to maintain their traditions as drought settled over the Animas Valley. Aztec East preserved many architectural traditions of earlier times, but there were changes, too—multiple plazas and many internal subdivisions—as the structure became more residential. What had begun with a bang continued as a sustained whimper, as some of Aztec's inhabitants strove to maintain the ritual usages and practices of earlier times, until as late as 1268/9, when renovation was still under way in Aztec East.

Another important Chacoan great house and outlier also rose on the San Juan River, 3 miles (4.8 km) west of Bloomfield, New Mexico, and 45 miles (72 km) north of Chaco (see plate 13). The Salmon great house was bracket-shaped, but flood waters from the nearby San Juan may have removed part of what was once a classic D-shaped structure. There were about one hundred fifty ground-floor rooms and as many as one hundred second-story compartments. Salmon was built between about 1088 and 1100, just before Aztec, with minor remodeling until 1130. In the late 1180s, people making Mesa Verde–like ceramics remodeled the pueblo, finally departing in the late 1200s. The Great North Road may have connected Chaco to Salmon.

Everyone agrees that Aztec was a major ritual center, perhaps the successor to Chaco in a time of drought and social upheaval. We don't have data yet on the extent of its world, or sphere of influence. The Mesa Verde and Montezuma regions lie to the northwest, some of the most thoroughly explored archaeological territory on earth, but there are effectively no signs that the leaders of Aztec presided in any political way over them. Certainly Aztec's architecture mirrors that of the canyon, albeit with some differences. It was the largest settlement in the north, more extensive than Yellow Jacket, the largest of the Montezuma Valley pueblos. Thousands of Mesa Verde Black-on-White potsherds come from Aztec and Salmon, and from a vast area of the northern San Juan, but they do not necessarily mean that Aztec was the center of some form of chiefdom. Like Chaco before it, Aztec was a ritual center, whose leaders' power depended on their authority, prestige, and ritual acumen. Aztec replaced Chaco during the late twelfth century and remained a major population center for a hundred years.[11]

THE CHACO MERIDIAN?

Chaco Canyon, Aztec, and then a pueblo far to the south, Casas Grandes: Was there a grand design behind Chaco and later centers of population? There's a sequence of major centers, or so Steve Lekson believes. He points out that Chaco and Aztec are north–south of one another, lying approximately on longitude 107° 57' 25", a centerline defined at the canyon by the alignment of Pueblo Alto and Tsin Kletsin (figure 12.6). He calls this the "Chaco Meridian" and extends the north–south line far to the south to encompass another, later pueblo—Paquimé in Chihuahua, Mexico, often known as Casas Grandes—which also lies on the same general meridian.[12]

Casas Grandes lies in relatively high altitude basin and range country, centered on a wide, fertile valley. By the fourteenth century, the valley's farmers had congregated in a large settlement, originally of house clusters surrounding a central plaza. Eventually Cases Grandes became a pueblo of multistory adobe apartment complexes, housing as many as 2,250 people. A ceremonial precinct, complete with I-shaped ball courts, stone-faced platforms, mounds, and a market area lay outside the residential area (see plate 14). This was a thriving pueblo, whose inhabitants had produced copper bells and ceremonial axe heads. They

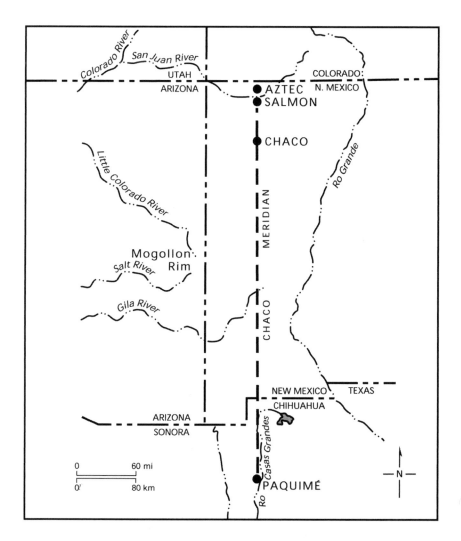

Figure 12.6   Map showing the Chaco Meridian. *Data from Lekson (1999).*

also turned marine shells into trumpets, beads, and ornaments. One compound contained rows of rectangular boxes apparently used for breeding macaws for their colorful feathers. Casas Grandes may have been one of the sources of such feathers for settlements far to the north.

At the height of its prosperity, Casas Grandes lay at the center of a small region, its influence extending about 18 miles (29 km) from the pueblo. A small group of privileged families may have controlled both trade and ritual activities for a while, but after a generation and a half the pueblo gradually fell into disrepair and was deserted by the early fifteenth century.[13]

This, then, is the third center on Lekson's Chaco Meridian, separated from Chaco by 391 miles (629 km). His total meridian line extends 447 miles (719 km), the three sites said to be on the same line, although the longitudinal measurements differ considerably. But, says Lekson, this is unimportant, for the Chaco Meridian was "a constructed feature not a geodetic line." He argues that this alignment was intentional, that power passed from Chaco to Aztec, then on to Casas Grandes in the fourteenth century. Lekson bases his arguments on the Great North Road, which most experts agree links Chaco and Aztec, and on sighting measurements between Chaco and Casas Grandes that involved "11 to 13 separate measurements [on ridges crossing the route] for 11 to 13 segments of relatively equal length."[14] He believes that such surveying was well within the capabilities of the Chacoans and others, to the point that there is only about a 0.2 mile (0.3 km) separation between Chaco and Casas Grandes along his meridian.

If it existed, the Chaco Meridian spanned a huge tract of the Southwest. One may legitimately ask if Chacoans, or others, could have even known of the existence of Casas Grandes, particularly since some forbidding terrain separated the two in the Mogollon Uplands and elsewhere. Lekson argues that the areas to the south of Chaco were booming during Aztec's closing decades, that the flow of exotic goods between north and south meant that people living along the Chaco Meridian were well aware of their neighbors to the north and south and traded with them.

But why establish a meridian at all? Lekson follows others in seeing the roads, however segmented, as "time bridges, symbolic umbilicals that linked one age to another." He believes they "legitimized the ritual and social roles of post-Chaco great houses and pueblos by a material landscape referenced back to a locus of mythic and historic power." The Great North Road projected the "Chaco Meridian; the Chaco-Paquimé alignment prolonged that same meridian." Lekson believes the chronology fits, too. Chaco was followed by Aztec, Aztec by Casas Grandes. Lekson concludes: "Times changed, but one idea remained, proclaiming political continuity: meridian alignment."[15]

Is the Chaco Meridian pure coincidence, or was it a deliberate formulation? Lekson believes it was deliberate, beginning with Chaco's key location, not as an unusually diverse environment but because of its central location relative to the far richer margins of the San Juan Basin. In contrast, Aztec rose in an environment with plenty of trees and permanent river water. There were plenty of places nearby where one could build it, but its founders chose a spot on the meridian, north of Chaco, at the end of the Great North Road. Casas Grandes also flourished in a nice location, again one of many locally that could have been chosen. Lekson believes it rose by the banks of the largest river in the area and that its rulers came from the north. There were other attractive rivers nearby, but Casas Grandes flourished where it did because of the Meridian. As each settlement rose to prominence, so agricultural methods became more sophisticated beyond the simple water-control systems at Chaco, to some irrigation agriculture at Aztec and then a full-blooded canal system at Casas Grandes.

Lekson believes that the Chaco Meridian was an attempt by Aztec and Cases Grandes to link themselves symbolically to the first center at Chaco. This was an issue of legitimacy, with new leaders calling on mythic and ritual power derived from elsewhere (Chaco) to strengthen their own positions. Under this argument, the Chaco Meridian was a monument, a tactic aimed at legitimizing authority with reference to the landscape and sacred places. By the time Casas Grandes was founded, Chaco had become the stuff of legend, an ancient society that had transformed Southwestern life. Any group, any leader, now had to incorporate this shared memory into history. Lekson sees the Chaco Meridian as a grand event in history, an alignment undertaken as "a performance for all Southwestern peoples to see." He adds: "Imagine the effect of a procession marching 630 km south from the ancient city of Chaco, cutting trees for lines-of-sight, lighting flares and bonfires for backsights, performing ceremonies and rituals."[16] All of this was done to "convince and persuade the ruled."

Lekson's Meridian theory rests on a combination of observations and assumptions, as follows. The Chacoans constructed, and indeed projected, roads to map out historical and sociocultural connections between communities. Of these roads, the so-called Great North Road is the longest and best marked. Furthermore, north–south orientations and their associated symbolism were important in Chacoan society, indeed throughout the San Juan. North–south orientation, north–south asymmetry, and east–west bilateral symmetry structure the design of the kiva, the household unit, the settlement, and also the layout of great houses and great kivas at Chaco Canyon, something the archaeologist John Fritz pointed out many years ago. Lekson believes it is not unreasonable to expect the Chacoans would extend their central north–south axis to encompass other regions they influenced and depended upon. Other societies, such as the Maya, and the Khmer of Cambodia, thought of the landscape in cosmological terms, even copied it in their cities and ceremonial centers as a mnemonic of history. Could not the Chacoans, albeit a much less complex society, have done the same?

Few archaeologists involved with any of the three sites accept Lekson's alignment as historical reality. Yes, the three sites are close to another in longitude, but is this mere coincidence or a matter of deliberate design? As Lekson himself points out, Chaco, Aztec, and Casas Grandes were "profoundly local." He believes that political developments in each affected not only local populations but people over much larger regions. There was a shifting center—from Chaco to Aztec to Casas Grandes, each occupied by a small elite, who maintained their power through architectural and landscape symbolism.

Chaco, Aztec, and nearby Mimbres set the stage for Casas Grandes. Almost no one except Lekson visualizes close connections, the existence of a symbolic meridian. He believes there was more intensive trade, greater interaction over large areas in the context of a "prestige-power economy" reflected in exotic objects and commodities at a considerably larger scale than archaeological reality suggests. Such a scale of interaction could have seen export of Chacoan architecture and ways of doing things, or just emulation by local centers, at considerable distances from the canyon.[17] As we saw in chapter 11, this "prestige-power economy" is built on very insecure archaeological foundations: there is almost no evidence outside Chaco for large numbers of exotic goods. The Chaco Meridian is almost certainly an archaeological myth, which has no solid grounding in historical reality. Nevertheless, it's a valuable piece of thinking, which encourages everyone working on Chacoan sites to think boldly, and out of the box, essential if our knowledge of Chaco is to advance.

What was historical reality? It was an ancient one, a way of life finely tuned to an environment of unpredictable rainfall and marginal conditions for any form of agriculture. It was a way of life where people survived by being flexible, by blending agriculture and religion into a seamless, intensely symbolic existence, living, as they did, in the midst of a vast cultural landscape, a landscape of mind.[18] Above all, as Lekson points out, Chaco, Aztec, and other great houses were profoundly local phenomena, whatever elaboration they acquired through ritual acumen or food surpluses. During the decades of plenty, Chaco Canyon society acquired more powerful leaders, a great economic, social, and political sophistication. But behind all the panoply of carefully engineered rituals, lavish ceremonies, great houses, and public display lay an eternal verity of the Ancestral Pueblo world—the endless rhythm of the seasons, of rain and drought, held together by agriculture and religion. And when this rhythm broke down, and the credibility of the social contract between farmer and leader broke down, Chaco readjusted and its people quietly departed.

By 1150 Chaco Canyon was virtually deserted. For a century, Ancestral Pueblo society flourished north of the San Juan River, only to readjust in the face of yet another, even more severe drought. In chapter 13, we trace the legacy of Chaco in the north and witness yet another implosion of Pueblo culture, which marked the final chapter of Chacoan history.

13 ∴ CHACO'S LEGACY

> We, the Pueblo people of today, are the caretakers
> of these places now. Even though people moved on,
> these places are sacred because people lived there
> and performed songs, prayers and ceremonies here.
> We respect this and are awed by this. Our people
> still come back to these places.
>
> Pueblo oral tradition[1]

Sand Canyon, Colorado, AD 1280: Mother and daughter carefully sweep
the empty room. They pile heavy items in the center of the floor, add
some small items to the bundles stacked in the shade outside. The
mother looks at her much-beloved metate, too heavy to carry on the
journey that lies ahead. She sighs quietly; they are leaving the pueblo
forever, to journey southward, away from the parched canyon. She's
buried three infants here, but the living must move away to a place
where there is water and crops can grow once more.

Soon afterward, the heavily laden family walks down a familiar path
away from the canyon, the husband armed and watchful, against those
who prey on laden travelers in a ruthless quest for food. Several families
travel together, accompanied by two men who have made the journey
several times—to trade, to visit with relatives. No one feels apprehen-
sion, for they know their kin at the other end expect them and will feed
them until their crops are harvested. . . .

∴ ∴ ∴

AZTEC AND SALMON AGAIN

The drought of 1130–1180 had brought Chaco's great houses to their knees a generation after Aztec rose near the San Juan River. While Chaco emptied, Aztec and Salmon were still major centers.[2] Between 1080 and 1100, Salmon's builders had used juniper, also rarer ponderosa beams, obtained from 50 miles (80 km) to the north and east, in the mountains of southwestern Colorado. A generation later, after 1120, Aztec East was built in stages, initially using ponderosa, then almost entirely juniper beams, which grow in abundance within a 6-mile (10-km) radius. Aztec's leaders seem to have made a valiant effort to perpetuate the architectural blueprint of earlier, more prosperous times, to maintain the existing social and political order once characteristic of Chaco. Despite their efforts, Aztec's leaders no longer had the drawing power of their predecessors, the ritual charisma to attract pilgrims, to assemble large labor forces to build great houses. The scale of life had shrunk to local parameters.

The farming population of the north clustered into two broadly defined groups, one centered on the Totah region, the other around Mesa Verde in the Four Corners area.[3] There appears to have been a depopulated zone north of Aztec after 1150, perhaps a sign of constant hostility between the two areas. Interestingly, burial data shows that the Central Mesa Verde region had more men than women, whereas Totah communities had more women than men. It may have been that the northern communities raided the Totah for women, but the samples are small and comprise little more than a tantalizing historical possibility.

PUEBLOS IN THE NORTH

After about 1075, Chaco-style great houses had appeared over a wide area of the northern San Juan, from the Totah region north of Aztec to southwestern Colorado and southeastern Utah. All of them were built within about sixty years, construction ending during the social disruption and hardship caused by the drought and widespread crop failures. The same drought that decimated Chaco also descended on the Mesa Verde region. Building on any scale came to a virtual halt. We know this because one archaeologist, Mark Varien, has assembled beam-cutting data from the Central Mesa Verde area and shown a slowdown in tree felling around 1160 fully as significant as the slowdown of the 900s, described in chapter 6.[4]

In contrast to Chaco, northern San Juan communities depended on dry maize farming, mainly on loose-grained soils at elevations over 6,000 feet (1,829 m) above sea level. Even in drought years, these soils could support many more people than actually lived in the region. The most effective way to farm such soils was to live in dispersed communities, often a small block of five to ten residential and storage rooms and a semisubterranean kiva. But settlement aggregation increased during the late 1100s through the 1200s. By the early 1200s, many communities were now villages, often with multiple room blocks, surrounded by dispersed homesteads and hamlets, each for one or more households. Some room blocks had several stories, but they were nothing like Chacoan great houses.

Between 1225 and 1290, more and more communities moved near canyon heads (smaller settlements being located in the canyons themselves), where springs bubbled forth in canyon heads, forming small streams. Many of these settlements were walled, perhaps to protect the precious water source from outsiders. By the late 1200s, most people in the region lived in villages boasting of fifty or more structures.

The villagers were thrifty folk, so they continued to use their great houses, which still retained considerable importance in the social and ritual life of their local communities. Their size, layout, and general formality contrasts with the humbler buildings around them, as if conveying the message that those who lived in them had exceptional powers. In time they became residential pueblos, remodeled for purely utilitarian purposes. Most northern settlements were still dispersed dwellings, but some now had a nucleus of room blocks, occasionally incorporating the original great house.[5]

The great houses themselves no longer retained such intense ceremonial associations. Their sanctity waxed and waned as people moved around, even in small areas. For instance, a community based in Woods Canyon in southwestern Colorado shifted its political and ceremonial center between three locations (figures 13.1, 13.2). In the late 1000s and early 1100s, a Chacoan great house rose in a highly visible location at

---

Facing page, top
Figure 13.1   Wood's Canyon Pueblo from the air, looking northwest. *Courtesy Crow Canyon Archaeological Center.*

Facing page, bottom
Figure 13.2   Artist's reconstruction of the rim complex at Wood's Canyon Pueblo. *Drawing by Charles "Pete" Peterson. Courtesy Crow Canyon Archaeological Center.*

what is now called the Albert Porter site. The house served as the nucleus of a widely dispersed Woods Canyon community until the late 1100s and early 1200s, when the hub of activity moved 1.2 miles (2 km) west to the Bass site, then to the Woods Canyon pueblo in the mid-1200s. The histories of the three pueblos overlapped, but the nucleus shifted significantly over two centuries. Settlements such as Woods Canyon were very different from the architectural styles found at Aztec, reflecting new ritual practices, although the Chacoan pattern persisted in other areas.

By the mid-1200s, numerous independent communities flourished in a northern San Juan world that was increasingly violent and competitive, a reflection of greater population densities and pressure on farming land. Raiding of neighbors for grain, for control of trade routes, and to achieve political power were symptoms of a time when, increasingly, there were not enough resources to go around. At the same time, almost no imported objects come from the pueblos, as if exchange networks throughout the region had broken down. No pilgrimage systems were now operating; no great houses attracted hundreds of visitors for major ceremonies.

Many northern communities now moved into easily defendable locations in canyons, partly in response to the greater prevalence of warfare in the region. They were generally single-story residential sites, a far cry from Chacoan great houses, organized around small household kivas. Some were room blocks, where households lived close together, others more dispersed. The more compact settlements protected themselves with masonry walls and often included a D-shaped multiwalled building, a plaza, a tower complex, and sometimes a great kiva.

By the thirteenth century, warfare was an accepted fact of life around Mesa Verde. This is reflected in the move to canyon locations, also in finds of war casualties, some of them mutilated or even consumed. These were times of fear, of widespread violence. One imagine communities living in dread of sudden nighttime attacks, of quick violent forays by armed men with deadly bows and spears, of flaming brands tossed into rooms and kivas, entire families slaughtered as the raiders make off with baskets of precious grain. There's a cluster of such incidents recorded for the difficult years between 1130 and 1160. Intercommunity warfare led to large numbers of casualties at the Cowboy Wash pueblo. An entire community was butchered at Castle Rock Pueblo, a small community in the Sand Canyon area, in the 1270s. Both aggregation and a shift toward canyon locations were probably defensive measures.[6]

This was the era of the Cliff Palace and other world-famous Mesa Verde pueblos, whose spectacular settings have tended to overshadow the importance of major pueblos elsewhere (see plate 16). It is these latter sites, away from the deep canyons, in the Mancos and Montezuma Valley, that give us a clearer picture of what happened in the north, largely because they've been investigated with the full panoply of modern archaeological methods. Here farmers inhabited large drainages, where population densities rose rapidly, from thirteen to thirty people per square kilometer (0.4 sq mile) to as many as one hundred thirty people three centuries later. At the same time, average village size doubled from six to twelve rooms.

This population growth came at a price. Environmental scientist Carla Van West has created environmental models of potential agricultural productivity in the region.[7] She estimates that the area could have produced enough maize to support 31,360 people at a density of twenty-one people per square kilometer (0.4 sq mile) over a four-hundred-year period. Her figures show that the twelfth-century drought that undermined Chaco had little effect in the Mesa Verde region, where there was still enough land to support a dispersed farming population. However, agricultural productivity varied considerably from place to place and year to year. The farmers tended to locate near the most consistently productive soils. They could survive the harshest of drought cycles *if* there were no restrictions on mobility or on access to the best soils, and *if* they could acquire food from neighbors when crops failed. However, their ability to move was severely restricted once population densities approached the carrying capacity of the land and the people had cultivated effectively all the most productive soils. By 1250, population densities in the Mesa Verde region were dense enough so that surviving extreme short-term climatic change was infinitely harder.

SAND CANYON PUEBLO

Growing population densities, a need for defense, much closer living quarters: Years of excavation at Sand Canyon Pueblo, near modern-day Cortez in southern Colorado, give us a telling portrait of a short-lived pueblo at a time of crisis.[8]

Sand Canyon Pueblo was one of the largest communities in the northern San Juan, its layout carefully planned to include a great kiva, a D-shaped structure, and an enclosed plaza. The plan of the village on either side of a stream is well balanced and clearly was carefully planned, strategically placed near the canyon head and its water sources, then fortified. The Sand Canyon excavators believe that some form of central authority was responsible for the layout of the settlement. Construction began there in the 1240s and continued until 1280. As many as seven hundred people lived in its room blocks and dispersed households. Around 1250 the residents erected a huge enclosure wall, which may have taken thirty to forty people two months to build. Over the next thirty years, they added more than twenty separate room blocks, which incorporated at least ninety kivas and about four hundred twenty rooms. Each household maintained its own identity, with its own cluster of structures—a living space, a storage room, a place to eat, and access to a kiva, just as they had done in their original, more dispersed settlements (figure 13.3).

When research began at Sand Canyon Pueblo in 1983, everyone assumed that the site was a great house and a ceremonial center where relatively few people lived. In assuming this, they were strongly influenced by contemporary thinking about Chaco great houses. To their surprise, excavators Bruce Bradley and M. J. Churchill discovered abundant traces of household occupation and a wide variety of domestic activities in and around every structure they excavated. The detritus of domestic activities dominated daily life at Sand Canyon, while ritual

Figure 13.3   Sand Canyon excavations. Block 500 with kiva looking northwest. *Courtesy Crow Canyon Archaeological Center.*

played a much smaller part than originally suspected. People lived in the room blocks of this large pueblo year-round. Current estimates calculate that between eighty and ninety households lived in Sand Canyon's room blocks, kivas, and associated hamlets.

Sand Canyon Pueblo was built, occupied, then left empty within the short span of forty years, a far shorter period of time than the use cycle of other northern pueblos. Despite its apparent planning, many people lived around it rather than within it. The D-shaped building was built on a cliff and could be seen from anywhere in the settlement. The flat face of the building is oriented 23° east of north, the azimuth of the rising sun in mid-May, traditionally the time of planting in the north. Judging from historic custom, D-shaped buildings like the one at Sand Canyon were associated with sun watching and the observation of the solstice by sun priests. This building, with its clear view of the eastern horizon, may have been the place where Sand Canyon Pueblo's leaders observed the passage of the sun at the solstices. At the same time, there's clear evidence that the structure was used both for daily living and for ritual observance. There are also indications from the clay vessels found in the pueblo that communal feasting was associated with major ceremonies.

In 1280, after forty years, Sand Canyon's inhabitants faced the crisis of a drought more profound than any in their experience.

THE GREAT DROUGHT

In 1276 tree rings chronicle the first below-average rainfall figures in the far northwest, while the remainder of the Southwest enjoyed above-average precipitation. Over the next ten years, very dry conditions spread over the entire Southwest, especially the northwest. An epochal drought—it was nothing less—settled over the Four Corners region after 1280. As we saw in chapter 3, most of the rainfall variation occurred in the northwest with its irregular summer and winter rains, just as it does today. The southeastern part of the Southwest always enjoyed relatively predictable summer rainfall, as it does today.

The long-term pattern broke down completely between AD 1250 to 1450, when an aberrant pattern of severe droughts and complex, unpredictable precipitation settled over the northwest, while the southeast remained stable. After the 1260s, pueblo construction slowed and ceased altogether by the 1290s. Within a generation, the northern San Juan was effectively depopulated.[9]

We have enough data to allow us to experience the crisis at Sand Canyon. Tree-ring-dated beams tell us that construction continued right into the 1270s, certainly until 1276, when the great drought descended over the north. The inhabitants of Sand Canyon, like other northern pueblos, faced the great drought of 1280, made more vulnerable after generations of steady population growth and depletion of local eco-systems by thousands of years of human exploitation. After three hundred and fifty years, they were now faced with a need for major change. Just as at Chaco a century earlier, their options were limited. They could not fall back on wild plants, which had already been depleted by expansion of cultivation. Animal populations suffered from overhunting and habitat destruction by human settlement. Dense populations and rigid ideologies may have inhibited efforts to develop new water-control systems. Even if they had freedom of action, the people had effectively eaten up the best land and much marginal acreage as well. Nor were there any technological solutions to the crisis.

Inevitably, the people resorted to ancient social strategies that had served them well in the past. They had already moved into densely packed settlements close to reliable and defendable water supplies. Social problems had mushroomed as more and more people moved into crowded pueblos. Increasing competition for food and water triggered conflict both within and outside communities large and small. The conflict prevented people from moving into potentially cultivable areas.

Sand Canyon was constructed so that it controlled its water supply and lay behind a stone enclosure wall, as if defense from outsiders was a consideration. We know there was violence at the very end of the occupation. The remains of thirteen individuals came to light in the excavations, many of whom had not been formally interred. These were mostly women, adolescents, and young adults. Eight of them died violently, seven of them found in kiva suites associated with towers built against the outside of the enclosure wall. The dead lay close to the spring, and were associated with large numbers of animal bones, perhaps from a communal feast.[10] Whatever the context of the killings, the casualties are compelling evidence for social conflict as the Sand Canyon community dissolved.

Just as at Chaco, high infant mortality rates and reduced birth rates owing to health problems must have caused local population densities to fall. Even then, the social and technological strategies to alleviate the crisis were inadequate. There remained one option—to move away into better-watered areas to the east, south, and west, where environmental conditions were more favorable, and where there were already communities capable of supporting large populations.

Excavations have documented the final years of the pueblo, when the uses of community structures changed as the pueblo shrank. Parts of it fell into disuse and became trash heaps. Many kivas stood empty until their roofs were burned, dismantled, or otherwise destroyed. Some contain traces of termination rituals, as if their owners made a deliberate decision to move elsewhere. People moved away without fuss, probably household by household. Large numbers of clay pots and stone tools, also heavy grinding stones, still lie where their owners left them. By 1290 Sand Canyon was deserted.

Sand Canyon is a microcosm of a troubled Pueblo world—rapid aggregation into an easily defendable location with dependable water supplies. But, after forty troubled years, the inhabitants, like thousands of other northern communities, simply repeated history. They moved elsewhere. More than three hundred years earlier, their ancestors had moved south across the San Juan River to Chaco and many other locations. This time, they migrated south once again, in a logical adaptation that was their only defense against a harsh and unpredictable environment.

DISPERSAL

Generations of archaeologists described the move out of Chaco, and then from the Mesa Verde region, as a "collapse." It was nothing of the sort, merely an utterly realistic adjustment to a persistent drought of a type commonplace in Pueblo society, even if this movement was on a larger scale than normal.

The people of the north dispersed along well-established migration routes, established over many generations as informal social networks. Many northern farmers moved into pueblos along the Rio Grande, with which they had long maintained close ties.

An endless debate, largely focused on architecture and artifacts, surrounds the extent of Chaco's influence on the south, but I suspect that the influence was less than often claimed. For instance, the Acoma/Zuni area had Chacoan-style great houses, but the ties with the canyon were loose at best, except close to Chaco.[11] There was some emulation of Chacoan building patterns and architecture, but the houses were smaller, variable in design, and not all associated with great kivas. There was a trend toward aggregation, as there was in the north, but we do not know why. In the early 1200s, new community forms emerged near Zuni, nucleated communities with as many as fourteen hundred rooms, among the largest pueblos in the Southwest. The largest of these sites developed in areas where there were no Chacoan-style great houses, although some ideas derived from the canyon appear in the architecture.

There's a marked difference between these pueblos and those from the Mesa Verde region. In the Zuni/Cibola area, the individual household is submerged in massive constructions, as if it were seething beehives of people living at very close quarters. These pueblos had formal layouts with circular or rectangular ground plans. There are no small kivas, just formal plazas and only a few kivas, signifying a marked change in ceremonial life. Now residential blocks surround open plazas, the open space being defined by the surrounding community. Households architecturally are no longer visible, with the new pueblos representing a new conception of social life. They were purposefully built by communal labor in well-defined building events.

This aggregated living was an invitation for factionalism and strife on scales that may have been unimaginable in earlier generations. Steve Lekson and Catherine Cameron have argued that a new social mechanism developed to combat schism, that of the *kachina*. These community ceremonies, involving masked dancers, are thought to have developed as a way of fostering a collective identity and combating factionalism and destructive schism (figure 13.4). The origins of *kachina*

Figure 13.4   Public kachina dance, part of the Niman ceremony by the Hemis kachinas at the Hopi pueblo of Shungopavi in 1901. *Photograph by A. C. Vroman. National Anthropology Archives, Smithsonian Institution. Negative 42,189F.189F.*

ceremonialism are hotly debated, but may lie in the Mimbres region to the southeast of Chaco, where aggregated villages appeared as early as 1050.[12] This was an area where canal irrigation, with all its maintenance needs, developed to a high level of sophistication a farming system that favored larger communities, with as many as two hundred inhabitants. Scholars debate whether *kachina* imagery occurs in Mimbres iconography, but the association of such putative imagery with aggregated settlements may be no coincidence. Lekson and Cameron suggest that *kachina* ceremonialism was successful in fostering living at close quarters, a major factor in the survival of aggregated communities for so long.

By 1275 this Cibolan style of pueblo thrived throughout the Western Pueblo area. They were nucleated settlements, a consolidation of small groups that led, inevitably, to closer interaction between neighbors. These were the communities that received many of the immigrants from the north.

We know from excavations at Sand Canyon that many households left large, hard-to-carry objects such as metates behind them—suggesting that they planned a long journey *and* that they expected to find help at the end of it. We know, also, that the social networks to connect them to their destinations already existed. Archaeologist Alison Rautman has used ancient pottery styles and climatic data to study social networks at the extreme eastern edge of the Pueblo world.[13] She traced the distributions of different styles of trade pots to show how communities developed regular exchange relationships with villages living in quite different climatic zones. This was a logical insurance, as it were, in a harsh and unforgiving land. In another study, John Roney has shown how thirteenth-century pottery styles from the northern San Juan south-southeast to the Rio Grande Valley near Socorro display remarkable similarities.[14] If these studies are any guide, then the inhabitants of the northwestern pueblos moved southeast into the Little Colorado River drainage, the Mogollon highlands, and the Rio Grande Valley. Rautman used tree rings to show that these areas suffered little rainfall change during the critical decades when the northwest was under severe drought.

The ripple of emigration took place over more than a century, but the Ancestral Pueblo never set out to remake their society along new lines. There were no technological innovations, nor new crops. They continued to live as they always had. New religious beliefs, adapted to new social institutions and circumstances, seem to have had little effect on the old trade routes and the old mobility. In the words of a Tewa elder: "They started coming and moving, and then they settled and they stood up again and then they started moving again."[15]

THE WHITE HOUSE

Chaco was an important incident in Pueblo history; its greatest legacy is modern Pueblo Indian societies, whose vibrant traditions reach back far into the past. So do their agricultural practices and much of their architecture, ritual, and symbolism—to mention only a few facets of their societies. Chaco was a Pueblo society, but one separated from today by seven eventful centuries that saw depopulation of much of the Ancestral Pueblo homeland, by the Spanish *entrada* and European colonization, and the traumatic changes wrought by modern industrial society. Despite all these upheavals, we can still trace a basic continuity between Chacoan and historic Pueblo society, albeit a continuity blurred by the palimpsest of history. Puebloan oral histories are a rich mother lode of past events.[16]

In material terms, the legacy includes water-control practices that worked well to harness runoff in the canyon, to farm basins with fertile soils, and to cultivate arid upland areas. The diverse agricultural practices that supported the large pueblo towns of the Galisteo Basin in later times are reminiscent of Chaco; they appeared in the Basin abruptly, just as the towns developed, as if introduced suddenly. Today, Pueblo communities are politically autonomous and economically independent, even when they trade with one another, just as Chacoan communities were.

Chaco was remarkable for its dense population, living in close juxtaposition. That its leaders did so in apparent harmony is a tribute to their skill in using shared rituals and ceremonies to promote common identity and harmony. Today, pueblos interact through ritual sodalities and with the help of religious specialists, people connected throughout the Eastern Pueblo world by complex networks of shared knowledge and ritual paraphernalia. They even share training and may replenish each other's priesthoods if their survival is in danger. Above all, religious knowledge is deeply secret, shared only with other ritual leaders and not with other members of society or outsiders. Such ties between ritual leaders and specialists must have been commonplace in Chacoan times, indeed been the mechanisms by which the canyon first became a place of great ritual importance. At the other end of

Chaco's history, ties between religious specialists in different communities may have been one of the ways in which migration streams came into being. And, in a society where agriculture and religion went together, no community could exist or thrive without the rituals that needed to be performed at different times of the year—to mark the solstices and other events. This may have been one reason why Chaco was almost completely emptied during the twelfth century.

Ritual societies and ceremonial networks are perhaps Chaco's most powerful legacy, for they flourish, albeit in different forms, to this day. They allowed, as they do today, peaceful interactions through ritual leaders between people in different environments and diverse histories. Chaco was not a warrior state; it was a classic Pueblo society where the powerful undercurrents of ritual practice and tradition allowed farming societies to remain self-sufficient, while at the same time supporting one another. Such warfare as occurred was on a small scale, much of it staged as raids in times of scarcity, as we saw earlier in this chapter.

Chaco Canyon looms large in contemporary Pueblo oral tradition. The descendants of the Chacoans did not forget this intensely sacred place in their histories, which they passed down from generation to generation. Pueblo oral traditions are layered stories, shaped by many themes, among them cosmology and moral instruction. Such tales are metaphorical accounts of history, where the meaning is more important than historical detail. Oral histories provide common identity, promulgate ethics, reinforce values, and pass from generation to generation in infinite diversity.

Few archaeologists have grappled with the complex problems of studying oral histories, or of decoding them as a source of information about the past. One problem is the reluctance of many Pueblos to share their oral traditions with outsiders, leaving the researcher with only published versions or tantalizing fragments, often collected by early observers.

Chaco Canyon remains part of the ancestral memory of the Acoma, Hopi, Zia, and Zuni, a stopping place along their complex way in ancient times in search of the central place.[17] With the belief that places are also alive, Pueblo people visit the old ruins to breathe in the strength of the place and "those who have gone before." The Hopi live today in northeastern Arizona and have lived in their homeland for many centuries. Zuni Pueblo is 85 miles (137 km) southwest of Chaco, but at the time of Spanish contact the people dwelt in six villages. The Hopi and Zuni have a long tradition of trading with one another. An important

Chaco outlier, Village of the Great Kivas, lies within 10 miles (16 km) of Zuni Pueblo. So do other sites that show some affiliation with Chaco culture. There may have been some survival of great houses and roads in this region after the canyon was depopulated. The Navajo (or Diné), a non-Pueblo group, arrived in the northwestern part of the San Juan Basin in about 1400. Originally, they were nomadic hunter-gatherers, who raided nearby Pueblos for corn. After the Spanish *entrada*, they also accumulated large herds of horses and sheep. Under pressure from the Comanche and Ute, they moved southward into the Chaco region, settling on Chacra Mesa. Some Navajo claim they are related to the Ancestral Pueblo and that they are descendants of Chacoans.

A place called the White House figures prominently in Pueblo traditions, a location where seminal events affected the course of history. It was here that the kachinas lived with humans and fought with them, after teaching them the dances and rituals that enabled the Pueblo to communicate with the spiritual world. No one knows if the White House was a real place. Some Pueblo informants believe it refers to the Four Corners area, a logical explanation if you note how the White House appears in the histories of many groups. There are those who believe the White House was Mesa Verde, others that it was Chaco Canyon. Lekson believes that the Chaco attribution has some merit. After all, he argues, Chaco was the place that transformed the Pueblo world, which would account for the appearance of the White House in so many histories. He goes so far as to link it with Chaco and Aztec, places where major changes unfolded.

Real or not, the White House is a metaphor for early Pueblo history. Acoma oral histories record how the people left the White House. "They decided to go to the south, where lay a place called Ako. They wished to go there and raise parrots [macaws]."[18] The people traveled south carrying god-given blue and dun-colored eggs, those of a macaw and a crow. But the eggs could not be distinguished from one another. When they reached Acoma, they divided into two groups by choosing eggs. The blue-egg people knew they would stay at Acoma and thought they were macaws, but they turned out to be crows. So they remained and the macaw group moved on to the south. The Zuni have a somewhat similar tradition, but the Hopi do not.[19]

Navajo storytellers recount tales of Noqoilpi, the Great Gambler, who lived at Chaco Canyon. He ruled Chaco, reduced the surrounding communities to slavery by always winning gambling bets. He demanded that they build a huge pueblo as his residence. He was ultimately overthrown by the gods, and shot into the sky like an arrow. It's not clear whether Noqoilpi was a Puebloan or an outsider, even a European, but the moral of the story is plain.

Oral traditions, whether songs or stories, are important sources about human lives. They integrate and sustain communities, define the duties and responsibilities of everyone in society. They represent, and have always represented, continuity in the cosmos, continuity in the cycles of the seasons, and in the business of farming the land. Everything revolved around a closely interconnected set of reciprocal obligations and responsibilities to both fellow kin and to maintaining the rituals that sustained society. Perhaps the White House is part of this metaphor, a commemoration of important events deep in the remote Puebloan past, of ancient ancestors who transformed society in fundamental ways.

The story of Chaco as revealed by archaeology is a tale of people adapting constantly to the challenges of a demanding and unpredictable environment, of societies where agriculture and religion went hand in hand. This was not a world of great empires and states, nor of powerful chiefs who mounted punitive raids and controlled lucrative trade routes. Nor was it one where a few individuals devoted their lives to an ambitious quest for untold wealth. Rather, Chaco is a story of households and kin groups living in a multilayered cosmos, where the realms of the living and the supernatural passed insensibly one into the other. Ritual knowledge, ritual choreography lay at the center of community life, spiritual truths that were guarded jealously among a few and passed carefully from one generation to the next. Human existence depended on the meticulous performance of elaborate rituals and dances, on performance public and private, on the skill of the few people who were guardians of sacred knowledge. Chaco is remarkable because it achieved an extraordinary sanctity as a sacred place across a much wider world of the San Juan Basin, a sanctity that was ultimately powerless in the face of a capricious environment. This sacredness translated itself into great houses and elaborate rituals, into symbolic roads, and a new, nascent complexity of Pueblo society. Then came the droughts, and the entire façade imploded like a stack of cards. In the end, the rituals, so carefully performed, did not suffice.

Chaco still casts a profound spell, especially when the thunderclouds build and the silent great houses squat under the vast arc of the heavens. Then you remember: "When you are at these places, you should leave a prayer to the ancient ones and spirits."[20]

I always do.

• • NOTES AND REFERENCES

The academic and popular literature on Chaco Canyon, Pueblo Indian society, and Southwestern archaeology is so enormous that it's beyond the capacity of a single person to absorb it all. I wrote this book from personal experience and from a maze of monographs, edited volumes, and journal articles, so many that it's impracticable to list them all here. My narrative is referenced with carefully selected sources, all of which will lead the interested reader into the more detailed literature. What follows is but a beginning.

GENERAL WORKS

Kendrick Frazier's *The People of Chaco: A Canyon and Its Culture*, rev. ed. (New York: W. W. Norton, 1999) is a widely read account and excellent summary of major Chaco discoveries and archaeologists. David Grant Noble's *In Search of Chaco: New Approaches to an Archaeological Enigma* (Santa Fe: School of American Research Press, 2004) is an authoritative summary by leading experts. Robert H. Lister and Florence C. Lister's *Chaco Canyon: Archaeology and Archaeologists* (Albuquerque: University of New Mexico Press, 1981) is somewhat outdated but an excellent summary for its day. See Gwinn Vivian and Bruce Hilpert, *The Chaco Handbook: An Encyclopedic Guide* (Salt Lake City: University of Utah Press, 2002) for an admirable reference work, which tells you all you want to know about Chaco and more. A fluent and perceptive story of Chaco and today is David Stuart, *Anasazi America* (Albuquerque: University of New Mexico Press, 2000). For a more controversial view of the canyon, which requires some advance reading, read Stephen H. Lekson, *Chaco Meridian* (Walnut Creek, CA: AltaMira Press, 1999).

Southwestern archaeology generally: Linda S. Cordell, *Archaeology of the Southwest*, 2nd ed. (San Diego: Academic Press, 1997) is widely regarded as a definitive work. Stephen Plog's *Ancient Peoples of the Southwest* (London and New York: Thames and Hudson, 1997) is an excellent, well-illustrated summary.

There are two major syntheses of research at Chaco for more academic audiences: Stephen H. Lekson, *The Archaeology of Chaco Canyon: An 11th Century Pueblo Regional Center* (Santa Fe: School of American Research Press, in press) and Frances Joan Mathien, ed., *A Synthesis of the Chaco Project: Culture and Ecology of Chaco Canyon and the San Juan Basin* (Santa Fe: School of American Research Press, forthcoming).

∴ ∴ ∴

CHAPTER 1

1. Gwinn Vivian and Bruce Hilpert, *The Chaco Handbook: An Encyclopedic Guide* (Salt Lake City: University of Utah Press, 2002), xxiii.
2. Brian Swann, ed., *Coming to Light: Contemporary Translations of the Native Literature of North America* (New York: Random House, 1994), 684.
3. Austen Henry Layard, *Nineveh and Its Remains* (London: John Murray, 1949), 112.
4. *Wijiji* is named after the finely made baskets found with their burials by early archaeologists (see ch. 2).
5. Most excavation in Chaco's great houses has concentrated on a few sites, notably Pueblo Bonito. For this reason, I've used this, the largest of Chaco's great houses, as the framework for my story. Other sites such as Wijiji are mentioned, where appropriate, in the narrative, then briefly described in legends accompanying the illustrations.
6. Bruce D. Smith, *The Origins of Agriculture* (Washington, DC: Smithsonian Institution Press, 1998) offers an excellent summary of the origins of maize agriculture.
7. W. H. Wills, *Early Prehistoric Agriculture in the American Southwest* (Santa Fe: School of American Research, 1989) offers a useful summary of early maize cultivation in the region, although new discoveries have pushed the beginnings back considerably earlier, to around 1800 BC.
8. For the origins of the Basketmaker term, see ch. 2.
9. See Gwinn Vivian, *Chacoan Prehistory of the San Juan Basin* (San Diego: Academic Press, 1990), ch. 10.
10. Vivian and Hilpert, *Chaco Handbook*, 16–17.

CHAPTER 2

1. Lynne Sebastian, *The Chaco Anasazi* (Cambridge: Cambridge University Press, 1992), 1.
2. My historical account of Chaco is based on Gwinn Vivian, *Chacoan Prehistory of the San Juan Basin* (San Diego: Academic Press, 1990), and on Don D. Fowler, *A Laboratory for Anthropology: Science and Romanticism in the American Southwest, 1846–1930* (Albuquerque: University of New Mexico Press, 2000).
3. Josiah Gregg, *Commerce of the Prairies, or the journal of a Santa Fé trader: during eight expeditions across the great western prairies, and a residence of nearly nine years in northern Mexico* (New York: Henry Langly, 1844). His book did much to attract settlers to the West.
4. Quotations in these paragraphs from F. McNitt, ed., *J. A. Simpson, Journal of a Military Reconnaissance from Santa Fe, New Mexico, to the Navajo Country Made in 1849* (Norman: University of Oklahoma Press, 1964), 35–37.
5. Pueblo Pintado is an L-shaped great house about 3 miles (4.8 km) east of the head of Chaco Canyon and 16 miles (26 km) east of Pueblo Bonito. It was founded in the 1060s.
6. McNitt, *J. A. Simpson*, 36.
7. Ibid., 45–49.
8. Archaeologists commonly use the term *Mesoamerica* to refer to that area of Central America where pre-Columbian civilizations flourished.
9. Quoted by Fowler, *A Laboratory for Anthropology*, 54. The Welsh story, which is really irrelevant to Chaco, went as follows. In 1170 Prince Madoc of Wales led a group of colonists across the Atlantic to a "western land," left them there, and returned home, promising to return. The Madoc legend was politically useful, being cited as justification for claiming title to "all the Coasts and Islands beginning at or about Terra Florida . . . unto Atlantis going north."

The Welsh prince and his doings became a counter in the geopolitical struggle between England and Spain; Welsh Indians were sought on the Great Plains; at least fifteen Indian languages were claimed to be a form of Welsh. Inevitably, the legend spread to the Southwest, where the Zuni Indians were said to have "white skin, fair hair, and blue eyes" inherited from the wives of Welsh miners who had entered Zuni country and been massacred, while their spouses married the conquerors. Eventually the Mormons adopted the story. They believed that the pueblos seen by military expeditions had been the work of colonizing Nephrites from Mexico.

10. Jackson's report on Southwestern ruins: William H. Jackson, "Ancient Ruins in Southwestern Colorado," *Bulletin of the United States Geological and Geographical Survey of the Territories*, no. 1 (1875): 17, 17–30. His autobiography, *Time Exposure: The Autobiography of William Henry Jackson* (New York: G. P. Putnam's Sons), appeared in 1940. The steps quote is on p. 40.
11. Fowler, *A Laboratory for Anthropology*, 189–91 covers this interesting figure.
12. Ibid., 195–200.
13. Ibid., 187–201, assesses Wetherill and his doings.
14. George H. Pepper, *Pueblo Bonito* (New York: American Museum of Natural History Anthropological Papers 27, 1920).
15. Fowler, *A Laboratory for Anthropology*, 261–74, gives an excellent account. So does James E. Snead, *Ruins and Rivals: The Making of Southwestern Archaeology* (Tucson: University of Arizona Press, 2001).
16. Nels C. Nelson, 1919, "The Archaeology of the Southwest: A Preliminary Report," *Proceedings of the National Academy of Sciences* 5 (4): 114–20.
17. Snead, *Ruins and Rivals* has a comprehensive analysis of these rivalries.
18. Alfred V. Kidder, *An Introduction to the Study of Southwestern Archaeology* (New Haven: Yale University Press, 1924), 54–55.
19. Neil Judd, "Pueblo Bonito, the Ancient," *National Geographic Magazine* 44, no. 2 (1923): 99–108; and "Everyday Life in Pueblo Bonito," *National Geographic Magazine* 48, no 3 (1925): 227–62. His 1954 monograph on Pueblo Bonito is *The Material Culture of Pueblo Bonito* (Washington, DC: Smithsonian Miscellaneous Collections 147/1, 1954). He published a volume on the architecture of the site a decade later, also with the Smithsonian.
20. Earl H. Morris, *The Aztec Ruin* (New York: American Museum of Natural History Anthropological Papers 26, no. 1, 1919), 1–108.
21. Earl H. Morris, *Archaeological Studies in the La Plata District, Southwestern Colorado, and Northwestern New Mexico* (Washington, DC: Carnegie Institution of Washington Publications 519, 1939).
22. Alfred V. Kidder and Samuel J. Guernsey, *Archaeological Explorations in Northeastern Arizona* (Washington, DC: Bureau of American Ethnology Bulletin 65, 1919).
23. Described in Kidder, *An Introduction*. Pecos Pueblo lay atop a mesa overlooking what became the Santa Fe Trail. Today, we know that Pecos was founded in the 1300s and had become a large, multistoried pueblo with a central plaza and kivas by 1450. Some two thousand people lived at this strategic location where the inhabitants served as middlemen in trade between the Rio Grande pueblos and the buffalo hunters of the Plains to the east, who supplied hides, flint, and tobacco in exchange for maize, beans, pottery, and fine-grained obsidian (volcanic glass). The Franciscans built a church and convent at Pecos in the 1620s, which was finally vacated in 1838. For the Pecos Conference, see Fowler, *A Laboratory for Anthropology*, 315–18.
24. Florence M. Hawley, *The Significance of the Dated Prehistory of Chaco Canyon, New Mexico* (Albuquerque: University of New Mexico Bulletin Monograph Series 1, no. 1, 1934).

25. Gordon Vivian and Tom W. Mathews, *The Great Kivas of Chaco Canyon and Their Relationships* (Santa Fe: Monograph of the School of American Research and the Museum of New Mexico 22, 1965).
26. McElmo Style is a term used to describe great houses strikingly different from Pueblo Bonito and other earlier structures. Such great houses comprise one or two compact room units, each with one or two central kivas surrounded by several rows of rooms. They lack plazas and great kivas, typical of earlier great houses. The McElmo phase at Chaco dates ca. AD 1050–1125, to the closing stages of the canyon's heyday.
27. Gordon Vivian and Tom W. Mathews, *Kin Kletso: A Pueblo III Community in Chaco Canyon, New Mexico* (Albuquerque: University of New Mexico Publications in Anthropology 13, 1965).
28. Cynthia Irwin-Williams, ed., "The Structure of Chacoan Society in the Northern Southwest: Investigations at the Salmon Site, 1972," *Eastern New Mexico Contributions to Anthropology* 4, no. 3 (1972).
29. Steve Lekson, *Chaco Meridian* (Walnut Creek, CA: AltaMira Press, 1999).

CHAPTER 3

1. Gwinn Vivian and others, "Paleoenvironmental Reconstruction in the Chaco Canyon Region," in *Archaeology of Chaco Canyon: An 11th Century Pueblo Regional Center,* ed. Stephen H. Lekson (Santa Fe: School of American Research Press, in press).
2. Gwinn Vivian and Bruce Hilpert, *The Chaco Handbook: An Encyclopedic Guide* (Salt Lake City: University of Utah Press, 2002), 3.
3. This description is based on Gwinn Vivian, ed., *Chacoan Prehistory of the San Juan Basin* (San Diego: Academic Press, 1990), ch. 2.
4. William B. Gillespie and Robert P. Powers, "Regional Settlement Changes and Past Environment in the San Juan Basin, Northwestern New Mexico" (paper presented at the Second Anasazi Symposium, Salmon Ruin, Bloomfield, NM, 1983).
5. Vivian, *Chacoan Prehistory*, 25ff.
6. Don D. Fowler, *A Laboratory for Anthropology: Science and Romanticism in the American Southwest, 1846–1930* (Albuquerque: University of New Mexico Press, 2000), 298ff describes Douglass's work.
7. Described by Robert Silverberg, *The Moundbuilders of Ancient America* (New York: New York Graphic Society, 1968).
8. This section is based on Jeffrey S. Dean, "Dendrochronology and Climatic Reconstruction on the Colorado Plateaus," in George Gumerman, ed., *The Anasazi in a Changing Environment* (Cambridge: Cambridge University Press, 1988),119–67; also Jeffrey S. Dean and Gary S. Funkhauser, "Dendroclimatic Reconstructions for the Southern Colorado Plateau," in W. J. Waugh, ed., *Climate Change in the Four Corners and Adjacent Regions* (Grand Junction, CO: Mesa State College Press, 1994), 85–104. There is an important summary by Gwinn Vivian and others, "Economy and Ecology," in Lekson, ed., *Archaeology of Chaco.*

CHAPTER 4

1. Frank Cushing, *Zuñi: Selected Writings of Frank Hamilton Cushing* (Lincoln: University of Nebraska Press, 1979), 346.
2. Sir Edward Tylor, *Anthropology* (London: Macmillan, 1871), 231.
3. Account based on ethnographic records of western rabbit hunting. For the record, there are two rabbit populations in the Chaco area—jackrabbits (*Lepus*

californicus) and cottontail (*Sylvilagus auduboni*). They both have fairly distinctive habitats in Chaco. Whereas cottontail inhabit the canyon, jackrabbits occupy more open areas, including the wide gaps in the Chacra Mesa (e.g., South Gap, Fajada Gap) that border the canyon on the south. My thanks to Gwinn Vivian for alerting me to this esoteric distinction.

4. I'm reluctant to burden the reader with technical archaeological terms, but a few labels are essential and are, indeed, convenient. "Archaic" is a label given to diversified hunter-gatherer societies that flourished throughout North America after 6000 BC. There are numerous local Archaic traditions and cultures, among them the Oshara of the northern Southwest, identified in general terms at Chaco. See Cynthia Irwin-Williams, "The Oshara Tradition: Origins of Anasazi Culture," *Eastern New Mexico University Contributions in Anthropology* 5, no. 1 (1973).

5. Irwin-Williams, "The Oshara Tradition," 16. See also Larry L. Baker and Stephen R. Durand, eds. *Prehistory of the Middle Rio Puerco Valley, Sandoval County, New Mexico* (Albuquerque: Archaeological Society of New Mexico, Special Publication 3, 2003).

6. Here the terminological plot thickens. The term "Basketmaker I" was once applied to the Late Archaic (Oshara Tradition), but no more. So Basketmaker II is technically now the earliest Basketmaker culture. I use this widely adopted (and seemingly illogical) terminology here.

7. A summary of Los Piños appears in Gwinn Vivian, *The Chacoan Prehistory of the San Juan Basin* (San Diego: Academic Press, 1990), 93–99, where references will be found.

8. Frank W. Eddy, "Prehistory in the Navajo Reservoir District in northwestern New Mexico (parts 1 and 2)," *Museum of New Mexico Papers in Anthropology* 4 (1966).

9. Irwin-Williams and S. Tompkins, "Excavations at En Medio Shelter, New Mexico," *Eastern New Mexico University Contributions in Anthropology* 1, no. 2 (1968). Archaeologists often name ancient archaeological cultures after the sites where they were first identified. For more on these topics, see David Stuart, *Anasazi America* (Albuquerque: University of New Mexico Press, 2000). See also David and Rory Gauthier, *Prehistoric New Mexico: Background for Survey* (Albuquerque: University of New Mexico Press, 1988).

10. Discussion of this controversy in Vivian, *Chacoan Prehistory*, 105–9.

11. Michael Berry, *Time, space, and transition of Anasazi Prehistory* (Salt Lake City: University of Utah Press, 1982).

12. Climatic data from Vivian and others, "Economy and Ecology," in *The Archaeology of Chaco Canyon: An 11th Century Pueblo Regional Center*, ed. Stephen H. Lekson (Santa Fe: School of American Research Press, 2005, in press).

13. Alan H. Simmons, ed., *Prehistoric Adaptive Strategies in the Chaco Canyon Region, Northwestern New Mexico* (Window Rock, AZ: Navajo Nation Papers in Anthropology 9, 1985).

14. Alan H. Simmons, "New Evidence for the Early Use of Cultigens in the American Southwest," *American Antiquity* 51, no. 1 (1986): 73–89.

CHAPTER 5

1. Ruth Benedict, "Tales of the Cochiti Indians," *Bulletin of the Bureau of American Ethnology* 98 (Washington, DC: Smithsonian Institution, 1931), 249.

2. Frank H. H. Roberts, Jr., "Shabik'eshchee Village: a late Basketmaker site in the Chaco Canyon, New Mexico," *Bulletin of the Bureau of American Ethnology* 29 (Washington, DC: Smithsonian Institution, 1929).

3. My account is based on literature summarized in Gwinn Vivian, *The Chacoan Prehistory of the San Juan Basin* (San Diego: Academic Press, 1990), 121 ff; also

on W. H. Wills and Thomas C. Windes, "Evidence for Population Aggregation and Dispersal During the Basketmaker III Period in Chaco Canyon, New
Mexico." *American Antiquity* 54, no. 2 (1989): 347–69.

4. Discussion in Wills and Windes, ibid., 354.
5. Ibid. See also Kent Flannery, "The Origins of the Village as a Settlement Type
   in Mesoamerica and the Near East: A Comparative Approach," in *Man, Settlement, and Urbanism*, P. J. Ucko, R. Tringham, and G. W. Dimbleby, eds. (London: Duckworth, 1972), 23–53.
6. Julian H. Steward, "Ecological Aspects of Southwestern Society," *Anthropos*
   32 (1937): 87–104. The discussion that follows is based on Wills and Windes,
   "Evidence for Population Aggregations," 363ff.
7. Marshall Sahlins, *Social Stratification in Polynesia* (Seattle: University of Washington Press, 1958).
8. Kent G. Lightfoot and Gary M. Feinman, "Social Differentiation and Leadership Development in Early Pithouse Villages in the Mogollon Region of the
   American Southwest," *American Antiquity* 47 (1982): 64–86.
9. Discussion based on Wills and Windes, "Evidence for Population Aggregations."
10. David Stuart, *Anasazi America* (Albuquerque: University of New Mexico Press,
    2000), ch. 4.
11. Wills and Windes, "Evidence for Population Aggregation," 365.

CHAPTER 6

1. Richard H. Wilshusen and Ruth M. Van Dyke, "Chaco's Beginnings: The
   Collapse of Pueblo I Villages and the Origins of the Chaco System," in *The
   Archaeology of Chaco Canyon: An 11th Century Pueblo Regional Center*, Stephen
   H. Lekson, ed. (Santa Fe: School of American Research Press, 2005, in press).
2. This is the widely accepted scenario for the transition from pithouses to above-
   ground pueblos, which I see no reason to doubt.
3. This discussion is based on Wilshusen and Van Dyke, "Chaco's Beginnings,"
   in *The Archaeology of Chaco Canyon*. This important paper is a primary source
   for this chapter.
4. Mark D. Varien, "Persistent Communities and Mobile Households: Population Movement in the Central Mesa Verde Region, A.D. 950 to 1290," in *Seeking the Center Place: Archaeology and Ancient Communities in the Mesa Verde
   Region*, Mark D. Varien and Richard H. Wilshusen, eds. (Salt Lake City: University of Utah Press, 2002), 163–84.
5. Elizabeth Ann Morris, "A Pueblo I Site Near Bennett's Creek, Northwestern
   New Mexico," *El Palacio* 66, no. 5 (1959): 169–75. (Excavation by Earl Morris
   in 1932.)
6. Gwinn Vivian, *The Chacoan Prehistory of the San Juan Basin* (San Diego: Academic Press, 1990), ch. 7.
7. Peter J. McKenna and Marcia L. Truell, eds., "Small site architecture of Chaco
   Canyon, New Mexico," in *Publications in Anthropology 18-D Chaco Canyon Studies* (Santa Fe: National Park Service, 1989). I am grateful to Dr. Tom Windes
   for the information on larger Pueblo I sites south of the San Juan River.
8. Thomas C. Windes, *The Spadefoot Toad Site: Investigations at 29SJ629 in Marcia's
   Rincon and the Fajada Gap Pueblo II Community, Chaco Canyon, New Mexico*, in
   Reports of the Chaco Center, no. 12. (Santa Fe: National Park Service, 1993).
9. Ibid.
10. Thomas C. Windes, R. M. Anderson, B. K. Johnson, and C. A. Ford, "Sunrise,
    Sunset: Sedentism and Mobility in the Chaco East Community," in *Great House
    Communities across the Chacoan Landscape*, ed. John Kantner and N. M.

Mahoney, Anthropological Papers 64 (Tucson: University of Arizona Press, 2000).

11. Wilshusen and Van Dyke, "Chaco's Beginnings," in *The Archaeology of Chaco Canyon*.

12. Tessie Naranjo, "Thoughts on Migration by Santa Clara Pueblo," *Journal of Anthropological Archaeology* 14 (1995): 247–50.

13. Wilshusen and Van Dyke, "Chaco's Beginnings," in *The Archaeology of Chaco Canyon*.

14. J. M. Brisbin, A. E. Kane, and J. N. Morris, "Excavations at McPhee Pueblo (Site 5MT4475), a Pueblo I and Early Pueblo II Multicomponent Village," in *Dolores Archaeological Program: Anasazi Communities at Dolores: McPhee Village,* ed. A. E. Kane and C. K. Robinson (Bureau of Reclamation, Engineering and Research Center, Denver, 1988), 62–403.

15. Richard H. Wilshusen and Scott G. Ortman, "Rethinking the Pueblo I Period in the San Juan Drainage: Aggregation, Migration, and Cultural Diversity," *Kiva* 64 (1999): 369–99.

16. Known as *akchin* methods, after the Tohono O'odham word meaning "at the mouth of the wash." Such agricultural methods were widely used in arid regions of the Southwest for many centuries.

17. See Vivian, *Chacoan Prehistory*, 432ff for discussion.

18. My description here is, of course, much simplified. For a full account, see Alfonso Ortiz, *The Tewa World: Space, Time, Being, and Becoming in a Pueblo Society* (Chicago: University of Chicago Press, 1969).

19. Wilshusen and Ortman, "Rethinking the Pueblo I Period," 396.

20. Lynne Sebastian, *The Chaco Anasazi: Sociopolitical Evolution in the Prehistoric Southwest* (Cambridge: Cambridge University Press, 1992).

21. Mircea Eliade, *The Sacred and the Profane* (New York: Harvest Books, 1968).

22. See comments by Linda S. Cordell in Fred Plog and Walter Wait, eds., *The San Juan Tomorrow* (Santa Fe: National Park Service, 1982), 64.

CHAPTER 7

1. Stephen Plog, *Ancient Peoples of the Southwest* (London and New York: Thames and Hudson, 1997), 102.

2. Brian Swann, ed., *Coming to Light: Contemporary Translations of the Native Literature of North America* (New York: Random House, 1994), 660ff.

3. Inga Clendinnen, *The Aztecs: An Interpretation* (Cambridge: Cambridge University Press, 1991), 275.

4. Thomas C. Windes, R. M. Anderson, B. K. Johnson, and C. A. Ford, "Sunrise, Sunset: Sedentism and Mobility in the Chaco East Community," in *Great House Communities across the Chacoan Landscape*, ed. John Kantner and N. M. Mahoney, Anthropological Papers 64 (Tucson: University of Arizona Press, 2000), 56. The authors state: "Pottery of northern origins, exhibiting crushed igneous rock temper from the north, was also rare at the early East Community houses but relatively common in early houses at Pueblo Pintado." The "early houses" referred to are small house sites.

5. Emmanuel Le Roy Ladurie, *Times of Feast, Times of Famine: A History of Climate since the Year 1000* (New York: Doubleday, 1971).

6. For example, see Dabney Ford and Thomas C. Windes, "The Chaco Wood Project: The Chronometric Reappraisal of Pueblo Bonito," *American Antiquity* 61, no. 2 (1994): 295.

7. Nancy J. Akins, "The Burials of Pueblo Bonito," in *Pueblo Bonito: Center of the Chacoan World*, ed. Jill E. Neitzel (Washington DC: Smithsonian Books, 2003), 94–106.

8. Stephen H. Lekson, Thomas C. Windes, and Peter J. McKenna, "Architecture," in *The Archaeology of Chaco Canyon: An 11th Century Pueblo Regional Center,* ed. Stephen K. Lekson (Santa Fe: School of American Research Press, 2005, in press).

9. This estimate includes the inhabitants of both great houses and small settlements. The lower figures are based on the assumption that few people lived in the great houses. I'm grateful to Gwinn Vivian for discussion on this point.

10. Windes, "Spadefoot Toad."

11. This paragraph is based on discussions with Gwinn Vivian.

12. Lekson, Windes, and McKenna, "Architecture," in *The Archaeology of Chaco Canyon.*

13. Ibid.

14. Throughout this book, my accounts of Pueblo Bonito are based in large part on the admirable summary in *Pueblo Bonito*. The essays in this volume, most of which are cited in these pages, represent state-of-the-art Pueblo Bonito.

15. Gwinn Vivian and Bruce Hilpert, *The Chaco Handbook: An Encyclopedic Guide* (Salt Lake City: University of Utah Press, 2002), 94–95.

16. Anne Lawrason Marshall, "The Siting of Pueblo Bonito," in *Pueblo Bonito,* 10–13.

17. Stephen H. Lekson, *Great Pueblo Architecture of Chaco Canyon, New Mexico* (Albuquerque: University of New Mexico Press, 1984). This is a definitive account, which has only been modified slightly by later work, described in Lekson, Windes, and McKenna, "Architecture," in *The Archaeology of Chaco Canyon.*

18. For a summary of the results, see Thomas C. Windes, "This Old House: Construction and Abandonment at Pueblo Bonito," in *Pueblo Bonito,* 14–32.

19. This account of Old Bonito is based on John R. Stein, Dabney Ford, and Richard Friedman, "Reconstructing Pueblo Bonito," in *Pueblo Bonito,* 33– 60.

20. Neil Judd unearthed extensive low walls that extended far beyond the confines of the original buildings. They defined a much larger structure than the first room complexes. Steve Lekson believes the structure was, in some senses, a design tool, the clay platforms of Old Bonito a "scratch pad" for a full-scale layout of the as-yet-to-be-built room blocks, but it's only fair to say that this theory is controversial. He argues that right from the beginning the architects had some form of master plan, laid out with marked alignments and full-scale foundations. Lekson believes this because of the so-called northeast foundation (described in chapter 8), which coincides with the general orientation of the structure as a whole. See Lekson, *Great Pueblo Architecture.*

21. If you accept Lekson's hypothesis in note 20, then there's a possibility that a single architect designed Pueblo Bonito, or that all of downtown Chaco was the vision of one person. His blueprint was then rigorously followed by generations of successors, who used a carefully encoded plan, part of it alignments and already laid out foundations, the remainder preserved as mental templates held as arcane knowledge by a few individuals. I would not go as far as John Stein, Dabney Ford, and Richard Friedman, who remark somewhat controversially: "Pueblo Bonito was the vision of one man, made tangible and set in motion in a single lifetime." In truth, we will never know. See Stein, Ford, and Friedman, "Reconstructing," in *Pueblo Bonito.*

22. This analysis of Chaco agriculture is based on Vivian and others, "Economy and Ecology," in *The Archaeology of Chaco.* This is a shortened version of a much longer report, to which I had access for the writing of this chapter.

23. Anne C. Cully, Marcia L. Donaldson, Mollie S. Toll, and Klara B. Kelley, "Agriculture in the Bis sa'ani Community," in "Bis sa'ani: A Late Bonito Phase Community on Escavada Wash, Northwest New Mexico," ed. Cory Dale Breternitz, David E. Doyel, and Michael P. Marshall (Tucson: *Navajo Nation Papers in Anthropology* 14), 115–66.

24. Brilliantly described by David Lan, *Guns and Rain* (Cambridge: Cambridge University Press, 1985).
25. To obtain a sense of Cushing's work, see Frank Cushing, *Zuñi: Selected Writings of Frank Hamilton Cushing* (Lincoln: University of Nebraska Press, 1979).
26. For a full discussion, see Alfonso Ortiz, *The Tewa World: Space, Time, Being, and Becoming in a Pueblo Society* (Chicago: University of Chicago Press, 1989), 143, a book that has influenced me, and others, very strongly. The whole issue of Eastern and Western Pueblo organization is very complex. An important statement on Eastern Pueblo organization appears in Edward Dozier, "The Pueblos of the Southwestern United States," *Journal of the Royal Anthropological Institute* 90, no. 1 (1960): 146–60. Dozier, himself a Tewa, argues that Eastern Pueblo organization had deep roots and differs considerably from Western Pueblo, primarily because of major environmental differences and the use of irrigation in the east. Thus Eastern Puebloan organization structure was, and is, much more conducive to the needs of large corporate groups—as opposed to the more Western pattern of independent households operating within somewhat hierarchically organized clans and unified on the village level by clan ritual responsibilities for the entire village. The interwoven ritual and political links in Eastern Pueblo tend to reduce village fissioning, whereas these links are not as strong among Western Pueblos.
27. John M. Fritz, "Chaco Canyon and Vijanagra: Proposing Spatial Meaning in Two Societies," in *Mirror and Metaphor: Material and Social Constructions of Reality*, ed. D. W. Ingersoll and G. Bronitsky (Lanham, MD: University Press of America, 1987), 313–48.
28. John Ware, "Chaco Social Organization: A Peripheral View," in *Chaco Society and Chaco Polity*, ed. Linda Cordell and James Judge (Albuquerque: New Mexico Archaeological Council Special Publication 4, 2001), 78–87. Ware argues that most Chacoan archaeologists were strongly influenced by anthropologist Fred Eggan's theory that there was a Western Pueblo "protoculture." He believed that Eastern Ancestral Pueblo organizational structure was a result of "disruptive migrations" off the Colorado Plateau, economic shifts toward intensive irrigation on the Rio Grande, and profound European contact influences. Ware points out that "If one accepts Eggan's model of Pueblo social history, and an entire generation of Southwest archaeologists mostly did, the Eastern Pueblos are truly irrelevant for understanding pre-AD 1300 Pueblo societies" (81). Eggan was surely wrong. Interested readers should consult both Ware's fine paper and Fred Eggan's elegant statement on the subject in Alfonso Ortiz, ed., *Handbook of North American Indians*, vol. 9, *The Southwest* (Washington, DC: Smithsonian Institution, 1979), 288.

CHAPTER 8

1. Brian Swann, ed., *Coming to Light: Contemporary Translations of the Native Literature of North America* (New York: Random House, 1994), 657–63.
2. Once again, for this description I drew heavily on Stein, Ford, and Friedman, "Reconstructing," in *Pueblo Bonito: Center of the Chacoan World*, ed. Jill E. Neitzel (Washington, DC: Smithsonian Books, 2003), 33–60; also on Windes, "This Old House," in *Pueblo Bonito*, 14–32. For clarity, some detail is incorporated into the notes that follow rather than into the main narrative.
3. It may be, too, that a great deal of effort went into leveling and filling into long vanished adobe construction. Almost certainly, this developed through patient experimentation at Hungo Pavi in the early 1000s.
4. The new wall may seem to be continuous, but it might be that the builders deliberately left a gap at the point where the north–south axis bisects the

center, although there is no evidence for this. The back wall also enhanced the sunken-court effect of the central block. For some reason, the new rooms were attached to earlier blocks of rooms as separate units, with exterior doors to the outside or within the unit, but none connecting to the rooms of Old Bonito.

5. A great kiva (labeled Q today) was excavated west of the center axis. Perhaps the builders used the excavated soil to raise the level of the West Court. The extensive remodeling of this decade also raised the level of the West Court about 6.5 feet (1.98 m), burying the lowest story of Old Bonito and raising the roofs of the additional structures above the level of the earlier building.

6. Extensive repairs, using highly standardized timbers, remodeled the older western section, added new roofs, renovated walls, and rebuilt kivas. Sometime after 1103—the date is an estimate—the people built a great kiva partially into the southwestern corner of the East Plaza, its superstructure standing above ground level, opening into small rooms at its periphery. The entire configuration is rectangular and seems to define the southern end of the north–south axis.

7. John R. Stein and Stephen H. Lekson, "Anasazi Ritual Landscapes" in *Anasazi Regional Organization and the Chaco System,* ed. David E. Doyel (Albuquerque: Maxwell Museum of Anthropology, 95, fig. 8.9). See also: W. H. Wills, "Ritual and Mound Formation during the Bonito Phase in Chaco Canyon," *American Antiquity* 66 (2001): 433–51.

8. Wendy Bustard, "Pueblo Bonito: When a House Is Not a Home," in *Pueblo Bonito,* 80–93.

9. Ibid., 81–83.

10. Wollcott Toll and Peter McKenna, "The Rhetoric and the Ceramics: Discussion of Types, Function, Distribution, and Sources of the Ceramics of 29SJ627," in *Excavations at 29SJ627, Chaco Canyon, New Mexico,* ed. Frances Joan Mathien (Santa Fe: National Park Service Reports of the Chaco Center 11, 1992), 37–248.

11. Wesley Bernardini, "Reassessing the Scale of Social Action at Pueblo Bonito, Chaco Canyon, New Mexico," *Kiva* 64, no. 4 (1999): 447–70.

12. Windes, "This Old House," in *Pueblo Bonito,* 32.

13. Stephen H. Lekson, *Great Pueblo Architecture of Chaco Canyon, New Mexico* (Albuquerque: University of New Mexico Press, 1984), ch. 5.

14. Mary Metcalf, "Construction Labor at Pueblo Bonito," in *Pueblo Bonito,* 72–79.

15. Melissa Hagstrum, "Household Production in Chaco Canyon Society," *American Antiquity* 66, no. 1 (2001): 47–55.

16. Richard I. Ford, "An Ecological Perspective on the Eastern Pueblos," in *New Perspectives on the Pueblos,* ed. Alfonso Ortiz (Santa Fe: School of American Research, 1972), 19–26.

17. Timothy Earle, "Economic Support of Chaco Canyon Society," *American Antiquity* 66, no. 1 (2001): 26–35.

CHAPTER 9

1. Alfonso Ortiz, "Ritual Drama and the Pueblo World View," in *New Perspectives on the Pueblos,* ed. Alfonso Ortiz (Santa Fe: School of American Research, 1972), 143.

2. Larry Benson and others, "Ancient Maize from Chacoan Great Houses: Where Was It Grown?" *Proceedings of the National Academy of Sciences* 100/22 (2003): 13111–115.

3. Timber research is summarized by Julio Betancourt, Jeffrey S. Dean, and Herbert M. Hull, "Prehistoric Long-Distance Transport of Construction Beams, Chaco Canyon, New Mexico," *American Antiquity* 51, no. 2 (1986): 370–75.

4. The literature on Ancestral Pueblo pottery is enormous. This section is based on H. Walcott Toll, "Making and Breaking Pots in the Chaco World," *American Antiquity* 66 (2001): 56–78. For pottery classification, see Thomas C. Windes, "A View of the Cibola Whiteware from Chaco Canyon," in *Regional Analysis of Prehistoric Ceramic Variation: Contemporary Studies of the Cibola Whitewares*, ed. Alan P. Sullivan and Jeffrey L. Hartman (Tempe: Arizona State University Anthropological Research Papers 31, 1984), 94–119.

5. Stone tools: Catherine M. Cameron, "The Chipped Stone of Chaco Canyon, New Mexico," in *Ceramics, Lithics, and Ornaments of Chaco Canyon: Analyses of Artifacts from the Chaco Project, 1971–1978*, ed. Frances J. Mathien (Albuquerque: National Park Service Publications in Archaeology 18G, 1997), 997–1102.

6. The evidence for exotica at Chaco is described by Jill E. Neitzel, "Artifact Distributions at Pueblo Bonito," in *Pueblo Bonito: Center of the Chacoan World*, ed. Jill E. Neitzel (Washington, DC: Smithsonian Books, 2003), 107–26. For the interpretation of same, see Frances Joan Mathien, "Artifacts from Pueblo Bonito: One Hundred Years of Interpretation," in *Pueblo Bonito*, 127–42. In another perspective, Steve Lekson remarks that he thinks I have "turned time on its head. The question should be: 'Why do Hopi priests carry Chaco symbols of power, out of context?'" (letter to the author, 2004).

7. For ritual objects at great houses other than Pueblo Bonito, see also Gwinn Vivian, Dulce N. Dodgen, and Gayle H. Hartmann, "Wooden Ritual Artifacts from Chaco Canyon, New Mexico," *Anthropological Papers of the University of Arizona* 35 (Tucson: University of Arizona Press, 1978).

8. Turquoise: Jill Neitzel, "Artifact Distribution," in *Pueblo Bonito*, 107–25. See also Frances Joan Mathien, "Ornaments and Minerals from Site 29SJ627," in *Excavations at 29SJ627, Chaco Canyon, New Mexico*, ed. Frances Joan Mathien (Santa Fe: National Park Service. Reports of the Chaco Center 11, 1992), 265–318; Thomas C. Windes, "Blue Notes: The Chaco Canyon Turquoise Industry in the San Juan Basin," in *Anasazi Regional Organization in the San Juan Basin*, ed. David E. Doyel (Albuquerque: Maxwell Museum of Anthropology, 2001), 159–68.

9. J. W. Palmer, "Copper Bells from Anasazi Sites," *Blue Mountain Shadows* 13: 44–45 (1998). Also J. W. Palmer and others, "Pre-Columbian Metallurgy: Technology, Manufacture, and Microprobe Analysis of Copper Bells from the Greater Southwest," *Archaeometry* 40, no. 2 (1998): 361–82. For an analysis of trade patterns and an update, see Victoria D. Vargas, *Copper Bell Trade Patterns in the Prehispanic Southwest and Northwest Mexico* (Tucson: Arizona State Museum Archaeological Series 187, 1995).

10. Macaws remain the subject of much debate, one hampered by a lack of finds. There is currently no good evidence for macaw breeding in the Southwest. The closest area is the Paquimé (Casas Grandes) region of northern Mexico (see ch. 12), where there is good evidence for breeding of both the Scarlet Macaw and the Military Macaw. Of the some 150 macaw remains that have been recovered from the Southwest, only one is a Military Macaw—the macaw whose range is much closer to the region than the Scarlet macaw—yet both were bred at Paquimé. More discoveries are needed to decipher this enigma. For a discussion, see Mathien, "Artifacts," in *Pueblo Bonito*, 129.

CHAPTER 10

1. Brian Swann, ed., *Coming to Light: Contemporary Translations of the Native Literature of North America* (New York: Random House, 1994), 601.

2. P. G. Wodehouse, *A Damsel in Distress* (London: Herbert Jenkins, 1948), 23.
3. For a history of Chaco road research, see Margaret S. Obenauf, "A History of Research on the Chaco Roadway System," in *Cultural Resources Remote Sensing*, ed. Thomas R. Lyons and Frances J. Mathien (Washington, DC: National Park Service, 1980), 123–67. Two comprehensively referenced papers cover the fundamentals of roads and formed the basis for my discussion: Gwinn Vivian, "Chacoan Roads: Morphology," *Kiva* 63, no. 1 (1997a): 7–34, and "Chacoan Roads: Function," *Kiva* 63, no. 1 (1997b): 35–67. See also Chris Kincaid, ed., *Chaco Roads Project: A Reappraisal of Prehistoric Roads in the San Juan Basin* (Albuquerque and Santa Fe: Bureau of Land Management, 1983).
4. This discussion is based on Vivian, "Chacoan Roads: Function," 1–17. Additional Chaco road references include James Ebert and Robert K. Hitchcock, "Locational Modeling in the Analysis of the Prehistoric Roadway System at and around Chaco Canyon, New Mexico," in *Cultural Resources Remote Sensing*, 169–207. See also Frances J. Mathien, "Political, Economic, and Demographic Implications of the Chaco Road Network," in *Ancient Road Networks and Settlement Hierarchies in the New World*, ed. Charles D. Trombold (Cambridge: Cambridge University Press, 1991), 99–110.
5. John Kantner, "Rethinking Chaco as a System," *Kiva* 69, no. 2 (2003): 207–28. See also Keith W. Kintigh, "Coming to Terms with the Chaco World," *Kiva* 69, no. 2 (2003): 93–116.
6. http://sipapu.gsu.edu/html/chacoworld.html
7. Robert P. Powers, William B. Gillespie, and Stephen H. Lekson, *The Outlier Survey: A Regional View of Settlement in the San Juan Basin* (Santa Fe: National Park Service. Reports of the Chaco Center, 3, 1982), 66.
8. Descriptions based on Vivian, "Chacoan Roads: Morphology," 21–22.
9. Ibid., 20. See discussion, where references will be found.
10. Pueblo Alto: Thomas C. Windes, *Investigations at the Pueblo Alto Complex, Chaco Canyon, New Mexico*, 2 vols. (Santa Fe: National Park Service Publications in Archaeology 18F, 1987).
11. For example, in Stephen H. Lekson, *Chaco Meridian* (Walnut Creek, CA: AltaMira Press, 1999), ch. 4.
12. John R. Roney, "Prehistoric Roads and Regional Integration in the Chacoan System," in *Anasazi Regional Organization and the Chaco System*, ed. David E. Doyel (Albuquerque: Papers of the Maxwell Museum of Anthropology 5, 1992), 123–31.
13. Discussion in Kantner, "Rethinking," 212ff.
14. Summarized in Vivian, "Chacoan Roads: Function," where full references will be found.
15. For example, W. James Judge, "Chaco: Current Views of Prehistory and the Regional System," in *Chaco and Hohokam: Prehistoric Regional Systems in the American Southwest*, ed. Patricia L. Crown and W. James Judge (Santa Fe: School of American Research, 1991).
16. John Kantner, "Political Competition among the Chaco Anasazi of the American Southwest," *Journal of Anthropological Archaeology* 15 (1996): 41–105. Quote from p. 101.
17. Neil Judd, "Everyday Life in Pueblo Bonito," *National Geographic Magazine* 48, no. 3 (1925): 227–62. Quote from p. 234.
18. Thomas C. Windes, "The Prehistoric Road Network at Pueblo Alto, Chaco Canyon, New Mexico," in *Ancient Road Networks*, 111–31. Richard Loose's "Research Design," in Michael P. Marshall and others, *Anasazi Communities of the San Juan Basin* (Santa Fe: New Mexico Historic Preservation Bureau, 1979) is the first outlier study and identifies two types of "outlier" sites: "production sites" and "transportation sites." The latter are essentially small to very small sites located on roads that are in nonproductive areas (agricultur-

ally), which Loose believed were probably used as way stations on the road. Half House on the North Road is a possible example. Loose noted that such sites had a mean spacing of about 12 miles (19 km).

19. David R. Wilcox, "The Evolution of the Chacoan Polity," in *The Chimney Rock Archaeological Symposium*, ed. J. McKim Malville and Gary Matlock (Fort Collins: USDA Forest Service Rocky Mountain Forest and Range Experiment Station General Technical Report RM-227, 1993), 76–90.
20. Stephen W. Lekson, "Compared to What? Distance and Perception in Chacoan Archaeology" (paper prepared for a conference at Salmon Ruins, March 2004), discusses the scale of the Chaco world in much wider perspective.
21. John Kantner and Ronald Hobgood, "Digital Technologies and Prehistoric Landscapes in the American Southwest," in *The Reconstruction of Archaeological Landscapes through Digital Technologies*, eds. Maurizo Forte, P. Ryan Williams, and James Wiseman (Oxford: Archeopress, in press). Also, see discussion in Kantner, "Rethinking," 215.
22. The discussion that follows is based on Kantner, "Rethinking," 215ff.
23. Lekson, *Chaco Meridian*, ch. 2.
24. "regional exchange facilitator": see Kantner, "Rethinking," 215ff.
25. Ibid., 217ff.
26. See Steven Plog, "Exploring the Ubiquitous Through the Unusual: Color Symbolism in Pueblo Black-on-White Pottery," *American Antiquity* 68, no. 4 (2003): 665–95. Plog proposes that the hatching on Dogoszhi-style ceramics was used as a symbol for the color blue-green.
27. Kantner, "Rethinking," 218–19.
28. Ibid., 221.

CHAPTER 11

1. Brian Swann, ed., *Coming to Light: Contemporary Translations of the Native Literature of North America* (New York: Random House, 1994), 684. Hopi song-poem translated by David Leedom Shaul.
2. Alfonso Ortiz, "Ritual Drama and the Pueblo World View," in *New Perspectives on the Pueblos*, ed. Alfonso Ortiz (Santa Fe: School of American Research, 1972), 141. The discussion that follows is based in part on this important paper.
3. This section is based on Nancy C. Akins, "The Burials of Pueblo Bonito," in *Pueblo Bonito: Center of the Chacoan World*, ed. Jill E. Neitzel (Washington, DC: Smithsonian Books, 2003), 94–106. Her paper includes a detailed description of Pepper and Judd's burial discoveries.
4. Ibid., 102ff.
5. Michael Schillaci, "The Development of Population Diversity at Chaco Canyon," *Kiva* 68, no. 3 (2003): 221–245. Quote from p. 221.
6. James Judge, "Chaco Canyon—San Juan Basin," in *Dynamics of Southwest Prehistory*, ed. Linda S. Cordell and George Gumerman (Washington, DC: Smithsonian Institution Press, 1989), 209–61.
7. Lynne Sebastian, *The Chaco Anasazi: Sociopolitical Evolution in the Prehistoric Southwest* (Cambridge: Cambridge University Press, 1992).
8. David Stuart, *Anasazi America* (Albuquerque: University of New Mexico Press, 2000), ch. 4.
9. Wolcott Toll, "Organization of Production," in *The Archaeology of Chaco Canyon: An Eleventh-Century Pueblo Regional Center*, ed. Stephen K. Lekson (Santa Fe: School of American Research Press, 2005, in press).
10. For some examples, see Ruth L. Bunzel, "Introduction to Zuni ceremonialism," *Annual Report of the Bureau of American Ethnology* 47 (1932): 473.

11. David R. Wilcox, "The Evolution of the Chacoan Polity," in *The Chimney Rock Archaeological Symposium*, eds. J. McKim Malville and Gary Matlock (Fort Collins: USDA Forest Service Rocky Mountain Forest and Range Experiment Station General Technical Report RM-227, 1993), 76–90.

12. Polly Schaafsma, "Tlalocs, Kachinas, Sacred Bundles, and Related Symbolism in the Southwest and Mesoamerica," in *The Casas Grandes World*, ed. Curtis F. Schaafsma and Carroll L. Riley (Salt Lake City: University of Utah Press, 1999), 164–92. We do not have any evidence for Chacoan objects or commodities being passed southward into Mexican communities.

13. Lekson summarizes his main hypotheses in Stephen H. Lekson, *Chaco Meridian* (Walnut Creek, CA: AltaMira Press, 1999), the basis for the discussion here.

14. Ibid., 48.

15. Ibid., 50.

16. Ibid., 51.

17. Ibid., 164.

18. Colin Renfrew, "Trade as Action at a Distance," in *Ancient Civilization and Trade*, eds. Jeremy A. Sabloff and C. C. Lamberg-Karlovsky (Albuquerque: University of New Mexico Press, 1975). For recent discussions, see Colin Renfrew, "Production and Consumption in a Sacred Economy: The Material Correlates of High Devotional Expression at Chaco Canyon," *American Antiquity* 66, no. 1 (2001): 14–25; also Timothy Earle, "Economic Support of Chaco Canyon Society," *American Antiquity* 66, no. 1 (2001): 26–35.

19. Gwinn Vivian (personal communication) notes that Cushing described a single Zuñi pueblo with many associated small farming settlements. Before his time, there were many large Zuñi pueblos, which might give us a model closer to the Chacoan one.

CHAPTER 12

1. Kendrick Frazier, *The People of Chaco: A Canyon and Its Culture*, rev. ed. (New York: W. W. Norton, 1999), 212.

2. Oral tradition from an anonymous Pueblo informant. See Ian Thompson, "Native American Perspectives on Sand Canyon Pueblo and Other Ancestral Sites," in *Seeking the Center Place: Archaeology and Ancient Communities in the Mesa Verde Region*, eds. Mark D. Varien and Richard H. Wilshusen (Salt Lake City: University of Utah Press, 2002), 260.

3. Scenario based on diverse sources and my own reconstruction of events.

4. Nancy Akins, *A Biocultural Approach to Human Burials from Chaco Canyon, New Mexico* (Santa Fe: National Park Service. Reports of the Chaco Center 9, 1986).

5. Ibid., 61.

6. David Stuart, *Anasazi America* (Albuquerque: University of New Mexico Press, 2000), 119.

7. John Kantner, "Rethinking Chaco as a System," *Kiva* 69, no. 2 (2003): 207–28.

8. Steven Plog, "Exploring the Ubiquitous Through the Unusual: Color Symbolism in Pueblo Black-on-White Pottery," *American Antiquity* 68, no. 4 (2003): 665–95.

9. See Andrew I. Duff and Stephen A. Lekson, "Chaco: Notes from the South," in *The Archaeology of Chaco Canyon: An Eleventh-Century Pueblo Regional Center*, Stephen K. Lekson, ed. (Santa Fe: School of American Research Press, 2005, in press).

10. Earl H. Morris, *The Aztec Ruin* (New York: Anthropological Papers of the American Museum of Natural History, 26/1), and subsequent publications in the same series in 1921, 1924, and 1928 cover the early excavations at this

important site. I'm grateful to Tom Windes for allowing me to consult an unpublished summary of recent work on the site: Gary M. Brown, Thomas C. Windes, and Peter J. McKenna, "Animas Anamnesis: Aztec Ruins or Anasazi Capital?" (paper presented to the Society for American Archaeology's Sixty-seventh Annual Meeting, Denver, 2001). The discussion here reflects the conclusions in this paper.

11. A comprehensive series of papers on the northern San Juan appear in Varien and Wilshausen, *Seeking the Center Place.*

12. This section is based on Stephen H. Lekson, *Chaco Meridian* (Walnut Creek, CA: AltaMira Press, 1999), ch. 3ff.

13. Casas Grandes: The latest interpretations are in Michael Whalen and Paul Minnis, eds., *Casas Grandes and Its Hinterland: Prehistoric Regional Organization in Northwest Mexico* (Tucson: University of Arizona Press, 2001). See also Curtis F. Schaafsma and Carroll L. Riley, eds., *The Casas Grandes World* (Salt Lake City: University of Utah Press, 1999).

14. Quotes in this paragraph from Lekson, *Chaco Meridian*, 113, 119.

15. Ibid., 130–32.

16. Ibid., 140

17. For a discussion of emulation, see *Great House Communities across the Chacoan Landscape*, ed. John Kantner and N. M. Mahoney, Anthropological Papers 64 (Tucson: University of Arizona Press, 2000), 130–46.

18. Ruth M. Van Dyke, "Bounding Chaco: Great House Architectural Variability Across Time and Space," *Kiva* 69, no. 2 (2003): 117–40. See also Van Dyke's "Memory, Meaning, and Masonry: The Late Bonito Chaco Landscape," *American Antiquity* 69, no. 3 (2004): 413–31.

CHAPTER 13

1. Oral tradition from an anonymous Pueblo informant from the northern San Juan region. See Ian Thompson, "Native American Perspectives on Sand Canyon Pueblo and Other Ancestral Sites," in *Seeking the Center Place: Archaeology and Ancient Communities in the Mesa Verde Region,* ed. Mark D. Varien and Richard H. Wilshusen (Salt Lake City: University of Utah Press, 2002), 261.

2. Gary M. Brown, Thomas C. Windes, and Peter J. McKenna, "Animas Anamnesis: Aztec Ruins or Anasazi Capital?" (paper presented to the Society for American Archaeology's Sixty-seventh Annual Meeting, Denver, 2001).

3. *Totah* is the Navajo word for "rivers coming together." The area encompasses the region surrounding the confluences of the La Plata, Animas, and San Juan Rivers in the middle San Juan River Valley.

4. Mark D. Varien, "Persistent Communities and Mobile Households: Population Movement in the Central Mesa Verde Region, A.D. 950 to 1290," in *Seeking the Center Place.*

5. This section makes use of William D. Lipe, "Social Power in the Central Mesa Verde Region, A.D., 1150–1290," in *Seeking the Center Place,* 203–32.

6. Kristin A. Kuckelman, Ricky R. Lightfoot, and Debra L. Martin, "The Bioarchaeology and Taphonomy of Violence at Castle Rock and Sand Canyon Pueblo, Southwestern Colorado," *American Antiquity* 67, no. 3 (2003): 486–513.

7. Carla R. Van West, *Modeling Prehistoric Agricultural Productivity in Southwestern Colorado: A GIS Approach* (Cortez, CO: Crow Canyon Archaeological Center, 1994).

8. The analysis of Sand Canyon Pueblo is based on Scott G. Ortman and Bruce A. Bradley, "Sand Canyon: Pueblo: The Container in the Center," in *Seeking*

the Center Place, 41–78. References to Sand Canyon literature will be found in this paper and the volume in which it appears generally.

9. Jeffrey S. Dean and Carla Van West, "Environment-Behavior Relationships in Southwestern Colorado," in *Seeking the Center Place*, 81–99.

10. See Kuckelman and others, "The Bioarchaeology,"and Kristin Kuckelman, "Thirteenth-Century Warfare in the Central Mesa Verde Region," in *Seeking the Center Place*, 233–53.

11. This section draws on Stephen H. Lekson and Catherine M. Cameron, "The Abandonment of Chaco Canyon, the Mesa Verde Migrations, and the Reorganization of the Pueblo World," *Journal of Anthropological Archaeology* 14, no. 2 (1995): 184–202.

12. Stephen H. Lekson, *Archaeological Overview of Southwestern New Mexico* (Las Cruces: Human System Research, 1992). See also Stephen Lekson's *Chaco Meridian* (Walnut Creek, CA: AltaMira Press, 1999), 158–59. For long-term settlement history, see Keith W. Kintigh, Donna M. Glowacki, and Deborah L. Huntley, "Long-Term Settlement History and the Emergence of Towns in the Zuni Area," *American Antiquity* 69, no. 3 (2004): 432–56.

13. Alison Rautman, "Resource Variability, Risk, and the Structures of Social Networks: An Example From the Prehistoric Southwest," *American Antiquity* 58, no. 3 (1993): 403–24.

14. John Roney, "Mesa Verde Manifestations South of the San Juan River," *Journal of Anthropological Archaeology* 14 (1995): 170–83.

15. Tessie Naranjo, "Thoughts on Migration by Santa Clara Pueblo," *Journal of Anthropological Archaeology* 14 (1995): 103.

16. Chaco's legacy is discussed by David Stuart, *Anasazi America* (Albuquerque: University of New Mexico Press, 2000), ch. 9.

17. Lekson, *Chaco Meridian*, ch. 4, discusses these topics.

18. Ibid., 146. See also Leslie A. White, *The Acoma Indians* (Washington, DC: Bureau of American Ethnology, 1932), 145.

19. A recent important study of Hopi song and imagery stresses the importance of such ritual song texts to farming activities. See Emory Sekaquaptewa and Dorothy Washburn, "They Go Along Singing: Reconstructing the Hopi Past from Ritual Metaphors in Song and Image," *American Antiquity* 69, no. 3 (2004): 457–86.

20. Thompson, "Native American Perspectives," in *Seeking the Center Place*, 261.

INDEX

Page numbers in *italics* refer to illustrations. Page numbers in **bold** refer to entire chapters.

importation, 20, 60, 69, 176–77
infant mortality, 200, 222
inheritance, 104
interconnectedness, 60, 115, 145–48, 149–63, 190, 229
interdependence of Chaco, 177
irrigation, 19–20, 59, *127*
Irwin-Williams, Cynthia, 39, 65–66, 69, 71, 73

Jackson, William Henry, 28–29
Jackson Staircase, 7
Judd, Neil, 34–35; on age of pueblos, 38; and artifacts, 140; burial excavations, 184; on chronology, 51; on construction stages, 122; on great houses, 138; on low walls, 238; on Macaws, 162–63; on masonry, 124; on Old Bonito, 123; on Threatening Rock, 117; on timber usage, 175; water canals discovery, 118
Judge, James, 40, 187, 191
juniper trees, 47, 67, 84, 152, 207, 215

kachina, 131, 224, 224–25, 228
Kana'a Neckbanded ware, 156
Kantner, John, 175, 177, 178, 180
Kayenta region, 155
Kearny, Stephen Watts, 24
Kern, Edward, 24
Kern, Richard, 24
Kidder, Alfred, 34, 36, 37–38, 40, 64, 156
Kin Bineola Wash, 47, *98*, 115, 125
Kin Kletso, *7*, 11, 21, 39, 144, *160*, 163
Kin Klizhin Wash, 115
Kin Nabasbas, 6, *7*, 98
Kin Ya'a, 172, 176
kivas *(estuffas)*, 6, 37; abandonment of, 223, 224; Casa Rinconada, 10; ceremonial significance, 188; Chetro Ketl, 8–9, 38; and communication, 176; construction, 139, 141; discovery of, 25; exotic artifacts, 160, 161; great kivas, 107, 117, *135*, 141, 167, 205, 240; human sacrifice, 101, 103; labor requirements, 143; of outlying communities, 203; placement of, 21; privacy of, 130; proto-kiva, *94*; Pueblo Bonito, 27, *48*, 135; and roads, 167, 174; Sand Canyon Pueblo, 220; as signal stations, 21; and social structure, 87; of South Fork, 96; tower kivas, 115, 176; Una Vida, 26

labor requirements, 142–44, 147, 174, 204
Ladurie, Le Roy, 113
lagomorphs, 63–64, 198, 234–35
lake, 13, 102
landmarks, 114, 117–18, 172
lands, allocation of, 104
landscape, 41, 43
La Plata Black-on-White pottery, 156
La Plata settlement, 79–80, 88, 153
Late Archaic Period, *13*
Layard, Austen Henry, 4
leadership, 20, 87–89, 102–5, 183–93
legacy of Chaco Canyon, 214–29
Lekson, Steve: on architecture, 119, 122; on Chaco Meridian, 208–12, *209*; on Chaco system, 40; on exotic artifacts, 177; on great houses, 114; on *kachina*, 224–25; on labor requirements, 142–43; on low walls, 238; on outlying communities, 190–92; on roads, 168–69, *170*; on White House, 228
Leyit Kin, *7*
life expectancy, 200
Lightfoot, Kent, 87
limestone, 11
Lindbergh, Ann Morrow, 38
Lindbergh, Charles, 38
Lino Gray pottery, 156
Lister, Robert, 40
Little Colorado River, 225
Lizard House, *7*
Lobo Mesa area, 177
looting, 185
Los Piños, 66–69, *68*, 70, 71, 72, 79–90
Lyons, Tom, 39

macaws, 160, 162–63, 178, 191, 204, 228, 241
Maiz de Ocho, 15–16
maize, 14–15, *17*, 68; at Chacra Mesa, 89; and climate, 72; demands of, 86; dependency on, 198, 216; and drought cycles, 198; and En Medio groups, 70, 71; and foraging, 82; and hunter-gatherer lifestyle, 70; impact of, 75; and population requirements, 219; raiding for, 228; reliance on, 93; and ritual, 189; as staple, 150–51
Mancos area, 101, 219
Mancos River, 93
Marcia's Rincon, 96
marriage, 86, 88, 104